THE MOTION PICTURE
STUNT PILOTS
AND HOLLYWOOD'S CLASSIC AVIATION MOVIES

THE MOTION PICTURE
STUNT PILOTS
AND HOLLYWOOD'S CLASSIC AVIATION MOVIES

BY H. HUGH WYNNE

PICTORIAL HISTORIES PUBLISHING COMPANY
MISSOULA, MONTANA

LIBRARY OF CONGRESS
CATALOG CARD NUMBER 87 60073

ISBN 0-933126-85-9

First Printing: April 1987

Cover Art: James Farmer, Glendora, California
Typography: Arrow Graphics, Missoula, Montana
Layout: Stan Cohen, Missoula, Montana

PICTORIAL HISTORIES PUBLISHING COMPANY
713 South Third West, Missoula, Montana 59801

CONTENTS

Preface vi

Acknowledgments vii

I. EXHIBITION AVIATORS 1

II. THE WING WALKERS 9

III. HOLLYWOOD DOGFIGHTS 53

IV. THE ASSOCIATED MOTION PICTURE PILOTS 107

V. THE CLOSING OF AN ERA 143

Notes and References 165

Feature Films On Which The Stunt Pilots Worked 169

PREFACE

Library shelves are well stocked with books that document the contributions of the many different professions and occupations in the motion picture industry. Cameramen, writers, directors, actors, and most of the engineers, artists and technicians who work behind the cameras have been well represented, along with some of the later motion picture stunt flyers. But the work of one highly skilled group of contributors still remains hidden in obscurity. The original motion picture stunt pilots, who grew up with the industry, and invented the special techniques of motion picture flying, have been overlooked and almost forgotten. Where aviation was the theme or a significant part of the story, their work was just as important as that of any other discipline working on the picture. Without acting airplanes, the realism of yesterday's classic aviation movies would never have been achieved.

The total subject of motion picture flying, from its beginning to the present, is far too extensive to be adequately covered in one volume. Therefore this book is limited to the 1920s and 1930s, the period of the pioneer stunt flyers—the Associated Motion Picture Pilots. It ends with the end of the romantic era of aviation, which was the beginning of World War II.

The post-war work of Paul Mantz, Frank Tallman's colorful career, and the motion picture flying work of Frank Pine, Jim Appleby and others can be found in other books and publications.

While Hollywood's aviation movies are almost always saddled with technical errors*, and regardless of the term's connotation of reckless daring, "motion picture stunt flying" means highly skilled precision flying consisting of acrobatics, special stunts, camera flying and controlled crashes. It is a part of both the aviation profession and the motion picture industry, distinctly separate from the ballyhoo and hokum that permeates show business.

Motion picture stunt flying stands on merits of truth and reality, and should not be confused with the phony side of Hollywood. When forty airplanes came together over Oakland, California, in a gigantic milling dogfight for "Hell's Angels," the fact that it was only a sham battle made the danger of collision and death no less real for the men in the cockpits.

This work does not pretend to include every pilot who ever flew an airplane for a motion picture. Many pilots drifted in and out of motion picture stunt flying in the 1920s and 1930s. Some were unfortunately killed immediately, and a few worked in only one or two pictures before moving on to other careers. This book is con-

cerned with the small group of pilots who continued to fly for the studios during the 1920s and 1930s, and who were responsible for approximately 250 aviation films made during that time, which was the brightest era in Hollywood's history.

While much information in regard to motion picture flying in this period still remains to be uncovered, this is an attempt to accurately record the main events of those times, and to hopefully correct much of the false information that has become associated with some of these men.

Based on personal interviews, the story follows these events in chronological order, and wherever possible, the pilots and others are allowed to speak for themselves and describe these events in their own words.

The Associated Motion Picture Pilots lived during the times that have been defined as "Hollywood's Golden Age." Their profession appeared and thrived during the years between World War I and World War II, which may have been the best of all times in the United States of America. Society was centered around the home and family where most future citizens at least acknowledged God and were taught basic honesty, social courtesy, respect for the rights of others, the work ethic, self reliance and the pursuit of excellence. Crime, corruption, the use of drugs and sexual promiscuity existed, as they always have, but on a much smaller scale than today —and they were not being promoted as acceptable values by anti-heroes on the screen. Most Americans lived in an orderly and free society with a minimum of governmental control where front doors and automobiles seldom had to be locked. The people could enjoy their cities and parks without fear of being attacked by brutal predatory animals. And in most neighborhoods a girl could walk home alone at night in complete safety.

Society in the 1920s and 1930s wasn't perfect. No social system devised by man ever has been. But it was one of the few times in history when a society approached optimum levels of freedom, affluence and security for the majority of its members.

If this time can be called a high point in American culture, then it was reflected in its motion pictures. While the movie theater was no synagogue or church, heroines and heroes, on the screen at least, reinforced the moral characters of young people by exemplifying the higher and more civilized qualities of mankind such as honor, valor, marital integrity, respect for law and other virtues that can be found in healthy and peaceful societies.

The 1920s and 1930s were also the decades of fabric-covered airplanes, grass airfields and open cockpit flying. Aviation was still elemental and a great adventure where individual pilots challenged the mighty forces of nature with their frail flying machines. In an atmosphere where ordinary flying was still considered to be dangerous, and where any aviator was regarded as an extraordinary man, the motion picture stunt pilots stood as extraordinary aviators. Gifted with the marvelous coordination of champion athletes, and a calm courage that allowed them to risk their lives again and again, their exceptional sense of timing told them the exact split second in which to make their moves in situations where the slightest hesitation or anticipation meant losing more than just a game.

Aviators were heroes to many young people who eagerly watched the coming attractions at the local theater for the next aviation movie to come from Hollywood. Many of the pilots, engineers and executives in commercial and military aviation today can trace their flying interest back to the airplane films of the 1930s, and the thrills provided by the motion picture stunt pilots.

---

*It seems strange that film producers will faithfully and expensively produce ancient sailing ships, reconstruct the architecture of Babylon, Egypt, Greece and Rome, but fail in historical accuracy when it comes to aviation—particularly in aircraft types, markings and armament of World War I airplanes.

ACKNOWLEDGMENTS

The privilege of personal contact with some of the men who were first-hand participants in and directly responsible for many of the events described herein was enriched by their warm extensions of hospitality during the long period of research. Homes, memories and photograph collections were freely opened, turning that part of the work into pleasant periods of recreation. Grateful thanks are extended to the following ladies and gentlemen, whose kind cooperation and generosity made the recording of this special segment of aviation and motion picture history possible.

Howard and Rosemary Batt
Dick Grace
Garland and Pauline Lincoln
Harry and Fern Perry
Jerry Phillips
Moye Stephens
Wally and Ellen Timm
Frank and Ruth Tomick
Tave and Nettie Wilson

The following people, also related to this subject, generously furnished information and photographs which filled many gaps in the body of research. The author is indebted to: James Dunavent, artist, flyer and aviation historian for the use of photographs and transcriptions of his taped interviews with Jimmy Barton; Barney Korn, engineer and master craftsman who built many of the miniatures used in "Hell's Angels"; Leo Stratton Nomis, the son of Leo Nomis and a courageous military flyer in his own right; Gloria Dyer Seaver, daughter of Elmer Dyer, who still carries on with his film library; and G. Lawrence Hensey, nephew of the famous Al Wilson.

Additional aid was kindly given by William C. Aldridge, "Dusty" Carter, Sandra Duncan, Mrs. Elmer Dyer, K.O. Eckland, Robert G. Elliott, James Farmer, John M. Kennedy, Dr. Robert Knutson, Stacy and Ray McCullough, Marian McCarty, Owen McGrath, Nina Melcon, Art Ronnie, Arch C. Wallen, the Cecil B. DeMille Trust, the Academy of Motion Picture Arts and Sciences Library, the U.S.C. Library Special Collections, the U.C.L.A. Theater Arts Library, the Culver City Public Library, the Santa Monica Public Library, and the Los Angeles Public Library.

The photographs appearing herein were made available by the individuals and institutions noted and are not a part of the author's copyright.

The motion picture stunt pilots at the home of Florence "Pancho" Barnes in San Marino, Calif., on January 5, 1932, when they officially organized as the ASSOCIATED MOTION PICTURE PILOTS. Standing from the left: Earl Robinson, Frank Clarke, Garland Lincoln, Roy Wilson, Jack Rand, Howard Batt, Clinton Herberger, Oliver LeBoutillier, Ira Reed and three union representatives. Seated from the left: Earl Gordon, Dick Grace, Al Wilson, Florence Barnes, Tave Wilson, Dick Rinaldi and Joe Touhey, a public relations man. Leo Nomis and Frank Tomick were also charter members of the organization though absent from this meeting. Courtesy: Garland Lincoln

CHAPTER ONE
EXHIBITION AVIATORS

Glenn Martin, in center, with Mary Pickford and an unidentified actor in a scene from "The Girl Of Yesterday." Courtesy: First American Title Co., Santa Ana

WHILE THE AEROPLANE was still a powered box kite, and newspaper writers used the verb aviate, some obscure motion picture pioneer devised a situation that would involve his characters with a flying machine. A forgotten aviator was hired to pursue the villain, dive on the outlaw's hideout, or don a fierce mustache to become the villain himself and take off with the struggling heroine. This first time that the aeroplane appeared before the motion picture camera in an acting capacity technically marked the beginning of motion picture stunt flying.

Aeroplanes performed for motion picture cameras as early as 1905[1], if not sooner. The first aviator, producer and film title may never be identified because most early films no longer exist. But with a potential for comedy, peril and spectacle situations, the aeroplane became widely used in motion picture work and the unique profession of motion picture stunt flying was created.

Several years after the Wright Brothers historic flight, exhibition flying for audience entertainment was still considered by many to be the only practical use of the aeroplane. Even after designers produced machines that were capable of military and commercial functions, exhibition flying continued to develop separately from the mainstream of aviation. Exhibition aviators dominated the major air meets that began at Rheims, France, in 1909. John Moisant, a Chicago architect turned sportsman flyer, led a group of aviators on the first exhibition flying tour of the United States in 1910. Lincoln Beachey, a former exhibition balloonist, was the most daring of the stunt flyers who first capitalized on the show-business side of aviation. In a primitive Curtiss Pusher, he looped, rolled, flew upside down, plucked handkerchiefs off the ground with his wing tip, and brought cheering crowds to their feet with his vertical "death dive," which began at 5,000 feet and levelled off just above the ground in front of the grandstand.

The motion picture stunt pilots came from this general category of exhibition aviators. They grew up with the motion picture industry itself, in that part of Southern California defined by meteorologists as the Los Angeles Basin.

A rare combination of geographical features peculiar to that part of the Golden State produced the most comfortable climate in the nation, and attracted pioneer aviators as well as the early film companies. Mountains, deserts and the sea, all within one day's travel time from Los Angeles, offered the motion picture companies a variety of location backgrounds. Open pastures and fields with sparse tree coverage provided unlimited emergency landing fields for primitive temperamental engines. But the main attraction for both cameras and flying machines was an average annual 340 days of sunshine.

The first of many motion picture companies arrived in Los Angeles during the winter of 1907-1908[2]. Two years later the world's second international air meet took place at Aviation Park on the Dominguez Ranch, fifteen miles south of downtown Los Angeles. For ten days thousands of spectators witnessed daring, for the time, flights and maneuvers that established new altitude, speed and distance records. Enthusiastic magazine and newspaper reporters proclaimed to the world that aviation was here to stay. Motion pictures of the event were distributed among larger cities of the nation and Los Angeles was firmly established as an aviation center.[3]

Flying activity increased at Aviation Park. With the success of the 1910 air meet, organizers planned a second event and a flying school soon appeared. By January 1912 it was known as Dominguez Field and served as a base for twenty-four aeroplanes.[4] Film companies continued to move west for the good photographic conditions, and to escape the severe winters of New York and Chicago.[5] Thus the nucleus of two giant industries appeared in Southern California at the same time, and out of both came the unique discipline of motion picture stunt flying. Though film companies continued to operate in New York, and a few aviation scenes were filmed in that area with local aviators,[6] the main part of the industry, with its motion picture stunt flying spin-off, shifted to Southern California.

The first aviation incidents to appear in the locally made comedies, serials and novelties, which was the usual motion picture fare of the time, were photographed at Dominguez Field. Biograph released "A Dash Through The Clouds" in 1912, a comedy in which Mabel Normand flew in a Wright Model B aeroplane with an unidentified pilot. Mack Sennett used aeroplanes in several comedies including "The Sky Pirate," "Dizzy Heights and Daring Hearts," and "Saved by Wireless." Phillip Parmalee and Clifford Turpin worked for the Wrights at this time, and one of them probably flew the Wright Model B's used by Biograph and Sennett.

When the Griffith Air Field, located in the northeast corner of Griffith Park, was established in 1913, a second location for motion picture flying was available. Glenn Martin opened a flying school at the Griffith field, and performed as an actor and as a pilot in the 1915 Mary Pickford film, "The Girl of Yesterday." Lincoln Beachey and Frank Stites, a local aviator who learned to fly at Dominguez Field, flew for various film companies at this location, in addition to the one at Dominguez Field.

Various pastures and fields around the small city of Los Angeles served as aviation locales, in addition to the air fields at Dominguez Ranch and Griffith Park. The aviation activity was minor, and the aviators who

A suspended mockup aeroplane is photographed against a live background for a scene in the Mack Sennett comedy, "Saved by Wireless." Courtesy: UCLA Theater Arts Library

maneuvered their machines for these early films were not yet motion picture stunt pilots. A take-off, fly-by, and landing scene or two, mixed with closeups of the actors in crude flying machine mock-ups, was the usual extent of motion picture flying until after World War I. The young film companies hired the nearest aviator for a one- or two-time appearance, and then the flyer returned to his primary business of aviation.

The first flyers who can be called motion picture stunt pilots appeared among the exhibition flyers at Venice, California. An examination of stunt flying at this beach resort shows how some of these flyers drifted into the business of flying for the motion picture studios, and reveals the origin of the profession.

Located on the coast about fifteen miles southwest of downtown Los Angeles, and with canals and gondolas like its Italian namesake, Venice was a famous resort area with amusement piers and wide beaches that made it a popular location for conventions, vacations and picnics. Even before the first aeroplane arrived in Southern California, the Venice amusement pier owners hired exhibition balloonists to stimulate business. When exhibition flying appeared in Los Angeles, the early exhibition aviators came to Venice for the readily available audience of several thousand beach patrons.

There was no air field at Venice when Charles F. Walsh contracted with the Windward Avenue Pier for a series of exhibition flights in 1911. The local newspaper reported, "Ground is to be looked over in the next few days for a suitable place for the machine to make its ascensions."[7] But Walsh wrecked his machine at Dominguez Field while performing maneuvers for an Interna-

tional Pilot's License and never fulfilled this engagement.[8]

Advertisements then announced that the huge captive balloon "Peoria," with a capacity of forty-five passengers, would make ascensions from the Windward Avenue Pier. But when the owner, W.M. Morton, tested his balloon, the prevailing sea breeze moved the large bag so far inland that its cable touched the roof of a building across the street from the hoist.[9] The engagement was canceled.

Frank Champion made an exhibition flight over Venice in the autumn of 1911. He flew a Bleriot monoplane from Dominguez Field, executed dives, dips and spirals over the beach crowd, circled several naval ships anchored in Santa Monica Bay, and returned to his base at Dominguez. The Venice Daily Vanguard prophetically noted that Champion's flight indicated that the mighty warship was now vulnerable from the air.[10]

Well-known exhibition flyers Phillip Parmalee and Clifford Turpin dominated the first part of the 1912 beach season with a Curtiss Hydroplane. After each day's demonstration flight, passengers bought tickets for sight seeing rides, and entered the flying boat from the surf line at the Windward Avenue Pier.[11]

Competition soon appeared in Santa Monica, the neighboring city north of Venice. The Santa Monica Chamber of Commerce hired Frank Stites to perform a series of stunts over the Ocean Park beach area, which lay within the Santa Monica city limits. Stites landed on and took off from the beach sand along the surf line at the Fraser Pier. As an added feature, Gladys "Tiny" Broadwick made parachute drops from a balloon which

A Wright Model B aeroplane is suspended on wires for this scene in the Mack Sennett comedy "Dizzy Heights and Daring Hearts." The actor stands on top of a chimney mockup that rests on a rolling platform. As the chimney top is rolled beneath the stationary aeroplane, the actor grabs the undercarriage and the camera records the actor apparently being plucked from a stationary chimney by a passing aeroplane. Courtesy: UCLA Theater Arts Library

was fulfilling a separate engagement at the Fraser Pier.[12]

Parmalee and Turpin took their hydroplane back to San Diego, returned with a land plane, and countered Stites' performance with a parachute jumping stunt. The jumper was balloonist W.M. Morton, who sat on a seat beneath the pilot and between the two skids, with a large parachute folded in his arms. The first attempt failed when a large wave drenched Morton and his parachute as Parmalee made a takeoff run along the surf line where the sand was the hardest.[13] They succeeded a few days later when Morton jumped from approximately two thousand feet altitude. A speed boat cruised the bay to retrieve the jumper, but the wind carried Morton inland where his shroud lines caught on an electrical line, leaving him suspended ten feet in the air.[14]

The next exhibition aviator to visit Venice was Clodion Mulas, a French flyer who came to Judge Carrillo's (the father of actor Leo Carrillo) court to learn of any restrictive ordinances the city had in regard to stunt flying. He was informed by city authorities that Venice encouraged navigation of the air in general, and flights at the beach in particular.[15]

Aeroplane flights became a normal event for the 1912 season at Venice and the novelty soon disappeared. Parmalee, Turpin and Morton left for an extended tour of Canada.[16] Frank Stites went to Long Beach, where he entertained the crowds with dips, spirals, and "death dives."[17]

Balloonist Edward Unger then made a series of ascensions and parachute drops from the Fraser Pier, and organized a balloon race at the end of summer. Several days later the Fraser Pier and many buildings in the Ocean Park area were destroyed by fire. When the flames threatened his balloon, Unger cut it loose, but recovered the undamaged bag and basket several hours later after its dangling ropes wrapped around the trolley line between San Dimas and Pomona.[18]

While they were performing at Venice, Stites and Parmalee made frequent trips to Dominguez Field for the maintenance facilities there. For their local base of operations, they and other aviators who visited Venice used what was then called the Machado[19] field. This vacant agricultural plot was adjacent to Tiger Park, the local baseball field, which was located on the southwest corner of Washington and Venice boulevards.

Glenn Martin landed at the Machado field during the first part of 1913 while making a round-trip publicity flight from Pomona to San Diego.[20] Military aviators and students from the Curtiss School at North Island in San Diego always included the Machado field in their cross-country training flight itineraries, to be assured of an evening at the Venice amusement piers.

The Machado field became a fixed base of operations when Frank Stites returned to Venice and made a series of exhibition flights in the spring of 1914. A small shed on the field was the first hangar, which Stites used to repair his aeroplane after it was damaged by a forced landing in the surf.[21]

When Stites completed repairs on the machine of his own design, he resumed his exhibition flights over the beach. He mastered the technique of heading into a stiff sea breeze, and hovering almost motionless over the beach crowds. He devised a parachute jumping stunt with Rose Arnold, a local teen-ager, and the young girl made a successful test jump over the Machado field. But she was injured in a subsequent takeoff accident, and never made the jump in public.[22]

The Machado field became the Venice Flying Field some time after May 1914, when the Schiller Aviation School moved its operations from Dominguez Field to Venice. The Schiller School taught aeroplane construction as well as navigation of the air. Schiller erected a large building to house the school's facilities, which became the main hangar for the Venice Flying Field.[23]

Thomas J. Hill, one of the instructors at the Schiller School, performed dives and spirals for a motion picture company at the end of summer in 1914. The film title is unknown, but this appears to be the beginning of aviation stunts for motion picture purposes at the Venice Flying Field.[24]

Complex aeroplane stunts that were invented to fit story situations, as opposed to the exhibition stunts performed by Lincoln Beachey and others for live audiences, appeared on motion picture screens in 1914. Charles Gaemon, an early stunt man, is reported to have made the first aeroplane-to-train transfer during the filming of Mutual's "Out Of The Air," which was released in 1915.[25]

Frank Stites performed a bombing stunt for Universal at the Griffith field some time in 1915. He flew over an aeroplane mock-up, which was suspended on cables and loaded with explosives. The charge was ignited to coincide with the arrival of a dummy bomb dropped from Stites' machine. The aviator flew victoriously away after having apparently destroyed the other machine with a bomb.

Carl Laemmle and other executives were impressed with the resulting scene and decided to have the stunt repeated as part of the grand opening ceremonies at Universal City, Laemmle's new studio complex just north of Hollywood.

A few weeks before this event, Stites did some work for D.W. Griffith's "Hearts Of The World" at Dominguez Field (the air scenes were edited out of the final picture),[26] and probably would have continued with aerial motion picture work if he had lived.

While Stites prepared for the Universal City opening, Lincoln Beachey was killed at the Panama-Pacific Exposition in San Francisco. Beachey was performing acrobatics in a monoplane when the wings collapsed. He fell into San Francisco Bay and drowned before rescue boats could reach the wreckage.

Two days later, on March 17, 1915, five hundred guests assembled for the grand opening festivities at Universal City. Frank Stites took off from a field on Universal's back lot at 4:15 p.m., at the close of the rodeo events. He headed for Lankersheim, later named North Hollywood, and turned back to Universal City at a height of two thousand feet. He dived on the explosive loaded dummy aeroplane which hung on wires two hundred feet above a ravine. The explosive man was not ready. Stites climbed, circled Lankersheim again and dived on his dummy adversary. This time the explosive charge was detonated, but Stites was only fifty feet above the static aeroplane. His machine staggered, and turned nose down, out of control. He frantically tugged at the controls, but the machine continued down in an awkward spiral. Stites left his seat, climbed through the rigging and jumped from a lower wing just before the aeroplane hit the bottom of the ravine. He was rushed to the Universal City hospital, but the motion picture stunt flying career of Frank Stites ended when he died a few minutes later.[27]

If there is a category for the first professional motion picture stunt pilot, that distinction belongs to Al Wilson, who started his flying career at Venice. He was the first member of the group that later became the Associated Motion Picture Pilots to fly for a film company, and was also the first man of that group to become a pilot.

Al Wilson was born in Kentucky in 1895. Around the

turn of the century, his family moved to Southern California, where his father and two older brothers established a large jewelry store on Spring Street in downtown Los Angeles.

A daring nature was apparent in Al Wilson's early childhood. He often climbed high trees. After several falls resulting in broken arms on three different occasions, he continued to climb trees.

During the summer of 1913 he built an aeroplane, with the help of a friend, in the backyard of the Wilson home in Ocean Park. It resembled a Curtiss Pusher and was powered with a worn-out four cylinder engine they obtained from a farmer in Santa Monica. Al Wilson flew this machine at the end of summer, but could rise no higher than fifty feet. Each time he tried to turn, the crude flying machine came down hard with major structural damage to the frame. When it could no longer be repaired, the two young men abandoned their dreams of exhibition flying and sold the wreck to one of the film companies where it was suspended on wires and used as a prop.[28]

After doing odd jobs and a few minor acting roles for the film companies then settling around Hollywood and the Santa Monica Bay area, Al Wilson built the first wind machines used in the motion picture industry. With aeroplane propellers attached to automobile engines mounted on portable frames, he rented these windmills to create artificial wind, sand and snowstorms. When the film companies decided to build their own machines, he worked for his brother Herbert, who was now an optician and jeweler in Ocean Park. But the adventurous younger brother was drawn back to flying, and quit the jewelry business in 1914 when the Schiller School moved from Dominguez Field to Venice. Al Wilson obtained a maintenance job with Schiller for $7.00 a week and the privilege of practicing on the school's Bleriot machines.[29]

The Schiller School used the French method of flight instruction where the student was always alone in the machine. The instructor explained the controls to the student, who then practiced with the throttle fixed to allow the machine only enough power to taxi on the ground. After he was able to handle the controls on the ground, the throttle was adjusted to allow the machine to fly a few feet above the ground for a short distance. As the student mastered the controls and gained confidence, he was allowed to fly a little higher and farther until he learned the basic maneuvers. Graduation came after an altitude and cross-country flight.

Al Wilson worked for Schiller until a flying school at Riverside, California, obtained one of the new Curtiss biplanes. Under the instruction of "Swede" Meyerhofer, he completed his flight training at Riverside, and obtained a certificate from the Aero Club of America.

When Al Wilson returned to Venice, the Crawford-Saunders Aeroplane Company had leased the three land parcels on which the Venice Flying Field was located. It was now referred to as the Crawford-Saunders Field. The American Aircraft Company sub-leased a part of the field and established a flying school with Al Wilson as its chief instructor.[30]

In order to stimulate his students, Al Wilson performed acrobatic maneuvers over the field, thereby joining the elite group of aviators who went beyond the standard practice of straight and level flight.

Herbert Wilson, who was interested in the technical side of aviation, built a two-seat monoplane patterned after the Bleriot design. With Al as the pilot, the two brothers rented this machine to film companies on several different occasions. This was the beginning of Al Wilson's motion picture stunt flying career.[31]

As the First World War gathered momentum in Europe, aircraft design developed rapidly and the military flying hero appeared. Military aeroplanes, which were little more than a collection of various civilian types being utilized for scouting purposes in 1914, became specialized machines designed for the specific military functions of bombing, reconnaissance and fighting. Newspapers and magazines followed the daring exploits of military aviators, particularly the pursuit or fighter pilots. French reporters endowed their champions with the title "ace," after the highest playing card, and other nations soon followed this practice. A romantic aura collected around the World War I flyers, which was to supply the basic story material for the major aviation movies of the next two decades.

Along with the improvement in aircraft design, terminology also changed. The words "flying machine" and "aeroplane" were replaced in American speech and writing by "airplane."

Several films containing aviation incidents were made during America's participation in World War I. Though technically poor by today's standards, they were well received by audiences in the charged atmosphere of the time.

Thomas H. Ince released "The Zeppelin's Last Raid" in 1917. The plot was a rationalized situation where a group of Germans work against the Kaiser's war effort and enlist the aid of a Zeppelin commander who destroys his airship with dynamite.

"Berlin Via America" came out in 1918. Its highly imaginative plot took an American Secret Service agent into Germany where he conveniently became a flyer in the famous Richthofen "Flying Circus" in order to reveal upcoming German battle plans by dropping messages behind the American lines.

Bert Hall, who briefly served with the Lafayette Escadrille (a group of American volunteer aviators who fought for France before the United States entered the war), appeared on theater stages with the showing of "A Romance Of The Air." Primarily a drama, it contained newsreel scenes of military airplanes, and was supposedly based on Hall's experiences in the war.

"Flying With The Marines" was a documentary film produced by the Marine Corps. It showed flight training activities and contained several in-flight scenes where the camera was attached to the airplane and photographed the forward view as the airplane performed acrobatic maneuvers.

Some time in 1917 Al Wilson flew the Bleriot for a minor aviation sequence in Cecil B. DeMille's "We Can't Have Everything." The famous director had recently volunteered his services to the U.S. Army, but was turned down because he was over twenty-six. After a high-ranking officer informed him that the army was desperate for pilots, and that he would have a better chance if he knew how to fly, DeMille engaged Al Wilson as his flying instructor.[32]

Venice based aviators. This area later became Clover Field, and then the Santa Monica Municipal Airport.

Cecil B. DeMille became an accomplished pilot under Al Wilson's instruction and then took additional training from a military pilot. The war ended before his commission was issued by the army, but it was not the end of Cecil B. DeMille's career in aviation.

During the spring of 1918, a balloonist developed a parachute device at the Crawford-Saunders Field, in hopes of aiding the war effort. The system consisted of a large parachute that was packed in a bomb shaped container, and fired vertically from a mortar attached directly to the airplane. When the container reached the end of the shroud lines, which were attached to the airplane, a second charge exploded the housing, and a large parachute canopy opened to save the airplane. A smaller parachute was carried by the pilot in case the larger parachute failed.[34] Coordination of the various stages caused too many problems and the device was never perfected.

Another threat to the German war effort appeared a few weeks later when one of the flying instructors at

The Bleriot type monoplane built by Herbert Wilson as it appeared in "We Can't Have Everything." Al Wilson landed on and took off from the beach at Venice for this scene in the film. Mr. DeMille can be seen just below the rear seat control wheel, wearing a hat. Courtesy: Cecil B. DeMille Trust

With little spare time available from his responsibilities as the production head of a large studio, Cecil B. DeMille was never late for appointments. After driving all the way to Venice one morning, he was naturally disturbed to find that Al Wilson's part of the air field had been completely plowed in preparation for agricultural planting. A dispute erupted between Al Wilson and Harry Crawford, but it was eventually determined that Al Wilson's section of the field was not a part of the Crawford- Saunders lease, and had been legally rented from the Machado Estate by a Japanese farmer.[33]

DeMille completed his flight training at a large field three miles northeast of the Venice field, which was often used as an auxiliary landing and take-off area by the

Venice announced a camouflage scheme to confound the best eyes of the enemy. He proposed to cover an airplane with shiny aluminum, which would cause it to become a silvery blur in flight, thereby making observation by enemy eyes nearly impossible.[35]

Exhibition flying was curtailed in most parts of the country during World War I. Venice escaped this restriction for some reason as flying continued at the Crawford-Saunders Field. The Venice Chamber of Commerce hired Al Wilson to perform dives, loops and spins over the beach area as part of the Independence Day celebration on July 4, 1918.[36]

Just before the Armistice was signed, an unusual event took place over an Air Service training field in Texas; it was to influence exhibition flying in general, and motion picture stunt flying in particular. While flying at an altitude of several thousand feet, Lt. Ormer Locklear, an instructor who had developed a wing-walking act to encourage recruiting for the Air Service, climbed down to the undercarriage of a Curtiss JN-4 training plane, and dropped to the top wing of another plane flying several feet below.[37] This was the first time in the world that anyone had transferred from one airplane to another while in flight, and it opened the way for many daring motion picture stunts of the 1920s.

Looking north over the Venice Flying Field in 1918. The Fraser Pier can be seen at the top left. The Venice piers are out of the picture at the left. Courtesy: Frank Tomick

Looking east over the Venice field in the early 1920s when it was known as DeLay Field. The hangar has been relocated from its 1918 position. Courtesy: Frank Tomick

The Venice piers in the early 1920s. The triangular shape of the Venice field can be seen at the top left. Residential development has begun to take over that part of the field across the trolley tracks. Courtesy: Frank Tomick

CHAPTER TWO
THE WING WALKERS

Al Wilson struggles with the bad guy while Frank Tomick rescues the girl. A splintered prop has replaced the Jenny's good propeller as it rests on its nose in a previously dug hole. Courtesy: G. Lawrence Hensey

WHEN THE WAR ended, hundreds of pilots were discharged from the military services, and several hundred surplus training aircraft were dumped on the open market at low prices. Many of the young men who had learned to fly during the war bought these affordable airplanes and traveled across the nation, earning a few dollars from the sale of sight-seeing rides in the air. Known as barnstormers,[38] they appeared at state and county fairs, race tracks, amusement parks, and eventually flew from any cow pasture where a group of spectators could be assembled. Noted more for courage than for contributions to commercial aviation or achievements in aircraft design, these gypsy pilots performed stunts to attract their customers, and brought elementary aviation to the small town and rural areas of the nation. Performing barnstormers gave their audiences a taste for aviation stunts, and thereby opened a market for increasing numbers of flying stunts in Hollywood films.

The Curtiss JN-4, nicknamed "Jenny," was the most common military aircraft offered for sale as war surplus. It was a wood-and-fabric, two-seat biplane designed for training. But, as one of the stunt pilots observed, with a cruising speed of only sixty miles per hour, a narrow fuselage that a man could easily straddle, and a maze of wing struts, bracing wires, wing skids and top wing king posts, it seems to have been designed for stunt work.

Ormer Locklear remained in the army for a while after November 11, 1918, but soon resigned to take his plane-changing act on a tour of the larger cities in the nation. He was widely known for in-flight transfers, and for climbing and crawling all over a Curtiss Jenny while in flight. By the spring of 1919, Locklear was the leading aviation stunt man in the world,[39] and pioneered most of the aviation stunts that appeared on motion picture screens during the 1920s.

Southern California continued to develop as a major aviation center. Cecil B. DeMille established the Mercury Aviation Company and DeMille Field on forty leased acres of land at the corner of Melrose and Crescent (later named Fairfax) during the first part of 1919. With Al Wilson as vice president and general manager, Mercury Aviation hired additional pilots and offered flying instruction, sight-seeing rides, advertising flights, and charter trips to neighboring cities. In addition to the studio where DeMille worked (the Lasky Company which later became Paramount), other motion picture companies soon came to DeMille Field for airplanes and pilots when they had stories with aviation incidents.

While looking for surplus aircraft at North Island in San Diego, Cecil B. DeMille and Al Wilson offered employment to a young Air Service mechanic who was also an enlisted pilot. Garland Lincoln immediately applied for a discharge and joined Mercury Aviation as a mechanic and alternate pilot.[40] While not entering motion picture flying at this time, he gained later recognition as one of the more prominent motion picture pilots, and contracted with the studios to furnish airplanes and pilots for many aviation movies.

Garland E. Lincoln was born in Ukiah, California, on October 28, 1899. His grandfather was a cousin of Abraham Lincoln. His father, a building contractor, moved the family to Southern California during the economic boom of 1910, where the young Garland Lincoln saw Lincoln Beachey perform. Smitten with a love for flying, he skipped school to hang around the air fields and look for ways to become an aviator. His own words give the best description of his early flying career:

"I entered aviation at the age of twelve during the air shows of 1912 and 1913, which were held at Dominguez Field, and later at Ascot Park, which was located at Florence and Central Avenues in Los Angeles. Since there were few air fields as such at that time, the aviators often flew from cow pastures. For obvious reasons, the undersides of the wings and sometimes the aviator himself needed cleaning. Performing this task for Lincoln Beachey was my first job in aviation.

"Another responsibility of mine was to move the airplanes out into the sun about two hours before a flight. In those days fabric on the wings and tail surfaces was doped with a mixture of formaldehyde and glue. During the night moisture loosened this concoction and the fabric sagged loosely by morning. A crowd always gathered before a flight, and the aviator, who was a showman and quite conscious of his audience, would critically tap the fabric all over the machine. He would carefully note the position of the sun and instruct me to turn the aircraft a few inches this way or that so the sun's rays would be exactly perpendicular to the surface in need of drying.

"Glenn Martin had a flying school in the Griffith Park area near Hollywood, and I was employed there in the maintenance of aircraft. I became quite a specialist at repairing punctured tires which resulted from the many cactus in the area. I used a steel forked rod with a cross bar that was wrapped with rubber bands. The rubber bands were painted with rubber cement and the fork was inserted through the cut in the tire. The rubber bands were pulled loose from the cross bar and the forked rod was pulled from the tire. After the cement had set the excess rubber was trimmed. The tires were single ply with no inner tube.

"About the time of the San Francisco Exposition of 1915 I was employed as a roustabout with Langley Airship Productions at Ascot Park. Two lighter-than-air ships were being built for Marshall Nielan to be used on a scheduled airline between San Francisco and Los Angeles. Only one flight was ever made to San Francisco and it took twenty-seven days.

"I joined the Aviation Section of the Army Signal Corps at North Island on December 27, 1917. I became one of several roving trouble shooters who traveled on motorcycles to downed aircraft in need of repair. I was given flying instruction from time to time and soloed while at North Island."[41]

According to Garland Lincoln, one of Al Wilson's first students at DeMille Field was Frank Clark, a nineteen-year-old cowboy fresh from the ranch.[42] Other sources indicate that Clark learned to fly at Venice under the instruction of "Swede" Meyerhofer. Whatever the exact truth may be about his flying lessons, Frank Clark can be definitely placed at DeMille Field during its beginning. He is easily recognized in a photograph that appeared in the May 11, 1919, issue of the Los Angeles Examiner, showing Cecil B. DeMille, Al Wilson and the new group of pilots hired by Mercury Aviation.

Frank Clark was born in Paso Robles, California, on December 29, 1898. Handsome and proud of his part Cherokee heritage, he was considered to be a man's man by his fellow stunt pilots. His family moved to a ranch in the central part of California, east of Fresno, where he grew up with horses and cattle. Frank Clark was blessed with an uncanny sense of coordination and courage that enabled him to excel at roping and riding. Had he not turned to aviation, this athletic potential could have developed into championship rodeo. He was content with a future in ranching until he saw an exhibition aviator at the Fresno County Fair in 1915. With a strong determination to become a flyer, he forgot all about cattle and moved to Los Angeles at the end of World War I.

Frank Clark's flying ability fell into that category frequently described as "natural born," where the control stick and rudder bar were almost physiological extensions of his arms and legs. He became one of the most daring and most famous of the motion picture stunt pilots.

DeMille Field was the base of operations for the first motion picture to feature a major aviation stunt. While it was not an aviation picture, and other films had included lesser aviation stunts, this was the most spectacular stunt attempted so far.

One incident in the script of "The Grim Game" called for the star, Harry Houdini, to climb down a knotted rope attached to the front mid-wing strut of one airplane, drop to the top wing of another machine flying just below, and make his way to the rear cockpit. When the stunt was filmed, it went contrary to the plan and turned out to be one of the most exciting air stunts ever recorded on film.

Word of the plane-changing job passed around local aviation circles as the Lasky Company searched for a stunt man to double for Houdini. No one responded because several stunt men had already been killed at air shows while trying to duplicate Locklear's famous stunt. Robert E. Kennedy, a former lieutenant and flying instructor in the Air Service, applied for the dangerous job and immediately received a contract.

The studio rented three DeMille airplanes and pilots,

and scheduled the flight for the calm air of early morning on May 31, 1919. Maintenance problems and a delay in mounting the camera held things up until after lunch. Finally three airplanes took off in the early afternoon. David E. Thompson and Christopher Pickup flew the stunt planes. Al Wilson piloted the camera plane with Irving Willat, the director-cameraman, riding in the back seat with his camera. They headed west into the prevailing wind and climbed to about 2500 feet.

In compliance with the flight plan, Pickup, with Kennedy aboard, flew straight and level while Thompson, with less weight and wind resistance, and better visibility in the lower machine, moved into position fifteen feet directly below. Al Wilson maintained a steady camera platform position to the left, and in line with the performing machines, so that neither his tail section nor wing tip appeared in the camera's field of vision.

By this time of day the air was rough and it was difficult for the pilots to maintain their positions. The three airplanes flew around for several minutes before Kennedy climbed down the knotted rope. The space separating the two machines varied from six to twenty feet as they bounced in the rough air. At one time Kennedy came very close to Thompson's whirling propeller, and had to double up his legs to prevent them from being ground to bits. Just before Kennedy released the rope to drop on Thompson's top wing, a gust or air pocket caused the two planes to collide. Thompson's wing tore into Pickup's landing gear and the two Jennies were entangled. Thompson's plane turned upside down and swung around until it was almost nose to nose with Pickup's machine. The pilots cut their engines as the shattered wooden propellers threw bits of wood, metal and fabric around the sky. With no parachutes the three flyers fell toward certain death as the enmeshed airplanes continued down in a flat spin. Kennedy dangled in space at the end of the rope while Thompson and Pickup frantically worked their controls in hopes of dislodging the two airplanes. Kennedy closed his eyes and waited for the inevitable end.

Suddenly Kennedy was aware of a change in the forces acting on his body and a difference in the speed of the descent. He opened his eyes. Approximately one thousand feet above the ground, the centrifugal force of the spin miraculously separated the two airplanes and the pilots regained control. Thompson's plane came down at 26th Street and Santa Monica Canyon, where it flipped over on its back. Pickup's machine, dragging Kennedy along the ground still clutching the knotted rope, landed in a bean field at 18th Street and San Vicente Boulevard in Santa Monica. Hundreds of spectators in the streets below watched the stunt and collision. A crowd soon gathered at both landing sites, but

Ormer Locklear demonstrates some of the stunts he invented while in the Air Service, on a Curtiss JN-4 "Jenny" piloted by Milton "Skeets" Elliott. Courtesy: U.S. Air Force

they could hardly believe that the only injuries suffered in the whole incident were a few bruises and abrasions inflicted on Kennedy as he tumbled in the dirt.

Willat recorded the spontaneous incident on film and the studio revised the script to include the mid-air collision. "The Grim Game" drew turn-away crowds when it was released in the fall of 1919.[43]

Unfortunately, show business hokum entered the situation and all publicity connected with the film's release led everyone to believe that Houdini, instead of the daring Kennedy, was at the end of the rope. Kennedy contacted the district attorney of Los Angeles County, but

was informed that he would have to file a civil suit since it was not a criminal matter. Lacking the necessary wealth for a prolonged legal battle, Kennedy declined this course of action.

After several barnstorming tours of Texas, Robert E. Kennedy joined with members of a Los Angeles-based bus company, Pickwick Transportation, in the formation of Pickwick Airways. Flying tri-motors, the new airline pioneered air routes into Mexico until Pickwick was absorbed by a larger airline. Kennedy continued flying until he went to work for Douglas Aircraft in 1934. After retirement, he lived in Anaheim until his death in 1973.[44]

Cecil B. DeMille at DeMille Field No. 2 in 1921. Courtesy: Cecil B. DeMille Trust

Looking north from the intersection (at extreme right) of Wilshire Boulevard and Crescent Avenue (later named Fairfax) in 1921. Chaplin Field is in the foreground, and DeMille Field No. 2 is across Wilshire to the north. Courtesy: Cecil B. DeMille Trust

Kennedy climbs down the knotted rope toward Thompson's top wing for the plane changing stunt in "The Grim Game."

As the airplanes are buffeted by the unstable air, Kennedy lifts his feet to avoid contact with Thompson's propeller.

After the collision, Kennedy dangles in space at the end of the rope as the airplanes start to descend. Courtesy: Marian McCarty

David E. Thompson after his crash landing on May 31, 1919. Courtesy: Cecil B. DeMille Trust

Robert E. Kennedy, standing behind actress Ann Forrest, expresses the joy of being alive. Standing along Pickup's damaged wing are from the left, after Miss Forrest, David E. Thompson, unidentified, Christopher E. Pickup, Al Wilson, Irving Willat, and unidentified. Courtesy: Cecil B. DeMille Trust

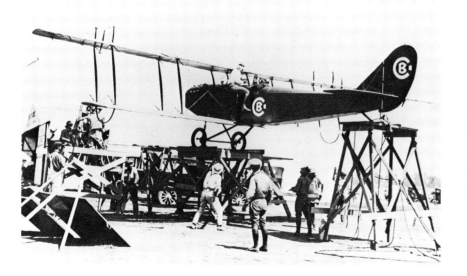

A scene from "The Great Air Robbery" being performed at DeMille Field No. 1. Though Locklear performed several stunts in the air, it was easier to film closeups on the ground. While Locklear confronts the pilot, the camera aims just above any trees or buildings in the background while prop men pull on the wing tips to simulate motion in the air. Courtesy: Cecil B. DeMille Trust

A closeup of Locklear on the wing of a DeMille Jenny during the filming of "The Great Air Robbery." Courtesy: Cecil B. DeMille Trust

Noting the financial success of "The Grim Game," Carl Laemmle foresaw the motion picture possibilities of Locklear and decided to make an aviation film with the famous stunt flyer in the leading role. With a story written around several wing-walking and plane-changing incidents, and the offer of a generous fee, Locklear signed a contract. Universal leased the facilities and airplanes at DeMille Field, and work began in July 1919. As head cameraman, Milton Moore went up in a Jenny to photograph the air scenes. He was assisted by a young cameraman named Elmer Dyer, who became a leading aerial photographer during the 1930s.

The plot revolves around Larry Cassidy, played by Locklear, the U.S. Air Mail's best pilot, and the activities of a society crook who secretly leads a band of aerial pirates, the Death Head Squadron.

Locklear's first aerial transfer takes place in the first part of the picture when he goes up with another pilot and changes to the airplane of a fellow air mail pilot who has become an alcoholic and is unable to make a safe landing. In a chase situation where a low-flying airplane matches the speed of a fleeing automobile, Locklear hung from the plane's landing gear and dropped into the back seat of an open car driven by the villain. After a brief struggle in which the stunt man driver was thrown from the car, Locklear grabbed the undercarriage of the hovering Jenny just as the speeding automobile overturned.[45]

Originally titled "Cassiday Of The Air Lanes," the completed film reached the theaters at the end of 1919 as "The Great Air Robbery." The first aviation feature film of any importance was a financial success and opened the door for additional features with an aviation theme.

Facilities for motion picture flying increased when Mercury Aviation expanded and DeMille Field No. 2 appeared on the northwest corner of Wilshire Boulevard and Crescent Avenue. Within a few weeks Emory Rogers and Syd Chaplin, the brother of Charlie Chaplin, opened Chaplin Field directly across the street. The intersection of Wilshire and Crescent now challenged Venice as the aviation center of Los Angeles.

With a recognition of aviation's potential, and extensive real estate holdings in the Santa Monica Bay area, motion picture producer Thomas H. Ince purchased the Crawford-Saunders Field. In an effort to counteract the competition from DeMille and Chaplin Fields, Ince offered a $50,000.00 prize for the first trans-Pacific flight that used Venice as a starting point. With B.H. DeLay as manager, the Crawford-Saunders Field was named the Thomas H. Ince Aviation Field in August 1919. The prize stimulated several attempts, but each one failed and Ince eventually withdrew his offer.

Al Wilson resigned from Mercury Aviation and resumed his career as an exhibition flyer. With a newly purchased Jenny he returned to Venice at the same time that brothers Otto, Wally and Reuben Timm arrived there from San Diego.[46] While Otto worked on an aircraft of his own design at the Ince Aviation Field, Wally Timm did maintenance work for Al Wilson in exchange for flying lessons. Reuben Timm was an exhibition parachute jumper, but his career ended prematurely with a fatal case of pneumonia.

Locklear returned to exhibition flying in the fall of 1919, after work on "The Great Air Robbery" was completed. While performing at the Minnesota State Fair, he met a young barnstorming flyer who was destined to play an important part in the making of aviation movies. This meeting with the famous Locklear caused Dick Grace to seek his future in Hollywood.

Richard V. Grace was born in Morris, Minnesota, on January 10, 1898. His father was a judge of the State Supreme Court, and Dick was attending the University of Minnesota when the United States entered the First World War. After joining the Naval Air Service and winning his wings at Pensacola, Dick Grace went overseas and served in France and Italy. When the war was over he returned to college, but found the pursuit of a legal career too tame. With a war surplus airplane, he worked the state of Minnesota as a barnstormer until the machine was damaged beyond repair. He arrived in Hollywood during the summer of 1920 and found work at the Fox Film Corporation as a stunt man. He dived from cliffs and burning buildings, leaped from speeding automobiles, and performed many other general motion picture stunts before specializing in airplane crashes.[47]

Though Frank Clarke[48] is reported to have performed balloon and wing walking stunts when he first came to Venice, his serious stunt flying career can be dated from October 4, 1919. In an effort to surpass the famous Locklear, two Jennies took off from Venice on that date and moved to a position 2500 feet above the crowded beach. Frank Clarke climbed to the top wing of the machine piloted by Howard Patterson, braced his feet against the wires and king post, and leaned into the wind. Al Wilson, in the other machine, moved to a position above Clarke so that he could grab Wilson's wing skid. On the first pass Wilson's Jenny came too low and the landing gear knocked Clarke to his knees, where he tore two long gashes in the top wing fabric. Clarke resumed his position and Wilson's second pass placed the wing skid four or five feet beyond Clarke's reach. Without stopping to consider the possibility of tumbling 2500 feet into Santa Monica Bay, Clarke sprang from his bent knee position, straight up, caught the passing wing skid with his hands, hooked his legs into the skid, and climbed onto the lower wing. Newspapers reported this in-flight transfer, without the use of a rope or rope ladder, as an aviation first. But Locklear had already made changes directly from one airplane to another without the use of ropes or ladders, though most of his public stunts were made with a rope ladder.

Frank Clarke repeated the stunt one week later,[49] and his name was forever linked with spectacular aviation stunts.

Al Wilson and Frank Clarke worked together for a while in a loose partnership arrangement. An ad in the October 10, 1919, issue of Billboard announced their availability for performance at fairs and other public gatherings where aviation stunts always attracted large audiences.

As the base of operations for much of the stunt flying in the southwest, the Venice field was busy during the latter part of October with preparations for the state and county fair season. While Al Wilson prepared for a barnstorming tour of California's Imperial Valley, Frank Clarke, Howard Patterson, "Swede" Meyerhofer, and Mark Campbell made final arrangements for engagements at fairs in Phoenix and Tucson, Arizona.

A race from Venice to Phoenix by Clarke, Patterson and Meyerhofer coincided with the opening of the Phoenix Fair. Frank Clarke provided additional publicity for the event by carrying a live rattlesnake in his cockpit. The newspapers failed to mention that it was de-fanged and borrowed from one of the pier attractions at Venice.

Visitors to both fairs saw acrobatics, wing walking, plane changing, and parachute jumps by Mark Campbell. At the same time, Al Wilson, with Wally Timm at the controls, thrilled residents of El Centro, California, with wing walking stunts.[50] The flyers returned to Venice at the end of December where they shared experiences and planned new stunts for the coming season.

When the newsreel became a standard feature in movie theaters, newsreel cameramen frequently turned to the stunt flyers for an eye-catching subject to add spice to their weekly programs. For a while the Venice stunt flyers earned as much from the newsreels as they did from the motion picture studios. Aviation films, or aviation sequences in films with non-aviation subjects, occurred sporadically. Weeks often passed before the next motion picture job came along. The Venice flyers supported themselves by barnstorming, flying lessons and local sight-seeing rides.

The stunt flyers at Venice shared a competitive spirit of daring, and stunts were sometimes executed when there was no audience or fee involved. As an example, Frank Clarke took off one day with Wally Timm in the front seat. They made one circle of the field and landed with Clarke in the front seat and Timm in the rear. While taking turns holding on to the control stick, they simultaneously climbed along opposite sides of the fuselage and exchanged seats to see if it could be done.[51]

Frank Clarke seldom flew straight and level when he was in the vicinity of the Venice field. His landings and takeoffs were always executed with a flourish. As soon as his Jenny was airborne, he made steep turns with a wing tip only a few feet above the ground. Landings were often made at the bottom of a loop or at the end of a spin. Wally Timm vividly recalls a time when they returned from a local barnstorming tour. Clarke went into a spin when they arrived at the field, and was below

the end of a perfect day [handwritten caption at top]

Clarke Field. [handwritten caption below photo]

Soon after he purchased his first Jenny, Frank Clarke hit the trolley wires at the Venice field while trying to land underneath the wires after coming out of a loop. Courtesy: Wally Timm

Aviators used their bottom wings to advertise everything from the latest movie to cigarettes and rubbing linament. When they had no contract they advertised themselves rather than let the space go to waste. Courtesy: Wally Timm

the top of the hangar when he levelled off to land.[52]

The possibility of another air field for the area appeared in December 1919. Emory Rogers and Fred Hoyt, a local Santa Monica boy who learned to fly during the war, presented a plan to the Santa Monica Chamber of Commerce for the establishment of a municipal aviation field in that city.[53] The enthusiastic members considered several sites, but all attention finally centered on the large field behind Ocean Park, already being used by several flyers, even though no hangars or buildings existed. One of these occupants of the field that became the next center of motion picture stunt flying was Leo Nomis, the leading professional stunt man in Hollywood.

Leo E. Nomis was born Ernest Simon in Indiana on May 5, 1892, the son of Michael Simon and Allie Rust Simon, a lady descended from the noble Sioux Nation. Unusually brave and gifted with marvelous coordination abilities, he left home as a teenager to become a professional acrobat. Appearing at fairs and carnivals, he was soon well known throughout the midwest for performing stunts and making parachute drops from a trapeze suspended below a hot air balloon. When his name appeared in the local newspapers, he decided to adopt the stage name of Leo Nomis, reversing the letters of his last name. He feared that some reporter would eventually write him up as "Simple Simon," in view of the precarious nature of his work, and he would be stuck with an unflattering name for the rest of his professional career. When he came to Hollywood in 1914 to do stunt work for the motion picture companies, his name was legally changed to Leo Ernest Nomis.[54]

In 1915 Leo Nomis worked for D.W. Griffith, showing armour-clad extras how to fall from the high walls of Babylon into safety nets below for the battle scenes of "Intolerance."[55] He specialized in motorcycle and automobile stunts for the early westerns, serials and comedies, perfecting the familiar stunt where a speeding automobile barely makes it across the tracks in front of an oncoming locomotive.

When the United States declared war in 1917, Leo Nomis joined the army and was assigned to flight training on the basis of his experience with hot air balloons. After completing ground school at the University of California in Berkeley, he went to Kelly Field for flying

instruction. Exhibiting superior flying ability all the way through training, he remained in Texas as a flying instructor after winning his wings and a commission. Serving in the same unit with Vernon Castle, Leo Nomis was also involved in a major crash with a student. He was seriously injured, but unlike Castle, he survived. He was confined to an army hospital for several months, and the war was over by the time he recovered from his injuries.[56]

Leo Nomis returned to Hollywood and resumed his profession as a stunt man. With a surplus Jenny purchased from the army, he gave flying lessons on weekends and added aviation work to his repertoire of automobile and motorcycle stunts. He performed his first aviation stunt for a Ruth Roland serial some time in 1919, and continued to provide all subsequent flying stunts for that company.

Leo Nomis, at the extreme right, on a motorcycle he rode for stunt work in an unidentified western made before 1917. Courtesy: Leo Stratton Nomis

Leo Nomis, kneeling in center with dark jacket, and members of the crew of a Ruth Roland serial pose with the star by Leo's Jenny. Courtesy: Leo Stratton Nomis

Mercury and Chaplin Fields thrived for a while and provided settings and bases of operation for many of the aviation sequences that appeared more and more in comedies and serials. Aviation stunt work was increasing, but exhibition flying, newsreel stunts and flying lessons continued to be the main source of income for the stunt flyers who worked from the dirt fields at Venice, Santa Monica, and the Wilshire Boulevard-Crescent Avenue intersection.

As manager of the Venice field and owner of several airplanes, B.H. DeLay contracted with many of the film companies and hired other Venice pilots when a script called for more than one airplane. Most of DeLay's motion picture work was limited to comedies and serials, including such titles as "Aerial Nut" with Al St. John, "Tiger Band" and "Broadway Bab" with Helen Holmes, "A Western Tenderfoot" and "Fighting Fate" with Bill Duncan, and "He Married His Wife" with Al Christie.

Frank Clarke worked with DeLay more than anyone else, but most of the other Venice pilots flew in at least one comedy or serial in the early 1920s. The names of the Venice pilots at this time can be seen from a news release that appeared in the January 22, 1920, issue of the Los Angeles Examiner. It noted that Venice pilots B.H. DeLay, Fred Hoyt, J.L. Littlejohn, E.L. Remelin, Otto Timm, Glen Boyd, Al Wilson, Frank Clarke, W.D. Timm, Reuben Timm and Waldo Waterman had offered their services to the California Air National Guard.

Venice stunt flyers provided the main attraction for an air show at the Ascot Speedway in the latter part of January 1920. Frank Clarke, Glen Boyd, J.L. Littlejohn and E.L. Remelin staged a mock dog fight between two Jennies. With Lewis machine guns firing blanks from the rear cockpits, the two Jennies dived, turned, looped and tried to outmaneuver each other at one thousand feet above the grandstand. Fifteen minutes later, Frank Clarke fell off into a spin in the "defeated" machine. The crowd watched anxiously as the distance between the ground and the spinning airplane quickly disappeared. When Clarke finally recovered and levelled off, the ground was less than one-hundred feet below the landing gear. The spectators indicated their approval with a standing applause. Al Wilson's in-flight transfer and wing walking stunts completed the program.[57]

After the financial success of "The Great Air Robbery," other film companies looked to the airplane and its ability to sustain a full-length feature. William Steiner, backed by the Sol Lesser Company, produced the next aviation feature film. With a working title of "Pirates Of The Air," the plot was primarily a love story that revolved around efforts to break up a ring of aerial pirates. With the same pattern used in "The Great Air Robbery," the producers rented two DeMille Jennies and hired stunt flyer Earl Burgess to act in the leading role and perform the aviation stunts. Though not as well known as Locklear, Burgess had also been a flying instructor during the war, and a barnstormer during the spring and summer months of 1919.

Released as "Sky Eye" in February 1920, the six-reel feature included a plane-to-plane transfer, a leap from an airplane to the top of a speeding train, and a fight between two men on the wings of an airplane in flight.

Earl Burgess would probably have been a well known motion picture stunt pilot, but his career ended on February 6, 1920, during the filming of a comedy by the Fox Film Corporation. The scene plan called for Burgess, who was doubling for Slim Summerville, to fight with a dummy on the airplane's landing gear; knock the "villain" from the spreader bar to fall to his doom, and then climb back onto the wing and eventually into the front cockpit.

Two previous takes of the scene failed to please the director, so the flyers went up for the third time on this same day for another enactment of the same scene. With Walter Hawkins in the pilot's cockpit of a DeMille Jenny, Burgess climbed down to the undercarriage, while Hawkins cruised at five hundred feet over Beverly Hills. Burgess struggled with the dummy in another mock fight and dropped the mannequin in compliance with the script. He worked his way along the leading edge of the lower left wing, hand over hand, toward the wing skid where he planned to again pull himself onto the lower wing. He could have gone directly from the landing gear to the lower wing where it meets the fuselage, but the long route along the length of the lower wing was apparently in the script to make the scene a little more dramatic.

When Burgess reached the wing skid, the pilot of the camera plane, A.C. Mann, and the Fox cameraman, P.H. Whitman, noticed that Burgess showed signs of fatigue. Mann immediately dropped behind and below Hawkins airplane in an attempt to get his top wing just below the exhausted flyer. Burgess struggled to pull his body up in order to place his legs in the Jenny's wing skid, but his strength was gone. According to news accounts of the incident, Burgess shook his head as he looked toward Mann's approaching Jenny. His arms straightened and held for a few seconds, suspending his body below the wing skid. But his hands released their grip before Mann could get into position, and he fell to the ground in the vicinity of the Beverly Hills Hotel. He was killed immediately.[58]

One week later, R.E. Goldsworthy, a new pilot at Venice, positioned his Jenny over a moving train, and Mark Campbell climbed down a rope ladder onto the top of a coach. After a brief pause, the cameraman, who was shooting to the rear of the train from a precarious position on top of the coach in front of Campbell, resumed cranking as Campbell climbed back up to the airplane. These scenes appeared in the First National picture, "Go And Get It," which starred Marshall Nielan. While the plot was not aviation, and portrayed the various adventures of a newsman, Campbell's transfer from the airplane to train and back was the feature stunt of the picture.

Many films of the 1920s contained a situation where either the hero or the bad guy transferred from an airplane to the top of a speeding train, and captured the outlaws on board if he was the good guy, or stole the valuables on board if he was on the other side. Fights were often staged on top of the rocking railroad cars with one man making his escape by way of a rope ladder suspended from a passing airplane.

The transfer from airplane to train was just as spectacular, and as dangerous, as the in-flight transfer between two airplanes, and required unusual skill on the part of the pilot. When making a transfer between two airplanes, one pilot maintains a steady position while the second pilot maneuvers into position for the transfer. At first, transfers were made from the center of the airplane by way of the landing gear. Later it was done from an outer wing tip in order to keep the stunt man and the machines themselves as far away from the propellers as possible. Aside from the awesome danger of the stunt man falling into space, or a mid-air collision as in "The Grim Game" accident, both pilots had some freedom of three dimensional movement. When approaching a train moving in only one dimension, the pilot had to maneuver to the exact same speed and position. A pickup was easier than a deposit as the airplane could pass reasonably close where the stunt man could grab the passing rope ladder or knotted rope. But when a stunt man climbed down from the airplane, the pilot had to hold a precisely exact position in relation to the moving train long enough for the stunt man to gain a secure footing on the vibrating railroad car before releasing his grip on the rope.

The location for most of the airplane-to-train transfers was a ten-mile-long stretch of perfectly straight railroad track near Riverside, California, that still runs along the western edge of March Air Force Base, then known as March Field. Civilian airplanes had relatively free access to army air fields in those days, so this particular section of railroad track was used because nearby March Field was available as a base of operations for the stunt and camera planes.

Frank Clarke and Al Wilson performed a stunt at this location for a Universal serial when Lt. Frank Tomick, a March Field pilot who was loaned to the studio, flew an

Frank Tomick in the uniform of the U.S. Army, Aviation Section of the Signal Corps. Photograph taken soon after his enlistment. Courtesy: Frank Tomick

army plane for one of the scenes. The army pilot impressed the film crew with his precision flying. After getting acquainted with Tomick at the officer's club that evening, Al Wilson and Frank Clarke recommended him to the studio executives. Frank Tomick became the next pilot to enter the profession of motion picture stunt flying.

The two Franks, Clarke and Tomick, became close comrades—rooming together, wearing each other's clothes, double dating, and sharing their last dime during the dark days of the Depression.[59] They also shared an unequalled skill in the handling of an airplane, but in different areas. Clarke became the master stunt and acrobatic flyer, while Tomick had no peers when it came to precision piloting ability.

Frank B. Tomick was born in Austria on September 8, 1897. His father preceded the family to North America, where he spent several years in the gold fields of the Yukon before settling in Seattle, Washington. He bought the Seattle Hotel and sent for his family in 1910. As a teenager Frank Tomick saw Lincoln Beachey at the 1915 Panama Pacific Exposition in San Francisco and decided to become a flyer. His father refused his pleas for flying lessons and sent him to the Montana School of Mines to learn a more practical profession. After graduation Frank Tomick tried to enlist in the Lafayette Flying Corps, an organization then recruiting American volunteers for the French Air Service, but he didn't have the money to pay his way to France. Working at the Bradley Mines in Colorado when the United States entered the war, he enlisted in the Air Service and was sent to Rockwell Field at San Diego. Despite a heavy German accent, unpopular at the time, he was placed on flying status and promoted to Master Signal Electrician after completion of his flight training. Assigned as a flying instructor, he remained in the service after the war and was a second lieutenant flying forest patrol at March Field when he was loaned to the Universal location company. Frank Clarke urged him to become a movie flyer where the earnings were quite a bit more than the pay of a second lieutenant. Tomick visited Frank McConnell at Universal Pictures and was hired immediately. He resigned his commission and signed a contract with Universal Pictures. One of his first jobs was to fly Carl Laemmle over Universal City so the studio boss could see his complex from the air. They took off from a dairy pasture that later became the site for First National and then Warner Brothers Studios.[60]

Howard Batt was the next motion picture stunt flyer to appear in Southern California. He came from Elko, Nevada, and was destined for the most diversified career of all the motion picture stunt pilots. In addition to being one of the leading movie flyers, he was also a barnstormer, an inventor, a stunt flyer at major air shows in the 1930s, a prominent aviation businessman, and a distinguished test pilot during World War II.

Howard Batt was a highly intelligent young man with ruggedly handsome features who was born in Salt Lake City, Utah, on December 21, 1900. His first contact with aviation came after his family moved to Elko, Nevada, where his father established a business that sold construction materials and supplies. The airfield at Elko, with its British canvas hangars, looked like a World War I flying field, but it was a base of operations for the DeHaviland mail planes that flew east to Salt Lake City and west to Reno, Nevada. While completing high school in 1919, Howard Batt worked part time for the Air Mail Service washing airplanes, changing spark plugs on the Liberty engines, and running errands for the pilots. The air mail pilots took him up for a flight now and then, and sometimes allowed him to handle the controls. In his own words, Howard Batt was "bitten by the aviation bug" and all of his subsequent activities were directed toward a career in aviation.

He learned the electrical trade in high school and worked for the Elko Power Company after graduation. Since there was no flying instruction available at the Elko field, Howard Batt came to Los Angeles for flying lessons. As a means of support he opened his own electrical shop on Santa Monica Boulevard, across the street from the Pickford-Fairbanks Studio. He maintained the studio's electrical motors, wind machines, etc., and was soon offered a position with the Pickford-Fairbanks Company. After selling his electrical shop, he went to work as a studio electrician and took flying lessons from Leo Nomis at the Santa Monica field on Sundays.[61]

The Venice flyers frequently devised new stunts to maintain public interest and to attract newsreel and newspaper coverage. Al Wilson made news in the middle of February 1920 with a double change of airplanes. He took off from the Venice field with E.L. Remelin as pilot. Fred Hoyt followed in a second Jenny, and they flew to a position over the Windward Avenue Pier on Venice Beach. Al Wilson climbed onto the lower wing and worked his way among the struts and wires to one end where he climbed to the top wing, and stood with his legs braced against the king post and bracing wires. Remelin held the plane steady as Hoyt slowly passed overhead. Al Wilson grabbed Hoyt's landing gear and pulled himself up onto the spreader bar, ever aware of the meat-grinding potential of the whirling propeller just a few feet away. He climbed onto the lower wing and again worked his way through the struts and wires to the end of the top wing, where he stood to await Remelin's plane. Remelin now moved into the top position as the two Jennies cruised up and down the beach. He made three passes before he came low enough for Wilson to grab the landing gear. As his hands clutched the spreader bar between the wheels, Hoyt's plane dropped away leaving him suspended from the undercarriage. Al Wilson pulled his body up, hooked his legs around the landing gear, and climbed up behind the lethal propeller onto the bottom wing. He then moved through the struts and wires back to the same cockpit he occupied during the takeoff.[62]

A week later, on Washington's birthday, Frank Clarke countered with a plane change while wearing handcuffs. He landed his airplane on the beach between the Windward Avenue Pier and the Center Street Pier, where he was handcuffed in front of a crowd by Chief Loomis of the Venice Police Department. With B.H. DeLay as his pilot, they took off and Clarke climbed to the top wing. He grabbed the wing skid of a second Jenny, pulled himself onto the lower wing, and made his way through the wires and struts to the front cockpit with the handcuffs on his wrists. The newspaper account

Al Wilson making an upside down transfer from his Canadian Jenny, flown by Wally Timm, to Frank Clarke's Hall-Scott powered Canadian Jenny, over Beverly Hills. Courtesy: G. Lawrence Hensey

Though damaged and out of focus, this photograph shows the wing tip transfer position favored by Al Wilson and Frank Clarke. Courtesy: G. Lawrence Hensey

Al Wilson hangs from his wing skid before making the upside down transfer to Frank Clarke's airplane. Courtesy: Wally Timm

Al Wilson stands on his head in the prop blast as Wally Timm flies the airplane. Courtesy: Wally Timm

Al Wilson at Venice in 1920. Courtesy: Wally Timm

the engine, forcing Clarke to ditch the airplane about one half mile from the Venice shore. A Japanese fishing boat was fortunately nearby, and it towed the airplane ashore, as well as rescuing the two occupants.[66]

Instrument flying was not unknown in those days. In an interview given years later, Frank Clarke recalled how he relied upon his tachometer and oil pressure gauge when flying blind through an overcast. When the tachometer showed that the engine was turning too fast, it meant your nose was down. If it showed a loss of revs, you were climbing too fast. The pilot simply watched his tachometer and kept the engine turning over at the right speed. When the oil gauge showed a loss of pressure, it was time to come down.[67]

Al Wilson signed a contract with the United Fairs Booking Association for a stunt flying tour of the midwestern fair circuit, and hired Fred Hoyt and M.E. Goldsworthy to fly the pickup planes. The trio left Venice in June for engagements that would last through November.[68]

When the 1919 fair season was over, Locklear signed a contract with the Fox Film Corporation for another aviation drama. Titled "The Skywayman," the story was again written around several Locklear stunts. DeMille Field No. 2 was selected as the base of operations, and filming of the air scenes began in June 1920.[69]

The only plane-to-plane transfer in the picture was made by Milton "Skeets" Elliott, Locklear's companion and pilot for most of his stunt flying career. A prolonged spin to the ground at night was planned in miniature, but Locklear insisted on doing the spin live, as he felt that a miniature would be recognized for what it was.[70]

Locklear made a plane-to-train transfer along the straight railroad track near March Field, and sat on the landing gear of a Jenny while exchanging blank shots with actors in a speeding car below. This sequence, where the hero and his companion pilot are pursuing a group of thieves, was filmed along Crescent Avenue all the way from Melrose to Wilshire Boulevard.[71]

The spinning scene of "The Skywayman" was made on the night of August 2, 1920, at DeMille Field No. 2. Five powerful studio arc lights were placed in a rough semi-circle around the field with their beams pointed upward to illuminate the airplane for the cameras. The plan called for four cameras to photograph Locklear and Elliott spinning down from two thousand feet with burning flares suspended below the airplane to simulate fire. They were to recover from the spin near the ground and come in for a landing. A previously filmed scene of Locklear and his companion climbing out of a wreck would be added to the spinning scene, which was to be cut just before the airplane recovered from its spin.

Attracted by the arc lights and studio trucks, a small

of this incident noted that Clarke was considered to be the most modest of all the Venice stunt flyers.[63]

Two months later Al Wilson went up with Gil Budwig, climbed out onto the lower wing and held onto a midwing strut while Budwig looped several times. Later in the day Wilson flew with E.L. Remelin, who rolled his Jenny several times while Al Wilson sat on the lower wing holding onto a strut.[64]

Frank Clarke survived two near-fatal incidents in the spring of 1920. Thick fog covered the Los Angeles Basin one afternoon when he and B.H. DeLay returned to Venice after flying for a Universal western at a location near Saugus, north of Los Angeles. The fog blanket was solid when they arrived over the Santa Monica Bay area. They flew around for an hour searching for a break in the thick cover. With no landmarks visible, they were lost by the time the fuel ran out. But just as the engine died, a hole in the fog blanket appeared in front of the airplane, and Clarke was able to see enough of the ground to make a dead-stick landing in a plowed field near Glendale.[65]

Frank Clarke encountered heavy fog a few weeks later when he was returning from Pasadena with Jimmy Hester, his mechanic at the time, in the front seat. It was also raining, and the combination of fog and rain killed

crowd of spectators gathered along the edge of the field as Locklear and Elliott took off. They climbed to the required altitude and circled the field for five minutes until the flares were ignited. This was the signal for the cameras to start turning, and for the beginning of the spin. The Jenny fell off on one wing and went into a spin at two thousand feet. The converging lights followed the white airplane as it came closer to the ground. When it was still spinning at five hundred feet, the Fox crew, and then the crowd of spectators, sensed that something was wrong. At about two hundred feet above the ground, the pilot tried to recover but it was too late. The Jenny crashed and burned at 10:00 p.m. near Crescent Avenue and Third Street. Both occupants died instantly.[72]

Two theories came from the film crew and the spectators. The pilot was either confused by the lights, or the engine failed to perform properly at the moment of recovery.[73]

One of the witnesses to the crash, assistant cameraman Elmer Dyer, was finding more and more work on aviation movies. He was born in Lawrence, Kansas, on August 24, 1892. After his father died, his mother moved to California in 1901, where she opened a small drygoods store in Long Beach. Nine-year-old Elmer sold newspapers on the street corners to help support his mother and sisters. His mother remarried, and Elmer Dyer inherited a small motion picture house in Los Angeles when his stepfather died. He operated this theater for several years, and married his pretty cashier in 1915. Wanting to learn more about the motion picture industry, he worked as a stage hand, and then in the Pathe laboratories, before joining Fox as an assistant cameraman.[74]

Ten days after Locklear's death, Al Wilson almost lost his life while making a plane change at the county fair in Decorah, Iowa. Sporadic rain showers were falling at the scheduled time of performance. With Goldsworthy and Hoyt flying the two airplanes, Al Wilson stood on the top wing of one Jenny, waiting to grab the wing skid of the other. Just before he was able to touch the rounded bar of the skid, the lower airplane dropped fifty feet in the unstable air. Suspended in the air for several seconds as the wing dropped away from him, Al Wilson faced a life shattering contact with the earth below. But his body followed the same path of descent as the airplane, and he landed on the same wing fifty feet below.[75] The three flyers finished the season at the end of October and completed all engagements in spite of bad weather on several occasions.

When he returned to Venice, Al Wilson made a widely publicized transfer from his own Jenny, piloted by Wally Timm, to Frank Clarke's Jenny. Hanging upside down by his knees from the wing skid, he dropped to Frank Clarke's top wing just below.[76] With a successful fair season behind him, and the satisfaction of accomplishing a new stunt, Al Wilson devoted his time to an extended vacation and investing his earnings in real estate.

Frank Clarke was now the leading stunt flyer at Venice. When he became the local distributor for the Hall-Scott L-6 engine, he installed one in his Canadian

Looking north along Broadway from the top of the Los Angeles Railway Building at 11th Street and Broadway during the filming of "Stranger Than Fiction." Frank Clarke can be seen entering his Jenny while Wally Timm has just stepped off the wooden take off platform in the foreground.
Courtesy: Wally Timm

Jenny, which proved to be an improvement over the heavier and less powerful OX-5. The Canadian Jennies, which were manufactured in Canada under license, were preferred by the stunt pilots for their better handling characteristics.[77]

As a promotion stunt to advertise the engine, Frank Clarke established a speed record by flying a Hall-Scott powered Fokker D.VII from Venice to San Francisco in three hours and forty minutes, not counting a fifteen minute refueling stop in Fresno.[78]

Frank Clarke's first important movie stunt came in December 1920 when he worked in the Katherine Mac-Donald film, "Stranger Than Fiction." The script called for an airplane to fly off the roof of a tall building. A nearly completed ten-story building in downtown Los Angeles was rented for the stunt because the concrete roof was clear of vent pipes and other protrusions, and formed a smooth but short takeoff deck. Clarke and Wally Timm spent several days at Chaplin Field tinkering with Clarke's Jenny until he was able to takeoff in less than one hundred feet, which was the length of the building.

One night the airplane was dismantled and hauled to the building where it was hoisted to the roof. By morning the Jenny was assembled on top of the nearly completed Los Angeles Railway Building, on the northeast corner of Broadway and 11th Street, with its wings hanging over the edge. Workers and shoppers arriving in the downtown area couldn't understand how an airplane had landed on top of the short building during the night.[79]

A wooden takeoff platform had already been built along the western edge of the roof with a small ramp that sloped up at the end. After two or three days of set-ups and close-up shots, the takeoff was scheduled. According to one of several different stories that came from this incident, building owners and city officials had second thoughts and decided to deny permission for the takeoff. In another version told around the hangars in later years, the city never intended for the airplane to take off—only for it to be photographed on top of the building. Whatever the truth may be, Frank Clarke took off on December 14, 1920. Newspaper photographers covered the event from the building itself and from the Goodyear "Pony" blimp. The tail of the Jenny was tied to the building with a rope. Wally Timm stood by the tail with a large knife while Frank Clarke revved the engine to almost full speed. When Clarke signalled that he was ready, Timm cut the rope and the Jenny lurched forward, tail high.[80] Since the platform was along one edge of the building, the wings hung over the edge, and the slightest deviation from a straight takeoff run could cause the airplane to fall to the streets below. Clarke stayed on the platform and the little ramp gave the Jenny

Frank Clarke clowns on his top wing ten stories above downtown Los Angeles while Wally Timm sits in the cockpit during one of the long waits between camera set ups. Courtesy: Wally Timm

Wally Timm third from the left, and Frank Clarke sixth from the left, pose with other unidentified members of the Katherine MacDonald Company at Chaplin Field during the filming of "Stranger Than Fiction." Courtesy: Wally Timm

a slight lift at the end. The airplane settled after it left the building and appeared to be going down for a crash. But Clarke picked up flying speed, and halfway between the top of the building and the street surface, he levelled off with full control and flying speed. He climbed to the west and headed for Chaplin Field where he landed several minutes later.[81]

"Stranger Than Fiction" was not an aviation film, but like "The Grim Game" and others, an aviation stunt was written into the script in order to attract a larger audience. The story was a melodrama of the criminal underworld in which Katherine MacDonald was a socialite who pursued a notorious criminal gang after they robbed her guests at a party. After several encounters and escapes, including one by airplane from the top of a

Frank Clarke coaxes the maximum power from his L-6 powered Canadian Jenny just before lift off from the Los Angeles Railway Building. Courtesy: Art Ronnie

Wally Timm and Frank Clarke at Venice in 1920.
Courtesy: Wally Timm

Participants in the parachute-grappling hook stunt pose before going up. Wally Timm is in the front seat, Roy Sauren in the rear, Frank Clarke is next and Ray Robinson is at the right. Courtesy: Wally Timm

building, the leader of the gang is forced to his death in a flaming airplane crash. The crash was made at Chaplin Field by Al Johnson, a stunt man and parachute jumper, who was to suffer a tragic death later. A Jenny was rigged with a device to start a fire, and Johnson, who was learning to fly, took it up to one thousand feet above the camera position. He set the fire and bailed out as the camera followed the burning plane to the ground.[82]

Wally Timm recalls an unusual stunt job devised by a screen writer one month later:

"The studio came up with this stunt, I forget the name of the picture, where a man would jump out of the airplane in a parachute, and another airplane was going to hook the chute with a four-prong grappling hook on the end of a rope. Of course the chute was all wired and reinforced. I took this jumper up and just about at the altitude of bailing out, there was another five hundred or a thousand feet to go, the engine quit. When it nosed down the engine started running again. When I would climb it would quit again, and it started up when I nosed down. It kept doing that. I couldn't figure out what was wrong. I just happened to look down, and the choke wire on Jennies was right alongside, exposed, and here I saw this choke wire coming back and the engine was dying. That was the first time I ever saw anybody literally get cold feet. He was choking the engine each time. He began to shiver and I could feel him shaking the airplane. I got him down and that was the end of his wing walking and jumping career.

"Then the studio got this other fellow who had been a parachute jumper in the army. I took him up, and Frank Clarke was flying the camera ship, and a fellow named Robinson was flying the pick up ship. On the first try, the jumper had a double chute, and the first chute had pins in it, the pins slipped out and let the chute go. Then he pulled his other cord and was coming down. The pilot doing the pickup didn't see this happen. So Frank flew in between him and the jumper, and stayed in there to keep him from hooking the chute that didn't have any reinforcing. Robinson didn't know what was going on. He got mad and we all came down.

"We tried it again, and this time Robinson hooked him and it held for just an instant. The jumper just pulled on through the harness and kept going. Then he pulled his second chute and came down all right. It was good enough so that they got a shot of him being caught and stopped for an instant, and then they cut to something else in the final picture before it showed him going on through the harness."[83]

Wally Timm joined Mercury Aviation as an instructor. One of his first students was Art Goebel, who flew in a few pictures later, before gaining fame as the winner of the Dole flight to Hawaii in the summer of 1927.

Paramount crews returned to DeMille Field in the latter part of 1920 for the aviation scenes in "Flying Pat." With Dorothy Gish in the leading role, it reached the theaters in January 1921. Aviation was a minor part of the picture, but the sight of an airplane was still a novelty at this time, even in cities like Denver, Colorado. As a promotion stunt for the opening of "Flying Pat" at Denver's Princess Theater, Paramount's publicity department arranged for the free use of an airplane and pilot, which the Curtiss-Humphres Company was glad to furnish for its own advertising benefits. When the airplane circled the city of Denver several times, newspapers noted the flight in glowing terms, thereby giving free publicity for the movie.[84]

B.H. DeLay dominated motion picture flying for the next year. He made several plane-to-train pickups, including one for the Fox film, "Skirts." His four Jennies at the Venice field, now called DeLay Field, were scheduled for months ahead by Thomas H. Ince, Chester Comedies, Vitagraph, Fox Sunshine Comedies, Brunton Studios, Western Comedies, Marshal Nielan, Jimmy Horn Comedies, Silver Productions, Ben Wilson Productions, Astra, Warner Brothers, Al St. John Comedies, and Helen Holmes Serials.[85]

Finding that he could not give proper attention to both motion pictures and aviation, Cecil B. DeMille sold his interests in Mercury Aviation to Emory Rogers[86] who had already purchased Syd Chaplin's interest in Chaplin Field. The Pacific Airplane and Supply Company of Venice then merged with Mercury Aviation to form Rogers Aircraft Incorporated.[87] Ten airplanes operated daily from the combined DeMille and Chaplin Fields, which was now known as Rogers Airport.

B. H. DeLay in one of his Jennies at the Venice field.
Courtesy: Wally Timm

Frank Clarke crashes a Curtiss Jenny for an unidentified motion picture in 1921.
Courtesy: Jimmy Barton

Roy Wilson in the cockpit of the Italian Balila that he and his brother Tave purchased from Frank Clarke.
Courtesy: Tave Wilson

At this time Moye Stephens was a senior at Holly-wood High School and Dick Rinaldi was a freshman at the same school. Both men were involved in motion picture flying at various times, and Dick Rinaldi became a member of the Associated Motion Picture Pilots. Moye Stephens was an airline pilot by the time the motion picture stunt pilots organized, and recalls his first experiences with aviation at Rogers Airport:

"I was born in Los Angeles, February 21, 1906. My parents took me to the Dominguez Air Meet in 1910, and it made an impression. I can't remember any details, but to this day I can close my eyes and see those pushers floating past the grandstand.

"When I learned to read I was constantly reading about flying. During World War I, I spent lunch time in the school library reading accounts of the World War I pilots.

"A buddy and I decided we ought to get into flying. We saved up our allowances, went out to Rogers Airport, paid our five bucks, and Gil Budwig took us up on our first flight.

"The thing that really got me started was when I hung around the field out there, and they put me to work. I worked 15 hours for a 15 minute lesson, which wasn't bad pay. Rogers was getting $25.00 an hour for instruction. This thing worked out to forty or fifty cents an hour, which in those days wasn't bad. Eddie Bellande taught me how to fly, and he usually stretched that fifteen minutes into a half hour.

"I started out washing motors and washing the airplanes, particularly the motors. Every Saturday morning we had to wash the engines very thoroughly with gasoline, and oil the rocker arms and valve stems. Before the first summer was out they had me rebuilding wings and doing top overhaul on the OX-5s.

-29-

"Dick Rinaldi was a freshman at Hollywood High. His folks were in the building contracting business and had moved out here from New York. He quit school and went to work washing dishes at "Tex" and Clara Newland's lunch stand there at Rogers Airport. They later put in a little restaurant on Melrose, and then a bigger one which was quite successful around 1928. Rinaldi met Leo Nomis there at Rogers, and when they sub-divided the first Rogers field, Leo Nomis and Vic Fleming moved down to what later became Clover Field. Leo took Dick with him—taught him mechanics and how to fly."[88]

Emory Rogers died in an airplane crash two months after the formation of Rogers Aircraft Incorporated. Moye Stephens recalls the circumstances of his death:

"Emory Rogers was killed in a C-1, which was a little racing monoplane with an OX-5 motor that Otto Timm built for him. Somebody else flew it in a race with a Nieuport 28 which Bud Creeth had been rebuilding when he was killed. Later on they finished it and fixed it up for smoke and used it for sky writing. Anyway, 'Remy' Remelin flew this Nieuport and beat the C-1, and Emory Rogers, who was recovering from malaria or something at the time, had stayed in the background and wasn't doing any flying that day. He couldn't stand to see his pet C-1 beat, so he challenged 'Remy' to another go. They made one turn just west of the tar pits (LaBrea Tar Pits), and he either blacked out as a result of his malaria, or else he pulled it up into an accelerated stall. He was killed."[89]

When "The Girl From God's Country" was released to the theaters in September 1921 audiences were impressed with several of the air scenes. The major part of the story dealt with the usual dramatic conflicts between people and the air action as a whole was minor. A stolen formula for "solidified gasoline," a trans-Pacific air race, and the formula's recovery after an air fight and crash into the sea provided enough air action to employ at least three aviators on the picture. The flyers have not been identified, but Dick Grace mentions this picture in his writings. Some of his accounts specifically mention films, flyers and locations, but many of his other writings are quite vague as to identities.

Frank Clarke flew the Hall-Scott powered Fokker D.VII at local air shows to promote the engine he was distributing. The owner of this airplane is unidentified, but L.C. Brand, a real estate developer, owned a Fokker D.VII at this time. A second Fokker D.VII arrived at DeLay Field in December from Kelly Field in Texas. Owned by the Crawford Airplane Company, it was then sold to Roy Page who had it rebuilt for stunt flying.[90]

An air field for Santa Monica was created in February 1922 when the Santa Monica-Ocean Park Chamber of Commerce met with Lt. H.A. Halverson of the War Department, and Winton M. Henry of Davis-Douglas Aircraft, to discuss the possibility of establishing a government air field. The location selected by all parties was one hundred and seventy-three acres of land south of what was then Central Avenue, at the easterly limits of Santa Monica. The Santa Monica City Commission received leases from the War Department in May and all paper work was signed by June. A government air field was officially established and work began on two steel hangars to house the military airplanes to be stationed there.[91]

The Chaplin Field portion of Rogers Airport was sold for subdivision, and Rogers Aircraft continued to operate on the north side of Wilshire Boulevard.

The air field at Venice continued to operate, but it was beginning to decline. The city of Venice had already pioneered aerial police work when "Swede" Meyerhofer was appointed as an aerial policeman before World War I. Aviators George E. Stephenson, Hubert Kittle and Frank Clarke were sworn in as officers of the Aerial Department, Venice Police Force on July 20, 1922. The cameras of Fox, International, Selznick and Pathe News recorded the ceremony as they received badges from Chief Cavanaugh. Seven airplanes were made available to patrol the bay, detect crime, assist in spotting fires and accidents, and to save the lives of shipwrecked persons. According to the local paper, Stephenson owned five of the airplanes, a K-6 Standard, three Fokkers and one Spad. Clarke used his Hall-Scott powered Jenny, and Kittle contributed his OX-5 powered Jenny for use in the effort.[92]

The plan of operations for criminal apprehension consisted of an airplane taking off with two officers on board with a description of the bandit's car. When the vehicle was spotted, one officer would climb onto the wing with a shotgun and parachute. He would pop his chute while standing on the wing, and be pulled off to land in front of the fleeing vehicle with his shotgun in the ready position.[93] The number of criminals captured by this procedure caused very little crowding at the Venice jail.

Minor aviation scenes appeared in "Maid Of The West" by Fox, "Ladies Must Live" by Paramount, "With Wings Outspread" by Camus Productions, and several westerns and serials produced at this time. Most of the flying work went to B.H. DeLay, Frank Clarke, Leo Nomis and Frank Tomick in his capacity as a staff pilot for Universal.

A lady daredevil joined Frank Clarke and Frank Tomick for a stunt with a twist, performed at an air show in Altadena, California. After some ballyhoo from an announcer with a megaphone, Sadie Kalishek climbed into the front cockpit of Clarke's Jenny. They took off with Frank Tomick close behind in a second Jenny.

When the airplanes reached 3,000 feet, the lady wing walker made a conventional transfer to Tomick's wing, and the crowd applauded. After she was apparently safe on Tomick's Jenny, the startled crowd saw her fall off and tumble into space. Unknown to the shocked spectators, she had strapped on a parachute previously placed in the front cockpit of Clarke's plane. Murmurs of relieved conversation and laughter passed through the crowd after she pulled the rip cord and they realized that it was part of the act.[94]

Two months later Tomick and Clarke made the headlines of the Venice newspaper. A sudden snowstorm had stranded a number of automobiles along the narrow and winding "ridge route" between Los Angeles and Bakersfield. Frank Tomick knew the terrain well from his

Cameraman Alvin Wykoff and pilot A. C. Mann in a DeMille Jenny, showing a typical aerial camera mount of the early 1920s. Courtesy: Cecil B. DeMille Trust

army days of flying forest patrol. After talking the situation over with Clarke, he contacted March Field and volunteered to fly one of the army D.H.4s which had been loaded with emergency supplies. When the storm broke, several D.H.4s took off from March Field into a strong headwind and lingering storm clouds. Frank Tomick was at the controls of one, with Frank Clarke and emergency rations in the front cockpit. More than two hours of flying into the strong head wind passed before they reached the area of LeBec, where most of the stranded motorists were located. After dropping the supplies, Tomick turned the D.H. 180 degrees, and with the strong winds now blowing from the tail, they were back at March Field in less than one hour.[95]

People with novel stunt ideas appeared at the Venice field from time to time, hoping to earn a few dollars from the newsreels, and a possible offer of motion picture

work from the resulting exposure. While not in the category of stunt pilots, they performed on or with the airplanes, and are worthy of inclusion in the overall field of motion picture aviation stunts.

One of the most unusual stunt men to wander into the Venice hangar was John Miller, a Cherokee Indian who went by the stage name of Chief White Eagle. After accepting an offer of fifty dollars from a newsreel photographer, he went up with Frank Clarke and climbed down to the landing gear. His long thick hair had been securely braided to a leather strap, which he now attached to the spreader bar. Chief White Eagle swung his body down from the landing gear, released his hands and hung several thousand feet above Santa Monica Bay, supported only by his hair, while a newsreel camera recorded the incident from another airplane.

The Santa Monica City Commission voted to reserve a portion of the new government airfield for civilian hangars and issued building permits to J.A. Montee, R.I. Short and Harry W. Kelly in October 1922.[96] The first hangar erected on the field, before the military hangars were completed, was one of the Chaplin Field buildings, which was relocated and re-erected by Ruel Short and Wally Timm.[97]

Dick Kerwood was an unusually daring stunt man who appeared at the Venice field some time in 1922. In one of his first local stunts, he joined with Frank Tomick for an aerial exhibition over the beach area designed to stimulate voter support for a proposed amendment to the state constitution. While Tomick flew the airplane, Kerwood hung by his feet from the bottom rung of a rope ladder that was attached to the front mid-wing strut of Tomick's Jenny. He then leaped several feet through the air and grabbed the landing gear. During Kerwood's performance, Tomick dropped leaflets from the cockpit, encouraging voters to support the amendment. When Kerwood climbed back into the cockpit, Tomick executed loops, rolls, and spins while Kerwood dropped leaflets.[98]

Several days later, Kerwood performed a stunt from Tomick's plane that, according to newspapers, had never been seen in Southern California, implying that it probably had been executed before elsewhere. One end of a rope, approximately half the length of the airplane's wing span, was tied to the landing gear. The other end

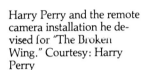
Harry Perry and the remote camera installation he devised for "The Broken Wing." Courtesy: Harry Perry

was tied to Kerwood. When they reached one thousand feet, Kerwood climbed to the tip of a bottom wing, and dived into space. He swung back and forth from one wing tip to the other. When the pendulum action lost its momentum, he climbed up the rope, hand over hand, to the landing gear, then onto the lower wing and back into the cockpit.[99]

Unable to stay away from the excitement of stunt flying, Al Wilson signed a contract for another tour of the midwestern fairs. When the season was over, he resumed his motion picture work with Universal, and continued in that capacity for several years. Frank Clarke was also under contract to Universal at this time, but he resigned, and then Tomick resigned when they discovered that more money could be made on a freelance basis. Clarke continued to barnstorm, and joined with Mark Campbell and lady parachutist Gladys Roy, for another engagement at the fair in Phoenix, Arizona.[100]

Jean Perkins was hired by Universal for an airplane-to-train transfer in the serial "Around The World In 18

Days," along with a pilot who had no previous experience in performing this difficult stunt. Though the pilot did his best, he was unable to place Perkins and the rope ladder directly over the train. At one time Perkins was bounced against the side of the coach. He fell to the ground by the side of the train, breaking both legs and suffering extensive internal injuries. Some reports say that he fell as a result of hitting the side of the coach, while others say that he tried to leap from the ladder to a handhold on the catwalk that ran along the top of the railroad car. Jean Perkins died four days later in a Riverside hospital.[101]

Frank Clarke crashed a Jenny on takeoff for the Paramount picture "Woman With Four Faces," but it was not in the script. Doubling for an actor, he was supposed to wave to actress Betty Compson as he took off. Clarke's attention became too engrossed with the acting part of the takeoff, and he failed to see that the airplane was drifting toward a tree on the edge of the takeoff run. The airplane was demolished but Clarke escaped uninjured.

Developers purchased the DeMille Field part of Rogers Airport in 1923, but just before it was covered with houses, stores, signs and telephone poles, an important development in aerial camera work occurred there. During work on an aviation sequence in Paramount's "The Broken Wing," Tom Foreman, the director, wanted a closeup shot of the leading man in the cockpit in the air, so it would appear that he was flying the airplane. With only two cockpits in the Rogers Jennies, there was not enough room for the pilot, the actor, the cameraman and his camera. The problem was solved by a young man who was just beginning an important career in cinematography. Harry Perry became one of the leading aerial cinematographers in the motion picture industry, as was shown by his original and outstanding work in the two aviation classics, "Wings" and "Hell's Angels."

Harry F. Perry was born in Kansas on May 2, 1888, and grew up in Colorado. After graduating from high school, he worked for the Denver and Rio Grande Railroad until 1917. When he was turned down for military service, he moved to San Diego and worked for the Hercules Powder Company. His motion picture career began in September 1918 when his brother Paul, who was chief cameraman for Famous Players Lasky, obtained a position for him as assistant cameraman.

Harry Perry solved the problem in "The Broken Wing" by adapting a Singer sewing machine motor to the drive mechanism of his camera. With a remote switch, the camera was mounted on the fuselage behind the rear cockpit with its field of vision just missing the pilot's head, and photographing the actor's head in the front seat. When the pilot turned and maneuvered the airplane, the camera photographed the back of the actor's head and the sides of his face, as he turned from side to side, against a tilting horizon beyond the nose and whirling propeller.[102] This was only the first of many innovations in the field of aerial photography to come from the fertile mind of Harry Perry.

Dick Kerwood almost lost his life during the filming of an incident for the Fox serial, "The Eleventh Hour." According to the plot, an airplane was to be hit by gun fire from a surfaced submarine and explode in the air. Arrangements were made for a U.S. Navy submarine and the location crew went to San Diego. A worn-out Standard was selected for the stunt, and Kerwood took enough flying lessons from Frank Tomick to fly the airplane from North Island to the submarine which was anchored in San Diego Bay. With a charge in the fuselage, placed by the studio explosive man, and a delayed timing device in the cockpit that was rigged to detonate the dynamite ten seconds after setting the switch, Kerwood took off. When he reached the submarine at a location off Point Loma, he was flying at 2800 feet. He unbuckled the safety belt and stood up in the cockpit before closing the switch, leaving only the act of going over the side. Within ten seconds he would be clear of the airplane allowing the cameras time to expose several feet of film between the time he left the picture and the actual explosion, since there was no escape by parachute in the script. He closed the switch, but something in the timing device failed to operate according to design. Before he could leave the cockpit an explosion ripped the plane apart and hurled Kerwood into the air. Stunned for several seconds and tumbling over and over in space, he lost all sense of the situation. But he suffered no injuries beyond a few

powder burns, and was able to regain his senses and pull the rip cord. The burning wreck staggered along and crashed into the sea, while a navy seaplane picked up Kerwood.[103]

Three days later he was able to perform another stunt for the same film by hanging from a rope ladder on Howard Patterson's Jenny, and seizing another stunt man who stood on the deck of a submarine, as the airplane passed over.[104]

The Venice field was also sold for real estate development and a tract office appeared on the site in March 1923.[105] Clover Field was officially dedicated a month later, being named for a Lieutenant Clover who was killed during the war. Lt. C.C. Moseley took command of the Army Reserve unit stationed there. The stunt flyers from Venice moved to Clover Field, where they were joined by some of the Rogers Airport flyers, to make Clover Field the new center of exhibition stunt flying.

The Wilson brothers appeared at Clover Field soon after its dedication. Roy became one of the most daring of the stunt pilots, and Tave became a skilled camera pilot. Together, they contracted for aviation films and operated the only airport ever licensed exclusively for motion picture work.

Tave Wilson was born December 7, 1899, in Manchester, Missouri. Roy was born in the same town on September 6, 1903. Their father manufactured special light-weight metal shoes for race horses throughout the United States, Canada and Mexico. Roy decided to become an aviator after seeing Lincoln Beachey and Arch Hoxie perform at St. Louis in 1912. Tave was fascinated with automobile racing, and after his army service in World War I, he was a regular competitor at race tracks in the Midwest. In 1922 he drove a sixteen-valve Ford Sportster to Los Angeles in order to participate in the dirt-track racing in the area. When Roy received a snapshot of his brother and a pretty girl, both in swim suits on Santa Monica Beach, taken on Christmas day, he left the snow and ice of the Midwest for the land of sunshine. They traded the Ford Sportster to Bob Lloyd for a Jenny at Clover Field, and Roy hired Frank Barber to give him flying lessons. He soloed after one and one half hours of dual time, and then taught his brother to fly. Tave Wilson describes their first cross country flight:

"Right after we got the Jenny we decided to fly up to the American Legion convention in San Francisco. We asked Mort Bach for the best way to go. We were new out here with just a few hours of flying time. We didn't know whether to fly up the coast or go inland through Bakersfield. Mort said, 'If you take my advice you'll go down to the Southern Pacific Railroad and rent yourself a flat car—put the dern airplane on it and haul it up there. You'll be sure to get there that way, with that roaring OX-5.'

"Well, we decided to go up the coast so we wouldn't have to climb over the mountains between Los Angeles and Bakersfield. What happened is that we got as far as Gaviota Pass and we got caught in a windstorm that kept blowing us out to sea. We were getting right over those islands and I didn't like the looks of that at all. I motioned to Roy and he headed her on back, and then we got down in the middle of that thing. One minute the wires on that Jenny were so loose you could tie knots in them, and the next minute they were tighter than fiddle strings. We got into the darndest tumult of air there. That hot wind was coming through the pass and hitting the cold ocean air and it was just in a whirl. I had some extra spark plugs on the floor and they bounced clear out of the cockpit. If it hadn't been for the safety belt I would have gone out too. It really gave us a shaking. I don't know to this day why it didn't shake the wings clear off.

"Roy finally got it in alongside the mountains to land, and just at that time we hit a downdraft. It was just like somebody took his hand and slammed you down. We smashed her up good. Here I was in the front seat with all four landing gear spars sticking right through the thing and me in the middle. Roy was in the back seat with the gas line broken. He had his finger on the tank trying to keep the gas from running all over him until he could get his seat belt unbuckled.

"We noticed a little white house when we were coming down which turned out to be a school house. This school teacher came over with an improvised stretcher and a bunch of kids. Here we were trying to get untangled and get out of that thing—the wings were down over us—and she came tearing up and asked my brother if we had crashed. I think he told her he was just practicing landings.

"Roy stayed with the airplane—got a truck and hauled it back down to Clover Field, and I caught a bus and went on up to San Francisco. I found out later that they sent sixteen DHs up there and only four of them made it. The other twelve had forced landings or cracked up when they got caught in the Gaviota Pass wind. I noticed that when we were in it there was a DH just standing there. You know a DH is 450 horsepower, and it was just standing there chewing the air like in a wind tunnel, and us trying to go through there with a ninety horsepower roaring OX- 5."[106]

B.H. DeLay's motion picture flying career ended abruptly in July 1923. After looping several times over Clover Field, his wings collapsed at two thousand feet, and he was killed, along with Ruel Short who was in the front seat, when the plane crashed at the edge of the field. According to the newspapers, friends of DeLay suspected foul play in the accident. Moye Stephens recalls that incident.

"Delay was killed with Short. Fiske had built this little airplane—what the heck was it called. Anyway, it had two sets of wings. One was his racing wings and one was his cross country wings. He told DeLay not to stunt the airplane with the cross country wings. But he went up with Short and stunted it, and the wings came off."[107]

Ten days later, Al Wilson's brother Herbert, was killed along with an engineer from Davis-Douglas, when their experimental seaplane crashed into the sea at Venice.[108]

Jerry Phillips was the next future member of the Associated Motion Picture Pilots to arrive in Southern California. Born Frederick Gerald Phillips in Baltimore, Maryland, on May, 22, 1902, he was a sophomore at the University of Wisconsin when he received a letter from his older brother, Clement, that caused him to turn to the profession of aviation. Clement K. Phillips came to Southern California after graduating from the University of Wisconsin, and would have also been a member of the Associated Motion Picture Pilots if he had not been killed before the organization was formed. Clem Phillips worked as a cowboy extra, shared a room with another extra named Clark Gable, and was taking flying lessons from Frank Tomick at Clover Field when he wrote a letter to his younger brother. When Jerry Phillips read about the warm climate, the abundance of pretty girls on the motion picture lots, and the thrill of flying, he forgot about a future in electrical engineering and joined his brother in California. He took flying lessons from Kenneth Montee at Clover Field and soloed on September 3, 1923.[109]

Dick Grace almost ended his career at its beginning while performing his first motion picture aviation stunt. Fox hired Grace to double for Tom Mix in the film "Sky High" by climbing down an eighteen-foot-long knotted rope, attached to the rear cockpit of an airplane. The director wanted the action to be photographed from the ground and again in the air from another airplane, which meant Grace would have to perform the stunt twice.

Bud Creeth, the pilot hired by Grace, flew over the camera position at five hundred feet, while Dick Grace climbed down the rope, and went through the motions of signalling to someone on the ground. While the camera recorded the action from the ground, Grace climbed back up the rope to the cockpit, and Creeth came in for a landing. When the camera was mounted on another airplane for the in-flight shot, the two airplanes took off and Grace repeated the stunt. The cameraman was not satisfied with his shot and signalled for another take. By now, Grace was feeling fatigue from going up and down the rope two times in a sixty miles per hour slipstream. He went down the rope for a third time, and slowly climbed back up toward the cockpit. He reached the fuselage and started to pull himself over the cockpit padding with what he felt to be his last surge of strength. But his upward motion was suddenly halted when the pistol belt he was wearing to double for the cowboy star caught on the bottom of the fuselage. If he released one hand to adjust the gun and holster, he would not be able to hold on to the cockpit edge with his remaining hand.

Bud Creeth saw the situation, and leaned out of the front seat to help Grace back into the rear cockpit, avoiding a repeat of the situation that killed Burgess.[110]

This was one of the few times that Tom Mix resorted to a double. He did all of his western stunts, and performed at least one airplane stunt in the Fox film "Do And Dare." In a staged struggle with the pilot of a J-1 Standard that was taking off, Tom Mix tumbled to the ground and rolled over several times as the airplane lifted off.

Frank Clarke and Howard Patterson signed a contract to perform several stunts for the comedy "Going Up," which was filmed at Brand Field in Glendale. One of the early airplane crashes deliberately planned for motion picture work was executed by Frank Clarke when he landed a Jenny on its nose for this film.[111]

As motion picture audiences grew, general stunt work and aviation stunts increased. Leo Nomis was in constant demand for a variety of stunts which included wing walking, plane changing, leaping from burning buildings, driving cars over cliffs, and crawling on railroad tracks between the wheels of moving trains.

Cecil B. DeMille engaged Leo Nomis for a stunt in "Manslaughter" that called for a motorcycle policeman to collide with an automobile. With mattresses placed on the opposite side of the car, out of camera range, Nomis hit the side of the vehicle at forty-five miles per hour, which was the speed he had estimated to propel his body over the length of the motorcycle and the width of the automobile after the impact. But the speed was too fast, and the momentum carried Leo Nomis beyond the mattresses. He landed on the pavement, breaking several bones.

When Los Angeles County enacted a set of basic air traffic laws in 1923, Leo Nomis flew too low over a football game at Hollywood High School during a halftime stunt, with fifteen-year-old Dick Rinaldi in the front seat, and had the distinction of being the first aviator to be arrested for violation of the new ordinance. His attorney promised to wage a legal battle to test the validity of the regulations that were unpopular with aviators.[112] The lawyer lost his case, but the matter was settled with a pleasant reprimand from the judge.

Howard Batt soloed after only a few lessons from Leo Nomis. After purchasing a Jenny from Clarence Prest in Arlington, California (near Riverside), where Prest operated a used airplane and parts business from a large citrus-packing warehouse, Howard Batt flew it back to Clover Field. He kept the Jenny in Leo Nomis' hangar along with Victor Fleming's L-6 Standard, Frank Tomick's Jenny, and a Jenny owned by Reginald Denny. Howard Batt recalls that Nomis' hangar was constructed mainly of Curtiss Jenny packing crates.

Howard Batt resigned from the Pickford-Fairbanks Studios at this time to accept a position with Edwin Carew Productions as their chief electrician. For location work the studios used large electrical generators that were hauled on trucks and powered with Liberty aircraft engines. In many situations a film crew did not require the amount of power that these giant motor-generator sets were capable of producing. While with Carew Productions, Howard Batt designed and built the first small portable motor-generator set used in the motion picture industry. But his love of flying caused him to leave this important position to become the chief pilot for California Aerial Transport.[113]

Clem and Jerry Phillips bought two Jennies after they learned to fly—one with an OX-5 and the other with a "Hisso" engine. They hauled weekend passengers on sightseeing rides, sold advertising space on their bottom wings, and flew for a motion picture now and then. Jerry Phillips flew his Jenny for an incident in a "Perils of Pauline" serial for his first aviation movie job. His second motion picture job came in the Ruth Roland picture, "Dollar Down." Wanting to learn more about flying, Jerry Phillips joined the Army Air Service as a Flying Cadet and departed for Kelly Field in Texas.[114]

After the Wilson brothers' Jenny was repaired, Roy flew it to Texas on a barnstorming tour, but sold it and then bought a Standard. His mother, who was in Texas at the time, flew back to California with him and sold tickets as Roy barnstormed all the way back to Clover Field. She had the distinction of being the first lady to cross the Rocky Mountains in an airplane, an event that was written up in the Santa Monica newspaper.

Tave and Roy Wilson bought an Italian Balilla from Frank Clarke and departed for an extended barnstorming tour of the Midwest. While they were in St. Louis, an airmail pilot named Charles Lindbergh admired the fast Balilla and its beautiful wood craftsmanship. He asked Roy for permission to fly the Italian fighter plane, but Lindbergh had bailed out of a mail plane one week before. While the bail out was necessary, Roy was hesitant to allow the unknown air mail pilot to fly the tricky Balilla, particularly when his bail out was still being discussed around the airport.

Several years later, after Lindbergh's famous solo flight to Paris, he met Roy Wilson again, in San Francisco while the "Hell's Angels" crew was working out of Oakland Airport. After a few laughs over the Balilla incident, Roy Wilson told Lindbergh that he felt it was now all right for him to fly his airplane.[115]

After Leo Nomis recovered from his injuries in the motorcycle stunt, his pretty wife, Geraldine, came out to Clover Field one evening to watch her husband make a night takeoff for a Gloria Swanson picture. Leo and

Geraldine agreed on everything except his love for flying. After much persuasion, Geraldine reluctantly agreed to double for Gloria Swanson, and occupy the front seat for the takeoff scene. Since the camera and lights were set up in front of his hangar, which was halfway down the field, Leo Nomis began his takeoff run from that position. As the Jenny neared a line of trees at the end of the field, it was well below the tree tops. Leo hit the throttle and pulled back on the stick as his wife turned and yelled, "You're not going to make it!" She was proven to be correct as the airplane mushed into the tree tops and ended up on the ground with its tail in the air. Neither occupant was injured, and the airplane suffered only minor damage. Geraldine's only comment was, "I told you so!", as she stalked off the field never to fly again.[116]

A refinement of the pendulum stunt performed by Dick Kerwood in 1922 appeared in "The Fighting American," which was released by Universal in 1924. It was directed by Tom Foreman and photographed by Harry Perry. The flying scenes were incidental to the non-aviation plot, but when they appeared on the screen many viewers refused to believe that they were real.

While Harry Perry photographed the action from the rear cockpit of Frank Tomick's Jenny, two stunt men fought on the lower wing of Leo Nomis's Jenny. After several minutes of animated struggle, one man fell from the wing, head first. Instead of continuing to the ground, several thousand feet below, wires attached to his ankles and the landing gear swung his body in an arc to the opposite wing tip, where he climbed aboard and continued the fight. How this unusual situation tied into the story is unknown, but it made a spectacular scene.

When Fern Perry saw the picture at a theater in Hollywood, the man sitting in front of her informed his wife that such a stunt was impossible, and could only have been accomplished by trick photography. Fern Perry lost no time in tapping him on the shoulder to inform the doubter that her husband was there, and had photographed the entire incident in reality.[117]

Moye Stephens' first motion picture job was with Leo Nomis and Frank Clarke in the Cecil B. DeMille picture, "Corporal Kate." Ever since the motorcycle stunt, DeMille always gave Leo Nomis the aviation work in his pictures. As the contractor for the aviation work, Leo Nomis flew a Standard painted up as a German bomber, and hired Frank Clarke to fly camera, while Moye Stephens was engaged to fly his own Thomas Morse Scout as a British Sopwith Camel.

At this time Universal was using airplane incidents in their films as much as all the other studios combined. Al Wilson obtained a feature acting role, along with several stunt jobs in two Universal serials. He made an in-flight transfer between two airplanes, and changed from Frank Tomick's Jenny to the top of a train for "The Eagle's Talons." A transfer from an automobile to an airplane in "The Ghost City" almost ended in disaster for Al Wilson. As the Jenny matched the speed of the car, which was approaching seventy miles per hour, Tomick positioned the rope ladder just to the side of Al Wilson so he could grab the ladder from his standing position in the car. When his full weight shifted to the rope ladder, the airplane settled, bringing Wilson into a bouncing contact with the ground. His first thought was to release the ladder, but he quickly realized that rolling and tumbling at seventy miles per hour would break both arms and legs, and possibly his spine. He held on and Tomick immediately hit the throttle when he saw what was happening, and Al Wilson was lifted from the ground with only a few bruises and abrasions.[118]

A few weeks later, Ben Wilson Productions hired Al Wilson to climb down to the bottom of a rope ladder suspended from an airplane, and fly parallel and close to a pair of running horses, one with a rider and one with an empty saddle. An actual transfer from the rope ladder to the saddle was not a part of the scene plan since that continuity of action would be accomplished by showing Wilson at the bottom of the ladder just above the horses, and then cutting to a closeup showing the actor in the saddle with a rope ladder dangling at the edge of the picture.

Al Wilson came down with influenza, and was still too weak on the day before the stunt was scheduled. Dick Kerwood was anxious to resume his career as a stunt man, and though not fully recovered from his back injury, he agreed to perform the stunt.

The crew assembled a few miles from Newhall, California, at the mouth of Pico Canyon, a location site used many times in western and aviation movies. The airplane was to fly into the canyon, turn and come back toward the camera with the stunt man climbing down the rope ladder above the galloping horses. Another shot of this scene, made from a camera car as it paced the horses and airplane, was to be made later. Al Wilson drove to the site to watch the action. Dick Kerwood's series of lucky escapes came to an end on October 15, 1924. Frank Tomick, who flew the airplane, tells what happened.

"Dick broke his back and was in the hospital, so I kept up the payments on his Cadillac as long as he was in the hospital. He had a few other problems, family and financial. This job came up, which was only five hundred bucks, but he needed the money and insisted he's gonna do it. I tried to talk him out of it on account of his back, but he said he was all right. Well, I figured if we come close to the horse and he didn't leave the ladder, it would be all right.

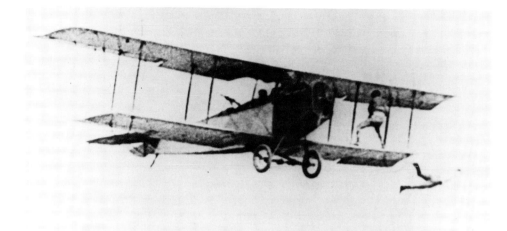

Former circus acrobat, Russell Benton, falls from the Jenny flown by Leo Nomis. With wires attached to his ankles and the landing gear, he will swing pendulum fashion, to the other wing tip and resume the mock fight with the other stunt man for a scene from "The Fighting American." Courtesy: Frank Tomick

From the left: Frank Tomick, Leo Nomis, director Tom Foreman, Russell Benton, Frank Clarke and Harry Perry at Clover Field after completing the air scenes for "The Fighting American." Courtesy: Frank Tomick

"When we were ready to go I told him to leave his money and everything down here, and I tapped him here, on the back. And he's got a gun, .25 automatic! I said, 'What the hell, you gonna shoot me up there?' He laughed and gave it to Al Wilson who was there, and his wallet and keys.

"When we started out he seemed all right and wanted to take off. I was teaching him how to fly, and he could take off and fly pretty fair. We got up in the air, and they gave me the signal down there, with the flags, when they were ready with the horses. I made a circle and he got down on the ladder. Well, with the wings and the fuselage, there's a blind spot for me to see the ladder from the back seat. Oh yes, when he got out he put his knee through my wing, and I told him he had to fix it when we got down. So he started down on the ladder and I couldn't see him any more. I got around, got ready to give her the gun to get down lower, and I banked so I could get a look at the ladder, but no Dick. I looked on the top wing. I thought he was hiding around, kidding me. But he wasn't on that airplane. So I came on down. Nobody saw him fall. I got on a horse

and several of us rode back to where I had been flying. Finally, after about forty minutes, we found him. He landed right on his head. Nobody knows what happened. Maybe he was too weak, maybe he had too many problems. We'll never know."[119]

Dick Grace crashed two airplanes in 1924 while working on the Fox picture, "Forest Ranger." One was planned and one was an accident. Two Curtiss Jennies, piloted by Dick Grace and Bud Creeth, flew up to the location in a forest area at Bonny Doon, near Santa Cruz. The planned crash was part of the story situation where an airplane crashes into the side of a barn and remains inside without going all the way through. For this stunt Grace positioned the airplane about five hundred feet from the barn, and opened the throttle. With its tail high and wheels on the ground, the Jenny smashed into the barn wall. In a swirl of boards, splinters, hay and dust, it came to rest against the opposite wall, still inside the building.

When all scenes of "Forest Ranger," which starred Tom Mix, were completed, Grace flew cameraman Norman Devoe around the area to obtain background shots from the air. As the Jenny came over the group of farm buildings that served as the set, the OX-5 engine died. Grace yelled to Devoe, who was standing up with the camera, to sit down as they were about to crash. Devoe continued operating his camera all the way to the ground. When Grace climbed out of the tangled struts, wires and wing panels, Devoe was sitting on one of the wing panels with his camera still in his hands.[120]

Charles Nungesser, the third highest ranking French ace of World War I, came to the United States in 1924 to lead an air circus on a barnstorming tour of North America. He also played the leading role in a motion picture that was apparently filmed in a New York studio and at Roosevelt Field. Titled "The Sky Raider," only the barest of information is available, but it has been reported that Nungesser flew a Nieuport 12 and a Hanriot, which he brought from France for the air circus, and that several Thomas Morse Scouts were painted with crosses to serve as German airplanes. Nungesser came to Los Angeles in 1925 and sold the Hanriot to Jim Granger at Clover Field, who used it for stunt flying at local air shows.

Dick Grace acted a leading role for "Flying Fool" which was released by Sunset Productions in September 1925. Grace played Donald Daring, an aviator who is late for his own wedding. The outraged bride returns home with her family, her jewels and the best man. When Donald Daring arrives at the house to explain, he is refused admission. He enters by an upstairs window but is knocked unconscious in the process, which gives the envious best man an opportunity to plant the family jewels on his unconscious and unsuspecting rival. After Donald is arrested, the best man persuades the girl to fly away with him to San Diego. But Donald Daring is bailed out of jail, and in another airplane, pursues and rescues his disillusioned fiancee. Donald is cleared of suspicion and the wedding takes place at the end of the picture.

The airplane chase was the only air sequence in the picture, but Dick Grace never mentioned this film in his books, and no records exist as to the extent of the flying scenes.

Some time in 1925 a group of stunt men, auto race drivers, pilots and cameramen formed an organization at Burdette Airport in south Los Angeles, that would cater to exhibition and motion picture stunt flying. Calling themselves the Thirteen Black Cats, they established standard rates for various stunts, which they submitted to studios, airport managers, and fair associations. Their schedule of fees indicates the range of stunts being practiced at that time.

Crash ships (fly into trees, houses, etc.)	$1200.00
Loop with man standing on center section.	150.00
Loop with man on each wing, standing up	450.00
Ship change.	100.00
Upside down ship change.	500.00
Change-airplane to train.	150.00
Change-automobile to airplane.	150.00
Change-speedboat to airplane.	250.00
Change-motorcycle to airplane.	150.00
Parachute jump.	80.00
Parachute races-two jumpers.	150.00
Parachute jump-ocean landing.	150.00
Double parachute jump-two men on one parachute.	180.00
Fight on upper wing-two men, one knocked off.	225.00
Upside down flying.	100.00
Upside down flying with one man on landing gear.	150.00
Delayed opening parachute-over 1000 feet.	150.00
Crash automobile into train.	150.00
Head on collision with automobiles.	250.00
Plane goes into spin to crash.	1200.00
Plane spins down on fire, does not crash.	50.00
Blow up plane in mid air, pilot chutes out.	1500.00

In addition to his ability as a skilled flyer and stunt man, Al Wilson also had an eye for business. He noted the intricacies of making motion pictures, and formed his own production company which made a series of aviation thrillers during the next five years. He wrote the scripts, performed the stunts, acted the leading roles, and included parts for the other stunt flyers whenever possible. His first film, "The Air Hawk," was released at the end of 1924. Al Wilson played the part of an aviator Secret Service agent who is assigned to investigate a gang of thieves who have been robbing a platinum mine on the Mexican-American border. The superintendent of the mine discovers a secret passage used by the gang, but is killed by the outlaws. His daughter assumes the running of the mine and falls in love with the flying Secret Service agent. When she is kidnapped by the gang leader, who escapes in a waiting airplane, the Secret Service agent gives chase in another airplane, changes to the bandit leader's plane in-flight and rescues the girl after a fight on the wings of the airplane.

Frank Tomick acted in one of the supporting roles and flew one of the airplanes. Frank Clarke flew the other Jenny, but the pilot of the camera plane for the in-flight scenes is unknown.

"The Cloud Rider" appeared in theaters during the first part of 1925. Al Wilson appeared on stage when the film was shown at the California Theater in downtown Los Angeles. In the story, he is again a flying Secret Service agent, but this time his assignment throws him in with a drug smuggling ring that uses a fleet of airplanes for its operations. The feature stunt of the picture takes place when a girl flyer loses one wheel on take off. When he

The original "Thirteen Black Cats." From the left standing: Sam Greenwald, Bon MacDougall and Art Goebel. Kneeling from the left: Fronty Nichols and Al Johnson. Sitting from the left: Paul Richter, Herb McClelland and Spider Matlock. Courtesy: Jerry Phillips

sees her predicament, Al Wilson takes off with another pilot and a spare wheel strapped to his back. While Frank Tomick flew the second airplane just below the one-wheeled Jenny, flown by Frank Clarke, Al Wilson stood on the top wing of Tomick's airplane, and installed the spare wheel on the axle. He then grabbed the wing skid and climbed aboard the Jenny flown by Clarke, who was doubling for the terrified girl, to supposedly bring the frightened girl's airplane in for a landing.[121] In addition to Clarke and Tomick, Boyd Monteith is listed in the credits as a pilot on the picture.

Al Wilson's third picture, "Flying Through," was released at the end of 1925. The plot revolves around the efforts of a barnstorming aviator to clear his wrongly accused father of a murder charge. Among several other stunts, Al Wilson changed from Frank Tomick's precisely controlled Jenny to a speeding automobile below, where he overpowers and captures the real murderer.

Paramount hired Frank Tomick for its 1925 production, "The Air Mail."[122] The airplane scenes, consisting mainly of landings and takeoffs, were filmed in the

Antelope Valley, north of Los Angeles.

Al Wilson chose the Air Mail Service as a background for his next picture, "The Flying Mail." Frank Tomick acted in one of the supporting roles, and flew the pickup airplane for Al Wilson's stunts. In one chase situation, he chases the villain's airplane on a motorcycle, grabs a dangling rope ladder, climbs aboard, and fights with the villains before capturing the leader.

Newsreel cameramen frequently appeared at Clover Field to photograph an ever-increasing variety of stunts. Couples sat in chairs attached to top wings several thousand feet in the air, while apparently playing cards. Others played tennis on the top wing with a tethered ball, and some performed the latest dance step on the wing ribs in a sixty mile per hour slip stream. One parachute jumper was strapped in a strait jacket, placed in a metal tube attached to the bottom of an airplane, and taken up to three thousand feet where he was dropped from the tube, descending to the ground head first while hanging from the shroud lines by his bound ankles.

In the spring of 1925, John Miller, known as Chief

A stunt by the "Thirteen Black Cats." From left: Paul Richter standing, Spider Matlock on the wing, Bon MacDougall flying the Jenny, Fronty Nichols on the right wing and Art Goebel on the ground. Courtesy: Jerry Phillips

Al Wilson prepares to rescue the heroine before the bad guy, closing from rear, can overtake her, as Frank Tomick carefully positions the Jenny. Courtesy: G. Lawrence Hensey

Al Wilson abandons his motorcycle to escape from a pursuing automobile while Frank Tomick pilots the pickup plane. Courtesy: G. Lawrence Hensey

Lunch break during work on an Al Wilson picture near Lone Pine, Calif. Frank Clarke is standing in front of the Jenny wing tip, Frank Tomick is kneeling to his right, and Al Wilson is the third person from the right of the picture. Courtesy: Frank Tomick

Al Wilson eludes his pursuers as Frank Tomick opens the throttle for a scene from the Al Wilson picture, "Three Miles Up." Courtesy: G. Lawrence Hensey

Frank Tomick carefully positions Al Wilson on the rope ladder for an encounter with a bad guy on top of a Santa Fe Railroad train near March Field. Courtesy: G. Lawrence Hensey

Lobby card for Al Wilson's "Sky High Saunders." Courtesy: G. Lawrence Hensey

Bad guys Frank Tomick and Art Goebel are restrained by badge wearing Roy Wilson and a cowboy, while hero Al Wilson holds the girl in a scene from an unidentified Al Wilson movie. Courtesy: Tave Wilson

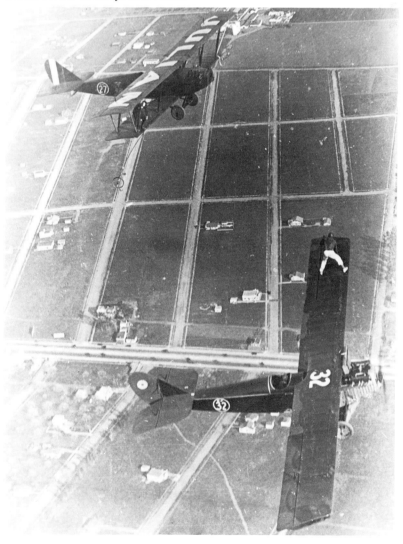

Al Johnson waits on Jerry Phillips' wing as Art Goebel moves into position for Ivan Unger to transfer the spare wheel. Julian was the name of a gasoline product being advertised by Goebel at the time. Courtesy: Howard Batt and Jerry Phillips

While Al Johnson lies blind-folded on Frank Clarke's top wing, Art Goebel moves into position for a newsreel stunt. Courtesy: Jerry Phillips

After Art Goebel "hooked" his bound feet, stuntman Al Johnson climbs aboard the Jenny. Courtesy: Jerry Phillips

White Eagle, made a tragic parachute jump for the newsreels that was supposed to surpass all previous jumps. Howard Batt flew the courageous stunt man in his J-1 Standard, while Frank Clarke flew the camera ship.[123]

Miller designed the stunt with the help of a balloon man and parachute jumper. A large sack containing ten parachutes was attached to the bottom of Batt's Standard, just behind the landing gear. Miller wore a special harness attached to each of the ten parachutes by a line and steel ring. When the Standard reached 2500 feet, Miller climbed down to the landing gear, hooked up and dropped into space pulling the ten parachutes from the sack. The plan of the stunt was for Miller to open a parachute, cut the line with a balloon knife which would separate him from the chute, open the second parachute, then cut it loose, and open the third chute and so on, finally descending in the tenth parachute. The plan

worked perfectly through four parachutes, but when he opened the fifth, he was less than one hundred feet from the ground. It was barely out of its pack when Miller hit the edge of Clover Field. He was rushed to the hospital at the nearby Sawtelle Soldiers' home, but Chief White Eagle died a few minutes after arrival.[124]

Another newsreel stunt that didn't go according to plan ended with happier results. Frank Clarke, Art Goebel and Al Johnson devised a situation for Pathe News where Al Johnson would lay flat on his back on Clarke's top wing, blindfolded and with his ankles bound together. While Johnson held his bound legs in a vertical position, Goebel would pluck him from Clarke's machine with a hook attached to the outer leading edge of his lower left wing. Johnson would then climb onto the wing and make his way to the rear cockpit.

The stunt became more complex when Jerry Phillips took off with a still photographer to record the action.

After the conclusion of the lost wheel incident the participants pose in front of Jerry Phillips' Jenny. From the left: Ivan Unger, Art Goebel, Frank Clarke, Bob Lloyd, Jerry Phillips, Al Johnson and the unidentified still photographer. Courtesy: Jerry Phillips

When he banked for a turn at 1500 feet, the left wheel fell from his Jenny onto a milk wagon in the streets of Santa Monica. Faced with a crash landing, Phillips circled the field to use up the one hour gasoline supply in his fuel tank.

The men on the field saw the wheel fall from the Jenny, and quickly devised a scheme to save the Jenny and its occupants from a crash landing. Frank Clarke took off with Al Johnson in the front seat. While Clarke moved alongside the one-wheeled Jenny, Al Johnson quickly climbed up to the top wing where he stood in a crouching position. Johnson motioned for Phillips to move in closer. When his lower left wing was just above Clarke's top right wing, Johnson transferred to Phillips' machine. With the agility of a cat, he moved through the struts and wires to the side of the pilot's cockpit, where he shouted above the engine noise that another plane was bringing up a spare wheel.

A few minutes later, Bob Lloyd, who had flown in several comedies and serials, took off in an L-4 Standard with Ivan Unger and a spare wheel attached to twenty feet of rope. While they climbed above the field, Johnson moved to the top left wing tip and waited for Bob Lloyd to move into position.

The Standard approached from above and behind, to the left of Phillips' Jenny, with Unger standing on the upper right wing holding the rope and wheel. In the turbulence, Al Johnson was unable to reach the dangling wheel as it bobbed up and down at the end of the rope.

When Lloyd pulled away and moved in for a second attempt, a gust or air pocket caused the Standard to bump, which resulted in a jerking motion of the rope. Thinking Johnson had grasped the wheel, Unger released the rope, but the wheel passed several feet beyond Johnson's hands as it fell to the field below.

Johnson climbed down and returned to the bottom wing by the pilot's cockpit. Shouting to each other, they decided to use up the remaining fuel and make a one-wheel landing with Johnson on the opposite wing tip to aid in centering the weight of the airplane on the single wheel. But the men on the ground had other plans. The frightened photographer sank lower into the front cockpit.

With another wheel on twenty feet of rope, but minus its tire this time to offer less wind resistance, Ivan Unger took off with Art Goebel in the latter's Jenny. Followed by Frank Clarke and a newsreel cameraman, Goebel and Phillips moved into position with Unger and Johnson on the wings. This time they were able to transfer the wheel, where Johnson placed it on the landing gear. But the hub was too large for the axle, and the holding nut would not keep the wheel in place. Al Johnson solved the problem by sitting on the lower wing above the wheel. Holding one foot under the landing gear strut, and pressing the other foot against the wheel hub, he was able to apply enough pressure to hold the wheel in place while Phillips brought the Jenny in for a safe landing.

No one was more relieved to be back on the ground than the bewildered photographer, but he went back up and photographed the originally planned stunt with Clarke, Johnson and Goebel.[125]

Frank Clarke, Art Goebel and Ivan Unger conceived

another lost-wheel incident for the newsreels a few months later. But this time, as in "The Cloud Rider," it was all planned for the cameras, and turned out to be one of the better aviation stunts to appear in the newsreels.

"The Great Mail Robbery," made in 1925 and revolving around an elaborate plot to rob a train, was not an aviation movie, but it contained two air incidents. Mark Campbell made a parachute jump into a ghost town in the Mojave Desert for one, while for the other Frank Clarke and Frank Tomick flew two Travelair biplanes as Marine aviators who strafe and capture the train after it has been taken over by outlaws.

These were among the first Travelairs to be used in motion picture work, and next to the Jenny, more Travelairs appeared in motion pictures of the 1920s and 1930s than any other aircraft type. Jimmy Barton was a young aircraft mechanic working on the airplanes used in "The Great Mail Robbery," and recalls the arrival of that airplane on the West Coast:

Looking northwest over Clover Field in 1924. The first hangar, after the two army hangars in the corner, was occupied by Bob Lloyd. Continuing to the left of the picture, the next hangar belonged to the Montee brothers, then Ruel Short's hangar, the hangar shared by Al Wilson and Howard Patterson, then Mort Bach's hangar which was moved up from Venice, Leo Nomis' hangar, Cross Aerial Photos hangar where Art Goebel kept his plane, and the Davis-Douglas hangar at the end. (Identification by Howard Batt.) Courtesy: Howard Batt

A planned lost wheel incident for the newsreels. Ivan Unger, with a spare wheel strapped to his back, takes off after Art Goebel purposely dropped a wheel over Clover Field. Courtesy: Jimmy Barton

Ivan Unger climbs to the top wing as Art Goebel moves into position for the transfer. Courtesy: Jimmy Barton

Unger attaches the spare wheel and the skit ends with a happy landing. Courtesy: Jimmy Barton

Another Clover Field stunt where Art Goebel is a little too high for Ivan Unger to pluck a handkerchief from the ground.
Courtesy: John Sloan

Al Wilson's replica Curtiss Pusher at a local air show. Courtesy: G. Lawrence Hensey

The location crew for an Al Wilson picture at the edge of Clover Field. The platform was called a "parallel" and allowed closeup shots to be made of the aircraft apparently in the air. Courtesy: G. Lawrence Hensey

"It caused a lot of comment when it first got here. Had better performance than a Jenny, and strong enough for acrobatics. Not nearly as good for wing walking, though—Jennies had a lot of bracing to hang from and use as handholds, so they stayed around for a while."[126]

Jimmy Barton came from Seattle, Washington, and worked as a motorcycle mechanic and construction equipment mechanic when he came to Los Angeles in 1921. After doing motorcycle stunt work in some of the early films, he hung around the Venice flying field and learned the profession of aircraft construction and maintenance. Jimmy Barton worked as an aircraft mechanic on every aviation movie made in Hollywood during the 1920s and 1930s, after his first job on "The Great Train Robbery."

Stunt flying was a precarious profession, and Howard Batt came very close to death during a barnstorming tour with the reorganized Thirteen Black Cats. Along with several other personnel changes from the original members, Jerry Phillips was also a member of the group on this particular tour. Howard Batt tells of his approach to eternity and the lasting lesson he learned from that experience:

"This is the story of the ill-fated flying circus and my dunk in the ocean in 1926. I made some strong rules for myself about flying without a compass and enough reserve fuel one cold night while clinging to the wings of an old Standard J-1 biplane, washing in the ground swells of the Pacific Ocean twenty-five miles off shore.

"Our flying circus, under the name of the Thirteen Black Cats, consisted of four ships. Two Jennies and the Standard were used for hopping passengers, wing walking, plane changing and parachute jumps. We used a Thomas Morse Scout for stunting and ballyhoo work.

"We were booked at various Pacific Coast towns north of Los Angeles all the way to the Canadian border. The pilots were Jerry Phillips, George 'Slim' Maves, who later flew for Wallace Beery, 'Loot' Barber, whose nickname came from his rank of lieutenant in the U.S. Army Reserve, and myself. Our stunt men were Ivan Unger, Freddy Osborn, and Spider Matlock.

"We opened at Bakersfield where Barber spun in

with a passenger in one of the Jennies. We left the Jenny in the junk yard, Barber in the hospital and moved on to Fresno where Maves made a one point landing with the Thomas Morse. We missed two other engagements while waiting for it to be repaired.

"Our next stop was Modesto where I administered the coup de grace by mushrooming the Standard into a vineyard with two passengers when the motor failed on takeoff. The promoter looked at the third major repair job and found other business ventures far away.

"Six stranded pilots and stunt men spent the next two and one half weeks repairing the Standard by day and standing off the hotel manager at night. The boys elected me as head man to see if we could salvage something from the collapsed tour. A cooperative show at Modesto gave us a few dollars for gas and we moved on to Sonora hoping to carry on with the original itinerary. We were rescued by a telegram from Hollywood offering steady work on a movie for all of us. We went back to Bakersfield to visit Barber, from where we would then fly on to Clover Field.

"On May 1, 1926, fog covered the Tehachapi Mountains and the Los Angeles area beyond. Jerry Phillips and 'Slim' Maves wisely decided to wait for the fog to clear. Ivan Unger remained with them. I was anxious to get to Hollywood and sign the contract for all of us, so I took off with Osborn and Matlock in the front cockpit of the Standard.

"I climbed to five thousand feet and the fog was up to the top of the mountain range. The old ship wouldn't take three of us over the top, so I landed alongside the highway at LeBec for Osborn to take the bus.

"Lacking a compass, my plan was to fly southeast using the late afternoon sun on my right as a guide, for an hour which would put me well in the Los Angeles area. Then I would drop down through a hole in the soup to a few hundred feet altitude and hedge hop home. I had a half hour reserve supply of fuel and thought it would be enough.

"At the end of the hour we were still flying on top of a thick, fleecy fog bank with no holes in sight. I kicked it into a spin. The Standard was the slowest spinning ship of its time, descending even slower than a parachute. My idea was to go straight down as slow as possible in case of a crash. I was afraid of a long glide or even a wide spiral because of the mountains around Los Angeles.

"We went down three thousand feet through the soup in what seemed like the same number of hours, hoping to break through and see the ground at each turn. Matlock saw the whitecaps before I did and yelled.

"I levelled off at 2500 feet and looked for the shoreline but it was nowhere in sight. With a quick glance at the low gas gauge I swung into a tight vertical until the tail was in the setting sun. By heading straight east and throttling back until we were barely flying, I hoped to get within at least a few miles of shore where someone could see us go down.

"Twenty anxious minutes later there was still no sight of land. Suddenly I thought Spider was out of his mind. He unbuckled his safety belt and climbed to the top wing center section, gesturing wildly to the north. About fifteen miles away, with its stern toward us, was a ship.

"Our only chance was to catch the ship, so I aban-doned our course for land and turned toward the ship. I motioned for Spider to take off his sweater and wave in hopes of catching the lookout's attention. This was no problem as he was a professional wing walker.

"The motor gave a final gasp and the silence was like a blow, but we had come closer to the ship and could still glide a few miles. Spider was still waving from the top wing and I yelled, 'Holler, Spider, Holler!' He shouted 'Ship ahoy!' several times at the wallowing lumber freighter ten miles away. He made me apologize later for laughing.

"Matlock was still waving his sweater when the wheels caught the crest of a wave and the nose went down. It doesn't sound very reverent now, but at that moment I whispered, 'God, this is Howard,' with all the sincerity that was in me.

"Matlock sailed off the top wing into the water. I kicked out of the cockpit and poked holes in the fuselage fabric with my toes, climbing toward the tail which was almost straight up. I looked for Spider, who was a good swimmer, and he was trying to swim straight up with his head and shoulders out of the water, still holding his breath. When I yelled to him he realized he was above water and yanked off his goggles which were full of water, causing him to think he was still below the surface.

"We hoped that someone on the ship had looked astern and had seen us go down. Each time the water-logged plane rose to the crest of a swell we looked anxiously at the ship, but it gave no sign of changing its course. After two hours we began to lose hope and took turns diving, trying to wrench a tire off the landing gear. We hoped to use an inner tube as a life preserver, as we knew the airplane would eventually sink. That hope vanished as we had no tools and our hands became so torn and bleeding that we had to abandon the effort.

"Just before dark Spider shouted that the ship was turning toward us. As we were slapping each other on the back, the ship swung away and we yelled in terrible desperation. The plane had settled until it was even with the surface of the sea. We stood on the top wing with the water lapping around our ankles.

"The ship came back or I wouldn't be able to tell this. The captain told us that he put the helm over hard when his lookout spotted us, which burned out a fuse in the steering mechanism, causing the ship to return to its original course.

"By the time the ship came within hailing distance we were up to our knees in water. Captain Charles E. Larsen of the S.S. Hamlin F. McCormick ordered a life boat over the side and even moved his ship alongside, rigged a boom and hoisted the old Standard aboard. Two days later we landed in San Francisco where the captain had another ship of his line carry the Standard to San Pedro from where it was trucked to Clover Field."[127]

By the mid-1920s, Leo Nomis, Al Wilson, Frank Clarke, Frank Tomick, Howard Batt, Jerry Phillips, Clem Phillips, Art Goebel, Roy Wilson, Tave Wilson, Dick Grace and Bob Blair were doing nearly all of the motion picture flying. Hardly a week passed without at least one of these men taking off from Clover Field for a

The "Thirteen Black Cats" by Howard Batt's Standard during the 1926 barnstorming tour. From the left: 1. George "Slim" Maves, 2. Freddy Osborn, 3. Howard Batt, 4. Ivan Unger, 5. Jerry Phillips, 6. Spider Matlock. Courtesy: Jerry Phillips

motion picture assignment.

Except for the Al Wilson pictures, aviation was usually incidental to the main plot, even when the title expressed an aviation theme. Flying scenes appeared in MGM's "Mike," First National's "Paradise," The Sky Pirate" distributed by Aywon, Sterling Pictures' "Wolves Of The Air," Pathe's "Pirates Of The Sky," "Daring Deeds" by Rayart, "Aflame In The Sky" distributed by the Film Booking Office, and Universal's "Hero For A Night." Dick Grace played his second lead in the Sunset Productions picture, "Wide Open." The plot revolved around a new aircraft engine design, its theft and eventual recovery in time to win the air race and a government contract.

Airplanes, almost always Jennies or Standards, continued to appear for a while in numerous westerns and serials where some airborne cowboy drops dynamite on a band of outlaws, buzzes a stampeding herd to turn them away from the local schoolyard filled with kids, or takes off into the sunset with the girl at the end of the picture. But the wing walking period of motion picture stunt flying was coming to an end. Script writers had contrived nearly every possible situation where men could walk the wings or change to another airplane, automobile, boat, motorcycle, train or horse. Newer, better performing and better looking sport biplanes by Travelair, Waco, Stearman, Fairchild, Bird and others were now common sights at Southern California airports, and readily available for rent to motion picture studios. The Jennies and Standards were deteriorating through age and use, and neither looked nor performed like the fighter planes used in the First World War which was about to be rediscovered as a story source for motion pictures.

Howard Batt's Standard after it reached port on the deck of the S. S. Hamlin F. McCormick. Courtesy: Howard Batt

CHAPTER THREE

HOLLYWOOD DOG FIGHTS

Earl Robinson's Speedwing Travelair just before it passed
through the explosion debris in "Dawn Patrol."
Courtesy: Frank Tomick

THE MOTION PICTURE studios avoided stories about World War I for several years after 1918 because the public was caught up in the "Roaring Twenties" spirit of abandon, and wanted to forget the recent war and its horrors. But Metro Goldwyn Mayer's 1925 war film, "The Big Parade," was well received and opened the way for a long series of feature films that utilized both the ground war and the air war as a background.

"Wings" was the first major motion picture to use large numbers of airplanes as a spectacle. The story was written by John Monk Saunders, who served as an army flyer in the training command during the war. The script called for squadrons of military airplanes to be photographed in formations and in dog fights. Airplanes were to be crashed, balloons were to be shot down, and a huge ground battle requiring thousands of troops was to be enacted. The army was the only source of men and equipment on such a scale.

Through acquaintances in Washington, Saunders contacted the War Department and presented the concept of a historically significant motion picture that would reflect the spirit of the nation's defenders. Two weeks later Dwight F. Davis, secretary of war, informed Mr. Lasky of Paramount Pictures that the War Department would extend its cooperation.

Camp Stanley, near Leon Springs, Texas, a former World War I training center thirty-five miles from Kelly Field, was selected as the main location site because of several military bases in the immediate area.

By the middle of summer 1926, army flyers and airplanes from Selfridge Field in Michigan, Crissy Field in San Francisco, and Langley Field in Virginia were on their way to Kelly Field at San Antonio, Texas. Observation balloons and crews came from Scott Field in Illinois, along with troops, trucks, tanks, barbed wire and explosives from nearby Fort Sam Houston.[128]

The story contained several crashes, spins and other air incidents that were beyond the army's agreement with Paramount. The studio hired Frank Tomick as chief pilot, and Ross Cooke as an assistant pilot.[129] Dick Grace contracted for two of the crashes, and Harry Perry received the assignment as chief cinematographer. William Wellman, who joined the Lafayette Flying Corps in 1916, (not to be confused with the Lafayette Escadrille) and served as a combat pilot with a French squadron for four months during the winter of 1917,[130] received the position of director.

Two other World War I flyers also worked on "Wings." Sterling Campbell, who flew with the R.A.F., served as a technical supervisor of flying sequences, and Edwin C. Parsons, an ace of the Lafayette Escadrille, served as a technical advisor and script writer.

Two special trains left Los Angeles for San Antonio,

Texas, in September 1926. In addition to actors, technicians, flyers, cameras, film, costumes, and thousands of other logistical items, four World War I airplanes for Dick Grace's two crashes were aboard. The script called for a Spad to crash in "no-man's-land," and a German Fokker D.VII to crash during a takeoff. As chief pilot, Frank Tomick recalls some of the details of the airplanes:

"I had worked for Paramount before, and they called me in to pick up some airplanes to go down to Texas. So I bought these planes, the two that Dick Grace cracked up, two Fokkers and a Spad. I got the Spad from Earl Daugherty in Long Beach—and I also got one Fokker down there, and I got the other one around L.A. somewhere. I paid $3500.00 for one, and $2000.00 for one, and $1500.00 for the Spad."[131]

A second Spad appeared in one of the lineups for "Wings," but its origin is unknown.

When the studio trains reached San Antonio, Texas, and all of the equipment had been trucked to Kelly Field, which served as the base of operations, Harry Reynolds took charge of the studio airplanes. Reynolds was the chief aircraft mechanic for Paramount, and worked in that capacity on several subsequent aviation movies. A member of the Naval Reserve, he rose to the rank of rear admiral during World War II. Working under his direction, along with several other skilled mechanics, was Jimmy Barton.

While six hundred local laborers, paid by Paramount but under the direction of army engineers, converted five square miles of the Camp Stanley artillery range into a replica of the St. Mihiel battlefield, work on the air scenes began. The army pilots were under the command of Maj. Frank Andrews, and included such other famous Air Force names as Hoyt Vandenberg, Harold George, Earl Partridge, and William Taylor.[132]

Harry Perry was busy devising special camera mounts, selecting camera positions, and planning assignments for twenty other cameramen, even before the location crew went to Texas.[133] Cameras with remote controls were mounted on airplanes to carry the audience into the air with the actors. Buddy Rogers and Richard Arlen, the two male leads, spent many hours in the air being photographed by remote cameras, while Frank Tomick and Ross Cooke flew the airplanes from second cockpits beyond the camera's field of vision.

After several test shots of the air action, Perry and Wellman realized that cloud formations were a necessary background in order to portray the immense three-dimensional depths of the air. Consequently, the air scenes had to wait for proper weather conditions. But the ground scenes continued without interruption.

The army assigned two hangars to Paramount for modification work on the studio airplanes, and for painting temporary Maltese crosses, roundels and camouflage on the army Curtiss P-1s, Thomas Morse MB-3s, D.H.4s, and Martin bombers used in the picture. Two Thomas Morse MB-3s were crashed with dummy pilots aboard. Jimmy Barton gives a good description of the devices employed in making those scenes:

"The studio bought, or got somehow, several old Thomas Morse pursuits from the army. They had been taken off the active list as being worn out, although they still looked good enough to me.

"Shooting was done mainly up at Camp Stanley, about thirty-five miles from Kelly Field, where the engineers had made a section of the field artillery range into a big battlefield set with trenches and dugouts. We had shipped several Jennies in, and two were bought locally for the training field scenes. You remember the one where Gary Cooper gets killed? Some of that was shot at Kelly in what they called the 'old field,' where they had a tent section and some of the old World War I hangars and buildings left. Some of the Jennies had been chopped up pretty well, so they had to be fixed back the way they was with original-style windshields, some new cowling and fabric where they was beat up. Two of 'em were Canucks, so we painted them like the Canadian air corps ships they used in Texas—the stripes and insignias.

"The special effects people staged the shot where Gary Cooper was supposed to be killed. Used good-size models, I think. It was done on the stage, not location. In the film it didn't show them coming at each other in the air—just shadows on the ground, then a quick cut to the ships grinding into each other.

"We used a track to wreck two—no, three of the Morses. The track was built like two troughs of planks, and a center guide grooved to take the tail skid. It was about 175 feet long, maybe a bit longer. Any shorter and the ship wouldn't get enough speed to fly off. We always located the tracks where we could take advantage of a little ridge or rise—give the airplane a little leeway in altitude—even a few feet was a help, because it really wasn't flying as it went off the end of the track—more like a powered glide. Sometimes they really wasn't flying when they went off the end of the track—just wallowing around through the air. You couldn't hardly send them off at full throttle—too much chance of jumping the track if a gust came along. The controls had to be lashed in place. Sometimes we had to put ballast in the ship fore or aft to correct estimated differences in static and dynamic balance. Some ships tend to be tail heavy at slow speeds—others just the opposite.

"If it was to fly into the ground you could lash a hair of down elevator into the control setting, or fix a time device that would release a holdback on the controls and dump it in—or stall it if you wanted it to fall off and go in.

"You couldn't depend on an engine cutting out when you wanted it to, just by limiting the gas supply. Even a quick shutting off of fuel won't do it. There's still gas in the carburetor that will carry it for sometimes close to a minute. It has to quit sudden, at the right place, or it'll be out of camera range.

"You had to have a way to make the engine throttle back, or chop the switch completely. We tried all sorts of things—timers, squibs to release springs, thin wire cable that would reel out and then jerk a restraining pin or clevis out. We worked a lot of things out as we went along."[134]

When the five square miles of Camp Stanley were covered with trenches, barbed wire and shell holes, Wellman scheduled the first crash by Dick Grace. An army pilot was killed the day before when he tried to make a turn too close to the ground.

Dick Grace carefully supervised the modification work on the Spad selected for the "no-man's-land" crash. A section of fabric was peeled from the fuselage and the wooden longerons of the framework were wrapped with tape to prevent them from splintering and acting as sabers at the time of impact. A steel framework was placed around the cockpit to prevent it from collapsing, and a special harness was attached.

In the story, Buddy Rogers is supposed to be shot down and crash in "no-man's-land." A camera was mounted behind the Spad's cockpit to photograph the action from the pilot's position. Several more cameras were hidden on the battlefield where the crash was to take place. At this particular spot, twenty-five feet of wood posts and barbed wire were replaced with balsa posts and twine.[135] Jimmy Barton recalls the circumstance of this crash:

"The way they was set up, Dick, the directors and the camera crews all got together and figured the best direction to come in—the light angle and the prevailing wind. They put up some posts, like they used for barbed wire, to tell him where to chop the throttle and put the ship down. Hung scraps of rag on 'em so's he could see them from the air.

"He made several passes at the place to get the feel of how it was going to be. During those they had a camera strapped to the turtleback, shooting forward past his head. Later they took the best parts of this footage and intercut it with footage of the actual crash. They took the camera off before he crashed it. They was Bell and Howell cameras, and cost several thousand dollars each, so they didn't want to bust one up.

"They got the Second Division engineers to work up the dirt where he was likely to hit—loose dirt being softer—then pile it back to look like it was before.

"When he came in he dropped a wing so's to catch the tip and make the airplane cartwheel and flip. They was some argument as to the right way to do it, but the main thing was to keep the ship from going in right on the nose, which is what it probably would do if he made a straight touchdown. Wipe the gear off, maybe drop the nose in a shell hole or go slithering across the ground. It wouldn't have made near as good action, and not been as safe either. Anytime you can slow a wreck up gradual, by breaking off pieces of it rather than all at once, you know—it's the sudden stop that kills you."[136]

The cameras ran for several seconds after the airplane came to rest, in order to insure complete coverage of the incident. Then Frank Tomick, being a fellow pilot who would best know how to quickly remove Grace from the cockpit in case of a fire, and other rescue personnel, left their fire extinguishers and cutting tools to climb from hidden positions in the trenches. Grace suffered no injuries, but discovered that he missed the balsa posts by seventeen feet and had crashed into hardwood posts strung with real barbed wire.[137]

In addition to a minor acting role, Frank Tomick flew the Fokker D.VII's for various parts of the air action. While flying below smoke bombs dropped from a higher plane to simulate anti- aircraft gun bursts, one of the bombs came too close and blew away one of Tomick's ailerons. The wing was also damaged, but he was able to make a safe landing.[138]

Several thousand troops came from Fort Sam Houston to re-enact the St Mihiel drive. While waves of doughboys and tanks threaded their way through planted explosive charges, squadrons of airplanes passed low over the battlefield. Cameras in airplanes, at various locations in the battlefield, and from the top of a one-hundred-foot-high tower, recorded the action from all possible view points.

Tave and Roy Wilson took time out from their barnstorming tour to visit Tomick, Grace and Cooke, and to attend some of the parties that took place almost every evening.[139]

One of the Fokker D.VII's was used in Grace's second crash. In the story, Richard Arlen has been captured by the Germans, but escapes by stealing a German airplane. As another German plane takes off in pursuit, Arlen circles the field and dives on the pursuer, causing him to crash during the takeoff.

The steel landing gear of the Fokker was partially cut, along with a part of the wing structure, to help the airplane break up for a more spectacular scene. Grace made his takeoff run while Lt. Thad Johnson dived on him in a Curtiss P-1. Apparently hit by machine gun fire, Grace slammed the Fokker into the ground from twenty feet in the air. Neither the wing nor the landing gear of the strongly built German airplane collapsed. The crash was successful as a scene, but the unyielding structure of the plane caused a fracture in Grace's neck at the time of impact, which required him to wear a neck brace for several months.[140]

After six months of work at Camp Stanley and Kelly Field, the location filming was completed. The Paramount crew returned to Hollywood, the War Department was reimbursed, and the army returned to its primary business of defending the nation.

The story of "Wings" opens in a small midwestern town where Buddy Rogers and Richard Arlen are unfriendly rivals for the love of Jobyna Ralston. Clara Bow is the tomboy girl next door who loves but is hardly noticed by Buddy Rogers. When war comes the two boys join the Air Service and are assigned to the same squadron in France where they become close companions. After some air action in their first dog fight, Buddy Rogers is forced to crash in no-man's-land, but is uninjured and makes his way back to the American lines. The two comrades are then sent on a mission in search of enemy observation balloons. After shooting down two of the gas bags, they are decorated and given leave in Paris. Clara Bow, who has become an ambulance driver in the meantime, also happens to be in Paris, but she is not recognized by the drunken Buddy Rogers. When she learns that all leaves have been canceled, she searches for Rogers and succeeds in getting him to a hotel room where she tries to sober him up so he can return to his unit without being court martialed. Her motives are mistaken by the military police and she is sent home in disgrace. Back at the front for the great offensive, the two boys take part in all of the air action and succeed in shooting down a bomber. Richard Arlen is shot down and captured, but escapes by stealing a German airplane. Buddy Rogers thinks he has been killed and takes off on a mission of vengeance. In his zeal for revenge he shoots down the German plane flown by Richard Arlen on his way back to the American lines, and his companion is killed. A sad Buddy Rogers returns home after the war as a hero, and finally notices Clara Bow as a beautiful girl and they fall in love.

"Wings" premiered in the spring at San Antonio where the aviation-oriented community demonstrated its hearty approval. It was released for a road show engagement with synchronized sound effects in August, and in a silent version for general distribution at the same time. Wherever it played, the theaters were filled, and the critics as well as the audience were generous in their praises.

The music and sound effects for the road show version were added after the filming was completed. There was no spoken dialogue, but Paramount leased General Electric's Kinegraphone System, and equipped twelve big-city theaters for the sound version. Kinegraphone was developed from the General Electric Pallophotophone System by which the voices of Calvin Coolidge and other famous people were recorded for radio broadcasts. The system utilized a sound track on the film[141] and was quite effective a few months before Al Jolson's voice was heard in movie theaters.

The music halted every so often to achieve full dramatic intensity. When airplanes were lined up for takeoff, the sound of motors and whirling propellers

Harry Perry in the rear cockpit of a Martin Bomber used as a camera plane during the filming of "Wings." Courtesy: Harry Perry

Frank Tomick entering the cockpit of a modified Fokker D.VII during the filming of "Wings." Courtesy: Frank Tomick

could be heard from the screen. Each time an airplane spun down in flames, a doleful high-pitched moaning accompanied the action. The whine and drone of motors came in two tones to denote the German and American airplanes.

Halfway through the first part of the sound effects version and during an air battle scene, the action switched to Paramount's Magnascope, where the screen and picture were enlarged to fill the entire stage of the theater. The same effect was utilized for the St. Mihiel battle scene in the second part.

Some of the Magnascope air battle scenes were further dramatized with color, where patient laboratory technicians had hand-tinted the sky, clouds, machine gun bursts, and burning airplanes in each individual frame of that sequence.

"Wings" reflected the highest quality of the motion picture arts at that time. In spite of the utilization of mostly post-war airplane types, the writing, direction, acting, editing, and particularly the aerial photography, were outstanding. "Wings" won the first Academy Award as best picture of the year.

One of the army pilots assigned to fly in "Wings" was Lt. Earl H. Robinson, who was born in Illinois on

From the left: Chief pilot Frank Tomick, Sterling Campbell, William Wellman, Dick Grace, Edwin C. Parsons, Norman MacLeod and John Monk Saunders at the Texas location for "Wings." Courtesy: Frank Tomick

The wooden track built for a crash scene in "Wings." With the engine running and a dummy pilot in the cockpit, the Thomas Morse MB-3 flew from a bluff at the end of the track and crashed into a river bed below. Jimmy Barton is second from the left and Harry Reynolds is on the extreme right. The ground crews often wore helmets and goggles to protect their eyes and ears from dirt and rock particles picked up in the prop wash. Courtesy: Jimmy Barton

September 19, 1903. Completing his Flying Cadet training two months before the Paramount location crew arrived in Texas, he flew one of the Martin bombers in the picture. Robinson liked the idea of flying for the movies and got well acquainted with Wellman.

Tomick, Grace and Cooke returned to Clover Field in the first part of 1927 to find that the Air Commerce Act had just become law. Interstate air traffic, the examining and licensing of pilots, and air safety were now under the jurisdiction of the federal government. Some of the more spectacular wing walking stunts would soon disappear, but "Wings" had opened the way for a series of aviation movies that would keep the motion picture stunt pilots busy for several years. Lindbergh's solo flight across the Atlantic at this time provided an even more receptive climate among audiences for motion pictures with an aviation theme.

Roy and Tave Wilson returned from their barnstorming tour about the same time that Davis-Douglas moved its plant to Clover Field. The resulting increase of air traffic limited the previously unrestricted use of the field for motion picture work. Hoping to attract motion picture contracts, the Wilson brothers established the Wilson Aero Service at the then less congested Glendale Airport, which had the added advantage of freedom from frequent marine fogs that often prevented shooting at Clover Field until the afternoon.[142] Roy Wilson obtained several flying jobs from Universal while Tave managed their fixed-base operations, which consisted of flying instruction, aircraft maintenance, charter flights, advertising flights, and the usual weekend passenger hops. Universal and other studios rented their airplanes and hangar as sets on several different occasions, but one of their first contracts was to advertise California Petroleum Products from the air.[143]

Al Wilson completed two more aviation thrillers, "Three Miles Up" and "Sky High Saunders," which were released by Universal in the fall of 1927. In "Three Miles Up," Al Wilson is a pre-war criminal who returns from France as a flying ace with a determination to end his life of crime in order to marry a girl from a nice family. Threatened with exposure by his old gang, he agrees to help the gang in one more robbery, but captures them after a climactic air battle. He returns the money, all is forgiven and he gets the girl. Art Goebel flew in the film and acted in a bit part.

In "Sky High Saunders," Al Wilson plays twins. While searching for his twin brother who was reported missing in an air battle in the recent war, Al Wilson finds him working with a gang of airplane smugglers. After a confrontation that ends with the shooting down of his errant brother's airplane, Al Wilson assumes the identity of his dead twin, joins the gang and captures the band of smugglers.

Universal released another Al Wilson thriller in the first part of 1928. In "The Air Patrol," Al Wilson is a captain in the government air patrol, but is dismissed after a misunderstanding. Frank Tomick plays the part of a suspected diamond smuggler. Frank Clarke and Art Goebel had lesser roles as aviators. Al Wilson again captures the gang of smugglers after changing planes and a fight in the air. He also rescues a girl who has been kidnapped by the criminals, and is restored to his position in the air patrol.

Lindbergh's flight influenced the story in Warner Brothers "Across The Atlantic" which was released in February 1928. In the story, two brothers love the same girl. She marries one who becomes a flyer in World War I. After being shot down in France, he loses his memory and becomes a wanderer. Eight years later he shows up as a test pilot at his unsuspecting father's airplane factory. While test flying a new airplane, he crashes and his memory returns. In the meantime his wife has promised to marry the other brother after one last trip to the spot in France where her husband was shot down and disappeared. Authorities refuse to believe that the amnesic brother is who he claims, and send him to an insane asylum. He escapes, steals an airplane and flies across the Atlantic just in time to be reunited with his wife.

Using the same slapstick comedy formula of "Behind The Front" and "We're In The Navy Now," Paramount took some of the leftover air scenes from "Wings" and made a third Wallace Beery, Raymond Hatton comedy titled "Now We're In The Air." In the story Beery and Hatton are cousins who become mixed up in the air war in France and drift over the German lines in a runaway balloon. Mistakenly honored as German heroes they are sent back to the American side as spies for the Kaiser. Captured and about to be shot, they are able to prove their identity at the last minute.

Frank Tomick served as chief pilot on the additional air scenes required for "Now We're In The Air." Paramount leased the Griffith Park field and the National Guard Jennies stationed there. The French Spad and German Fokker that were not crashed for "Wings" appeared in this movie at the Griffith Park field.

The director decided to make some air shots one afternoon after the National Guard personnel had gone for the day. The parachutes were locked up, and Frank Tomick, who was flying the camera plane, still flew without a parachute in spite of the new Air Commerce Act. Burton Steene, the aerial cameraman, was a cautious and practical man who believed in complying with that part of the regulations requiring parachutes. Tomick took the prop man aside and soon returned with a parachute that was strapped to Burton Steene. The airplane took off and the required shots were made in less

Glendale Airport in 1926 looking west toward Griffith Park. The large building is the hangar for the Slate metal dirigible. The two hangars in the center housed the Wilson Aero Service. The Los Angeles River flows at the top left, crossed by the Riverside Drive bridge. Courtesy: Tave Wilson

than one hour. When the camera plane landed, Tomick was smiling as he jumped from the front seat and eagerly assisted his surprised friend from the rear cockpit, purposely pulling the parachute release ring at the same time. Tomick could no longer control his laughter as the startled cameraman stood on the ground and stared at the pillow that fell from the dummy parachute he had been wearing.[144]

"The Sky Rider," released by the Chesterfield Motion Picture Corporation in the summer of 1928, contained very little flying. The story dealt with a nephew's attempt to do away with his aviation magnate uncle in order to inherit his millions.

Al Wilson provided another air thriller in "Won In The Clouds," though there was less air action than usual for an Al Wilson picture. Frank Tomick, Roy Wilson and Ivan Unger had parts as the bad guys, and Art Goebel played the role of Sam Highflyer. The story setting takes place in Africa where a crooked diamond mine manager is withholding gems for his own use. When the owner and his daughter travel to Africa to investigate, they are kidnapped. Al Wilson eventually rescues them after the usual air battle.

Universal's "The Cloud Dodger" again starred Al Wilson in another air thriller, as they were called by the publicity department. In this comedy drama, Wilson's

sweetheart deserts him for a wealthy suitor. But the jilted Wilson interrupts their wedding with his airplane, and chases them in their airplane. Transferring between airplanes, Al Wilson snatches the girl from the front seat and changes back to his own plane piloted by a friend. The girl realizes her mistake and the two lovers are eventually married in the air.

Despite its title, "The Flying Buckaroo" by Action Pictures was primarily a love story with a ground setting. However, one sequence shows the hero pursuing the outlaws in his airplane, and parachuting into their hide-out.

"Flying Romeos" was a comedy by First National in which Charlie Murray and George Sidney take flying lessons in an attempt to impress a girl. They accidentally perform stunts and eventually fly across the Atlantic, to find that the girl has married another.

Al Wilson almost lost his life in one of the pictures of this time. While filming closeups of himself with a remote camera installation on a Curtiss Pusher from Clover Field, the vibrating engine tore the camera from its mount and broke the fuel line. Flames immediately erupted when the fuel came in contact with the hot engine. With no parachute, fire in the air is a terrifying experience. But with a position in front of the engine, he was able to maneuver the burning machine down from three thousand feet and make a successful landing just before the pusher was consumed by the fire.[145]

Frank Clarke's handsome features won him the leading role in Pathe's ten-chapter serial, "Eagle Of The Night." Roy Wilson played a supporting role, and both men did all of the stunt flying. The plot revolved around the attempts of a smuggling gang to steal the "magic muffler," an invention which silenced the motor of an airplane. Of great value to their smuggling flights across the border at night, the gang eventually kidnaps the inventor and his daughter. After many flying incidents, aerial stunting situations, and a scene in which Frank Clarke lands his Jenny on the flat car of a moving train, he rescues the inventor and his daughter in the end.

The Dole Company offered a prize for the first successful flight from the mainland to Hawaii. Dick Grace tried to upstage the event by flying from Hawaii to the mainland, but he crashed on takeoff at Barking Sands Beach near Mana, Kauai, with no injuries. Art Goebel won the race a few weeks later, and seldom had time for motion picture work after the financial success and recognition he won from that and other pioneering flights.

After "Now We're In The Air" was released, Paramount started work on another World War I air film, "Legion Of The Condemned," again written by John Monk Saunders and directed by William Wellman. In the story, Gary Cooper finds his sweetheart, Fay Wray, in the arms of a German officer at a pre-war embassy party. Mistakenly thinking that she is being unfaithful, he later joins a French squadron composed of disillusioned flyers who want to escape painful incidents from their past with plenty of action and an honorable death. When Gary Cooper receives a suicide assignment to drop a spy behind the German lines, the agent turns out to be his former sweetheart, who can now reveal that her activities with the German officer were part of her duties as an underground member of French Intelligence. All is forgiven, but the lovers are captured. Just before they are to be shot, a bombing raid interrupts the firing squad and they are rescued by the Legion of The Condemned.

Most of the air scenes came from "Wings," but a D.H.9 appeared in several new scenes that were photographed at the Griffith Park field, and at an open field near Calabasas which was the location for the landing of the spy behind the German lines and the subsequent capture.

First National's "Hard Boiled Haggarty" appeared in the theaters at this time, and starred Milton Sills as an American aviator involved with twin French girls in Paris. Aside from a few brief air scenes in the beginning,

the rest of the picture dealt with Sills in Paris and mixups of identities with the twins.

Pathe's "Captain Swagger" opened with some good air scenes in France involving a Fokker D.VII and a Spad, but the main part of the story revolved around Rod LaRoque's post-war criminal activities in New York.

Universal released "The Lone Eagle," a World War I flying story that was partially filmed at an air field near San Diego.

Several other aviation pictures were in various stages of production when Howard Hughes entered the Hollywood aviation scene in 1927. Hughes had already been introduced to the motion picture industry through his novelist uncle, Rupert Hughes, who was engaged in screen writing during the early 1920s. With an almost unlimited income from the Hughes Tool Company in Texas, inherited from his late father, the young Howard Hughes financed Marshall Nielan's production, "Everybody's Acting." When this returned a handsome profit, Hughes organized Caddo Productions, and made a successful film titled "Two Arabian Knights." After seeing "Wings" several times, the young millionaire decided to make an aviation epic of his own.

Hughes purchased a story idea from Marshall Nielan,

When the Air Commerce Act became law, everyone was required to wear parachutes when flying. Ralph Douglas, an exhibition parachute jumper, gave instruction to some of the flyers and actors in "Hell's Angels." Posing in front of a Sopwith Snipe at the Mines Field location are from the left: Douglas, Leo Nomis, Frank Clarke, James Hall, Ben Lyon, Frank Tomick and Roy Wilson. Courtesy: Frank Tomick

Two of the Curtiss Jennies that were modified to resemble Avro 504 training planes, at the British training field location at Mines field for "Hell's Angels." Courtesy: Frank Tomick

Roscoe Turner's Sikorsky S-29 while it was being used to fly Curlee Clothes representatives to their sales territories. Courtesy: Source unknown

The Sikorsky S-29 at Caddo Field after it became a "Gotha" bomber for "Hell's Angels." Courtesy: Frank Tomick

The miniature Zeppelin constructed by Bill Butler, Lawrence Butler, Barney Korn and others. The model was photographed by Barney Korn in front of Bill Butler's home on Evergreen Street in the Magnolia Park area of Burbank. Courtesy: Barney Korn

The aluminum structural framework for the Zeppelin miniature photographed at the rear of Bill Butler's home in Burbank. Courtesy: Barney Korn

which grew into a basic script titled "Hell's Angels." Ben Lyon, James Hall and Greta Nissen were selected for the leading roles, and work on the dramatic portion of the film began in October 1927, at the Metropolitan Studios on Santa Monica Boulevard and Las Palmas, near the Caddo offices on Romaine Street.

Harry Perry was chosen for the position of chief aerial photographer. His selection of camera positions and the design of additional remote camera installations surpassed his work in "Wings" and was one of the main factors in the later success of "Hell's Angels."

Howard Hughes started taking flying lessons from the American Aircraft Company at Clover Field during the summer of 1927, and Moye Stephens recalls the circumstances when Hughes started his flying career:

"J.B. Alexander was sales manager for American Aircraft at this time. I had just gotten back from Stanford for the start of the summer vacation. The phone rang and it was J.B. who said Doc Whitney had told him I was back from Stanford and would I go to work for them. I said sure, and went down to see Doc. He gave me his very detailed description of how that airplane should be flown. No check out, he just took me over to the airplane. He was so methodical, this guy Whitney. When I started to work there was one stu-

The Los Angeles Metropolitan Airport in 1929 looking northwest. Caddo Field is indicated by the arrow. Courtesy: Frank Tomick

dent there, and I started giving him instruction. The following week they hired Charlie LaJotte. Doc had one of us come to work at 5:00 in the morning and fly till 12:30. The other one would come to work at 12:30 and fly till 8:00, to take advantage of all the daylight hours. Every week we would switch around.

"They had just started this thing and it was Charlie's afternoon hitch when Hughes came down to take his lessons. When we switched around and I showed up, Hughes took a look at me—and he had a very high voice and a hearing difficulty—Hughes said, 'I won't fly with him. He's too young!' So I was stuck with the morning shift for the rest of the summer."[146]

Moye Stephens later flew Richard Haliburton around the world, gaining international fame as an expert pilot. He then went to work for Maddux Air Lines, Transcontinental Air Transport, and eventually flew for many years as a captain for T.W.A.

Foreseeing the need for a manager to coordinate the many aviation aspects of "Hell's Angels," Hughes hired J.B. Alexander for this position. Frank Tomick tells how he was then brought into the production:

Looking northeast toward the San Gabriel Mountains with the two balloon sheds of the Ross Field Balloon School in the foreground. This photograph was made after one of the sheds was used for the Zeppelin sequence in "Hell's Angels." Columbia's arctic set for "Dirigible" can be seen at the left of the picture. Courtesy: Tave Wilson

Roscoe Turner by Frank Tomick's Fokker D.VII at Caddo Field during the filming of "Hell's Angels." Courtesy: Frank Tomick

Harry Crandall after spinning down in a Fokker D.VII with lamp black to simulate smoke for a scene in "Hell's Angels." Courtesy: Frank Tomick

Frank Tomick and cameraman E. Burton Steene stand by their Travelair camera plane at the Chatsworth location during the filming of "Hell's Angels." The Travelair is marked to fly in the formation and take pictures while other cameras in other airplanes are photographing the formation from a distance. Courtesy: Frank Tomick

Cowboy star Hoot Gibson landed at Caddo field to see Ben Lyon and turned on his nose. Here the "Hell's Angels" crew rights the airplane. Courtesy: Harry Perry

Roy Wilson was landing this Hisso Powered Fokker D.VII at Caddo Field when one of the bracing wires in the landing gear structure failed. From the left: Unknown, Roy Wilson, Phil Jones and Jimmy Barton. Courtesy: Frank Tomick

Camera extension on the nose of the Sikorsky whereby Ben Lyon photographed himself in the air with a remote switch in the cockpit. The man with the tool box is Phil Jones, who was killed in the bomber crash. Manuel Zamora, who was the explosives expert on the picture, is in the front cockpit. Cameraman Don Brigham is on the ladder. Courtesy: Frank Tomick

Harry Perry, at extreme right, waits for adjustments at Caddo Field while photographing machine gun hits on the tail of a mockup for "Hell's Angels." Courtesy: Frank Tomick

Four Fokker D.VII's lead the German squadron take off from the German airfield location at Chatsworth for a scene in "Hell's Angels." Courtesy: Jerry Phillips

Horseplay at Caddo Field during the filming of "Hell's Angels." From the left: Al Wilson, Roscoe Turner, Jack Rand, Roy Wilson (kneeling), Frank Clarke, Ben Lyon (on pony), Frank Tomick, Jimmy Barton (kneeling) and Harry Crandall. Courtesy: Frank Tomick

Frank Tomick and Burton Steene wait for their D.H.4 camera plane to be fueled at Caddo Field. Courtesy: Frank Tomick

Planning a scene for "Hell's Angels" at Caddo Field. From the left: Harry Perry, asst. director Freddy Fleck, Roscoe Turner, Frank Clarke, Al Wilson, Harry Crandall (kneeling), Roy Wilson, Frank Tomick and Jack Rand. Courtesy: Frank Tomick

The German squadron lined up at Caddo Field with Frank Clarke in the nearest of five Fokker D.VII's. The remaining six airplanes down the line are Travelair "Wichita Fokkers." Courtesy: Howard Batt

"I finished my flying for the 'Wings' in San Antone, finished with Paramount. I ran into J.B. Alexander who I had known before, and his company was teaching Howard Hughes to fly at the time. So he said, 'Howard is going to make Hell's Angels, why don't you come over with me and meet Howard Hughes.' So I went over to Caddo and met Howard Hughes. He wanted to know when I wanted to start work. He told me he needed a bunch of planes, Camels, S.E.5's, D.VII Fokkers. 'Get all you can.' So we went all over the country, wired and found out where they kept some planes. We got one D.VII in San Antone, or two, I forget now— one at Oakland, and two here. Anyway, we had five all total.

"He decided to get some Avros. So he wanted to know what the deuce we could use for Avros. You couldn't buy or find any in the United States. So finally we decided to buy three or four Jennies and cut off the wings to make it straight, upper and lower, and get some rotary motors, and make it look just like an Avro. We got Kinner Aircraft, he was in Glendale, not much of a business at that time. His wife worked as a seamstress, and they recovered these Jennies, and installed the motors, so we got three Avros."[147]

The modified Jennies, which were made to resemble the British Avro training plane, were taken to March Field for the first air scenes of "Hell's Angels." The giant World War I training field had been closed in April 1923, but a row of sixteen wooden hangars was still in place and served as an ideal location for a Royal Flying Corps training field.

In an effort to interject comedy into the flight training portion of the story, the Avro Jennies went through awkward maneuvers over the field. Two near accidents at this location came as the result of trying to depict the antics of green student pilots. Al Johnson, dragged a wing while flying close to the ground, and Bob Lloyd hit the top of a hangar with his landing gear.[148]

Hughes moved the training field location to Mines Field in Inglewood at this time, as a result of the War Department's decision to tear down the wooden hangars and replace them with steel hangars, when March Field was reactivated in 1927. The wooden hangar set that appeared at the Mines Field location looks exactly like the old March Field hangars, so it was quite possible that Hughes purchased some of the hangars and had them rebuilt at the Mines Field location.

Most of the training field sequence was edited out of "Hell's Angels," but some of the scenes appeared several years later in "Sky Devils."

Moye Stephens tells of flying Hughes to another location during the early days of making "Hell's Angels:"

"I flew Howard Hughes out to a location in the San Fernando Valley. Howard was quite a golfer. He was scheduled for a tournament at the San Gabriel Country Club. Al Johnson was going to flip this Jenny, rebuilt to

Howard Hughes sitting on the top step during the filming of "Hell's Angels" at Caddo Field. Courtesy: Frank Tomick

look like a British ship, on its back. Hughes wanted to see it, but he didn't want to miss the golf tournament. So they had me fly out to Ross Field in Arcadia, and get a taxi, go to the country club, find Hughes on the links there, follow him around till the thing was over, and have the taxi standing by all this time, and then get him to Ross Field, and he was going to fly the airplane out to this location. Where we were supposed to land was a newly subdivided tract. It was a city block with no buildings on it. We had to come in over some high-tension lines—northeast to southwest. We had to go between two oak trees. Howard had just soloed that summer. I figured it was okay to let him make the stab, but I was going to be ready to take over. He came in, but he saw he wasn't going to make it. He came around again, he made two stabs at it, then he pulled up and hollered, 'You do it!' So I had to come in over it, real high and fish tail it in. Just as we stopped rolling, Al Johnson came in and flipped this Jenny over on its back. They fixed it up, and without too much flying experience, Al was killed a short time later."[149]

Frank Tomick adds a few details of the crash that killed Al Johnson:

"Al Johnson was a stunt man, and he was helping to pick up parts. Kinner called and said one of the Avros was ready to deliver down to the airport. Howard Hughes rented a big field next to Mines Field, but to one side, built up big hangars like English. Al Johnson took off from Glendale Airport, hit those high tension wires in Griffith Park and burned up."[150]

"Hell's Angels" personnel at Caddo Field. Standing from the left: Earl Gordon (on wing), Frank Clarke, Ira Reed, Frank Tomick, Elmer Dyer and Roy Wilson. Kneeling from the left: Ross Cooke, Garland Lincoln, Howard Batt, unknown, Harry Perry, R.C. Merriman. Courtesy: Howard Batt

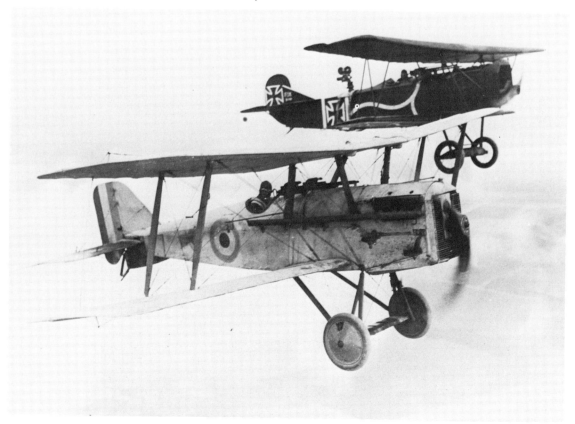

Roy Wilson in an S.E.5 and Frank Clarke in a Fokker D.VII with a remote camera installation shooting forward, controlled by a switch in the cockpit. Courtesy: Harry Perry

The pilots, cameramen and ground crews posed by the airplanes used in the main dogfight scene of "Hell's Angels." Courtesy: Harry Perry

Last minute briefings before taking off from Oakland Airport for the dogfight scene in "Hell's Angels." Courtesy: Frank Tomick

Frank Tomick and E. Burton Steene in the D.H.4 camera plane that was used to film most of the air scenes in "Hell's Angels." Courtesy: Frank Tomick

Otto and Wally Timm had recently established the Timm Aircraft Corporation at Glendale Airport, and Wally Timm was the first man to reach the burned Jenny which fell in the riverbed of the Los Angeles River. Al Johnson was not in the wreckage. After several minutes of searching the area, Wally Timm found him laying by a log in a gully. As he helped the injured flyer to his feet, Johnson begged to be put to sleep. When he collided with the electrical lines, the top wing tank ruptured and ignited, bathing the pilot's cockpit in flames. Johnson had inhaled solid flames into his lungs and was suffering excruciating pain. He died several hours later in a Glendale hospital.[151]

With only five Fokker D.VII's for the German squadron, Hughes decided to use the authentic airplanes in the foreground, though the markings and some of the minor modifications were not authentic, and fill in the background with Travelairs. The Travelair bore a strong resemblance to the famous German fighter plane, and they were easily available. Otto and Wally Timm did the modification work on the Fokkers and Travelairs. The Travelairs were christened Wichita Fokkers by the "Hell's Angels" crew—after Wichita, Kansas, the location of the Travelair factory. Travelair biplanes carried that name for many years in Southern California aviation circles.

Frank Tomick continues his account of the aviation side of "Hell's Angels" during the early stages of its production:

"Then we decided to get some T.M.'s (Thomas Morse Scouts) and make Camels out of them. So we picked up four or five, in fact I sold him one I had. We fixed these up like a Camel, cut out center section, bigger tails. We got two S.E.5's and two Sopwith Snipes, which didn't fly in the picture. They were considered too hot—used in backgrounds.

"Howard said, 'Frank, I want you to find me seven or eight pilots for this picture.' I said, 'How much you want to pay?' He saw all these young guys hanging around the airport who had just learned to fly, and they would work for nothing just to be in a picture. In the meantime he had just soloed and he thought anybody that soloed could fly anything. He said, 'I won't pay over ten dollars a day.' I said, 'You won't get much of a pilot for ten dollars.' He said, 'You get 'em, and you can teach them.' So I get a bunch of kids, or young fellows who just learned to fly. Howard said, 'I like to see their formation. You take them up and fly over the field, in T.M.'s, and see how they fly in formation.' I said, 'I'm not going to fly with that gang, that never been up in T.M.'s.' I didn't go, and I said to Jimmy Barton, who was a mechanic, 'Crank up that truck and get ready to bring those planes back.' I was kidding in a way.

"So I told them to make a formation and fly over the field. Howard was still belly-aching to me, 'Why don't you go out there and lead them.' Anyway, they never did get in formation, not what I would call formation.

Sure enough, two or three landed down in Wilmington, forced landing. One turned over in a plowed field, and one ended up in Long Beach. It took us two days to get the planes back. I said, 'There is your ten dollar pilots.' He said, 'That won't do. Get me the best.'

"So we got Frank Clarke, Roy Wilson, Leo Nomis, and a fellow named Loop Loop Murphy. He was a cartoonist with the San Francisco Examiner before the war. Murphy was one of the greatest T.M. pilots I ever saw. He could really make the thing talk.

"So we took those five T.M.'s out at the airport, but Murphy had a plane with a LeRhone and a rod to pull the gas on and off. So that rough field, you see—every time he got ready to take off, it would close the gasoline—bouncing, you know, would move the rod and he would have to come down. So three times he couldn't get off. Howard said, 'What are you talking about! He can't fly a T.M., he can't even take off.' But Jimmy Barton found out what was wrong and fixed it. I told Murphy what Howard said, and he was hot headed.

"We went up and flew in tight formation, no shooting, just so he could see, and he was very pleased. We all landed but Murphy. He spotted Howard down there, and kept diving at him for about ten minutes. He lay down in this plowed field, and Murphy came so low he was afraid to get up. He said, 'Fire him, Frank! He tried to kill me!' I said, 'He showed you he's the best T.M. pilot. Why do you want to fire him?'

"So anyhow, that's how we got the seasoned pilots.

The steady pilots all through the picture was Clarke, Roy and myself, the three of us. All the rest was off and on.

"It was the next week or so Howard wanted to fly a T.M. himself. I said, 'You can't fly a T.M. They got no carburetor, you got to mix your own air, and it's got a hell of a torque.' He said, 'You fly it, why can't I fly it?' I said, 'You're not a pilot yet.' That hurt him. He made up his mind, he's gonna fly, he's gonna show me.

"So Freddy Fleck, an assistant director, one of the finest fellows I ever knew, who was always kidding around, said, 'Don't let him fly until Monday. We got to get a check Saturday.' Howard was signing the checks then. So I marked with a pencil, where to put the gas and throttle. I said, 'Don't turn it this way or the torque will get you, until you get up high.' But he said, 'I see you do it.' I said, 'Never mind, don't you do it.' So he took off and turned—boom! Down on the nose. Howard Hughes is hard of hearing, you know. We ran down there and he was still in the cockpit. Broke his nose, that's all it did. Freddy Fleck said, 'Frank, ask him how is his right arm?' I said, 'Howard, how's your right arm? You gotta sign checks, you know.' But he didn't get the joke or didn't hear too good. He said, 'What the hell, my right arm? My nose, my nose!'

"So I had to go to his house on Mansfield, and draw the picture, why he did this or that—explain the torque and the forces working on the airplane. He wanted to understand completely."[152]

OPPOSITE PAGE:
The Caddo Field crew of pilots and cameramen, except for Roy Wilson, by the Sikorsky at Oakland Airport. Standing from the left: Roscoe Turner, Burton Steene, Frank Tomick, Billy Tuers, Ross Cooke, Earl Gordon, Garland Lincoln, Clinton Herberger, Jack Rand, Bob Starkey, Harry Crandall, J. B. Alexander and Jeff Gibbons. Kneeling from the left: Nate West, Burton Thomas, R. S. McAllister, Harry Reynolds, Ernie Smith, Ira Reed, Frank Clarke, Al Wilson, Elmer Dyer, Harry Perry and Don Brigham. Benny Colgren stands in the Sikorsky window. Courtesy: Garland Lincoln

BOTTOM:
The Caddo crew, except for Roy Wilson, with additional pilots from the Oakland area. Standing from the left: R. O. Shellaire, A. F. Mickel, John Penfield, unknown, C. F. Sullivan, C. E. Dowling, George Ream, unknown, Tom Penfield, Stuart Murphy, R. S. McAllister, Roscoe Turner, Burton Steene, Frank Tomick, Jack Rand, Harry Crandall and Elmer Dyer. Kneeling from the left: Harry Reynolds, Ira Reed, Ross Cooke, Julian Wagy, unknown, unknown, George Willingham, George Parker, Garland Lincoln, Bob Starkey, unknown, J. G. Walsh, Clinton Herberger, and unknown. Seated from the left: Harry Perry, unknown, unknown, J. B. Alexander, Billy Tuers, Jeff Gibbons, Frank Clarke, Ernie Smith, Al Wilson, R. A. Patterson and Earl Gordon. Courtesy: Frank Tomick

Ross Cooke in a two seat Fokker D.VII at Oakland Airport. Courtesy: Frank Tomick

Frank Tomick and the Hall-Scott powered Fokker D.VII that he flew in "Hell's Angels" as von Richthofen. The real von Richthofen never flew a Fokker D.VII in combat; he didn't have his name painted on the cockpit, and Fokker D.VII's didn't have headrests. Courtesy: Frank Tomick

Roy Wilson in one of the "Hell's Angels" S.E.5's. The faint handwritten reference to "War Correspondent" is incorrect as are the Marlin machine guns as armament for an S.E.5. Courtesy: Tave Wilson

Frank Clarke as Lt. von Bruen in "Hell's Angels."
Courtesy: Jerry Phillips

Part of the "Hell's Angels"
crew at Caddo Field. From
the left standing: Roy
Wilson, Al Wilson, Burton
Steene, Frank Tomick,
Roscoe Turner, Frank
Clarke, Harry Crandall and
Ira Reed. From the left kneel-
ing: Ross Cooke, Jack Rand,
Ernie Smith, Earl Gordon,
Harry Perry and Harry
Reynolds. Courtesy: Frank
Tomick

A Curtiss Jenny with dummy
engine nacelles, made to
resemble the Sikorsky and
originally planned for the
spinning and crash scene, but
it caught fire in the
maintenance shed. Courtesy:
Jimmy Barton

Ira Reed enjoys spoiling Roscoe Turner's picture as Turner poses in a Royal Flying Corps uniform. Courtesy: Jimmy Barton

Looking east along Hollywood Boulevard for the premier of Hell's Angels." Courtesy: Bruce Torrence Collection, First Federal Hollywood

One of the Fokker D.VII's flown in the movie was suspended at Grauman's Chinese Theater during the showing of "Hell's Angels." Courtesy: Bruce Torrence Collection, First Federal of Hollywood

While the Caddo Company was working at the Mines Field location, First National's "Lilac Time" crew shot its first air scenes at an elaborate Royal Flying Corps airfield set in the foothills between Santa Ana and San Juan Capistrano.[153] As the aviation contractor for the Royal Flying Corps scenes of the picture, Dick Grace was to execute three crashes, furnish seven airplanes to be used as the British formation, and furnish the pilots to fly the airplanes. He purchased and leased seven Waco 10 two-seat biplanes. After minor modifications to the engine cowling and front cockpit, and the addition of machine guns and insignia, the modified Wacos were of such proportions and appearance that they looked like authentic World War I airplanes, though they didn't resemble any specific type. Finding pilots to fly them proved to be more of a problem than locating the airplanes.

Most of the experienced pilots were already committed to other pictures. Ross Cooke and C.K. Phillips were the only available pilots, besides Grace himself, who had any previous motion picture flying experience. In addition to Cooke and Phillips, Grace hired five new men to become motion picture stunt pilots. Charles Stoffer, Frank Baker, B.M. Spencer, Lonnie Hay and E.D. Baxter were capable flyers and performed well in "Lilac Time," but for various reasons they did not continue as motion picture stunt pilots.

In order to provide a variety of scenes from which the film editors could choose, the seven Wacos were photographed from different angles while taking off, flying, and landing in formation. Before any of the crashes were made, they were also lined up in front of the hangars as a background for several scenes. Dick Grace appeared in a non-speaking role as one of the English aviators.

The basic plot of "Lilac Time" came from a Broadway play of the same name. In the film version Colleen Moore is a French girl, Jeannine, whose home and farm serve as a base for a Royal Flying Corps fighter squadron. She works in the squadron dining room where her table setting of lilacs is a symbol of her affection for the squadron. She is always on hand to count the airplanes as they return from a patrol. When Gary Cooper flies in as a replacement, he is forced to make a crashlanding to avoid Colleen Moore as she unknowingly crosses in front of his landing path. In a series of retaliatory confrontations, they eventually fall in love. But Gary Cooper is engaged to an English girl of noble birth. When Gary Cooper is shot down and severely wounded, Colleen Moore searches the hospitals. When she finally locates her sweetheart, Cooper's father intercedes and falsely tells the French girl that his son is dead, in order to preserve the forthcoming marriage. The French girl leaves a bouquet of lilacs which Gary Cooper recognizes. The father changes his mind and the two lovers are reunited.

The story setting for the first crash takes place as the squadron returns from a patrol, and a wounded pilot crashes while landing on the field. The entire location crew, along with principles Colleen Moore and Gary Cooper, gathered at the camera position to watch the action.

Grace took off into the wind and came around the field to again put his nose into the prevailing breeze. The Waco came in low over a row of eucalyptus trees that bordered the agricultural field as a wind break. Grace touched the ground with his wheels, then with a wing tip, and finally the nose in order to distribute the force of impact among as many points of contact as possible. When the nose touched the ground, the tail went up and hesitated in the extreme vertical position, before continuing over as the airplane settled on its back. When the cameras stopped turning, Grace released his belts and lowered himself to the ground from the inverted cockpit with no injuries.

Several days later the crew assembled near the same area for the second crash. Grace again came in over the trees and touched down in a rough three-point landing. He bounced twenty-five feet in the air, kicked left rudder and pushed the stick hard to the left. The Waco turned in the air after the bounce, and the lower left wing tip touched the ground, followed by the wheels and then the tail skid, coming to rest with the nose pointing in the direction from which the airplane came. Opal Boswell, the stunt girl doubling for Colleen Moore, crossed the landing path almost directly under Grace while he was turning in the air. A bruise to his side was the only injury Dick Grace received from this crash.

The third crash was from a taxiing position in which the airplane remained on the ground. The Waco had to pass between two trees at high speed and shear off its wings. In one of his books, Dick Grace notes that he was in Los Angeles on business at this time, and Charles Stoffer volunteered to do the crash in his place.

Cameras waited for the third crash in several different locations on each side of the eucalyptus wind break. Stoffer started his taxi run in one of the repaired Wacos used in the previous crash scenes. He was approaching fifty miles per hour when the airplane entered the ten-foot space between two of the trees. Stoffer aimed for the center of the opening, but with only the rudder for control, a taxiing airplane can't be as precisely steered as might be expected. The nose was off center and the right side of the fuselage passed within inches of one tree, shearing the break-away wings, which had been constructed without internal bracing wires, even with the fuselage. The left wing panels touched the other tree and were intact except for the wing tips, which were clipped

The second crash in "Lilac Time." Opal Boswell, the stunt girl, is running this way, crossing barely in front of the Waco 10 flown by Dick Grace. Courtesy: Dick Grace

Grace applied left rudder and bounced, causing the airplane to turn 180 degrees. Courtesy: Dick Grace

when Stoffer roared through the wind break. The fuselage fell on its right side at fifty miles per hour and would have ground Stoffer's head into the dirt if he had not ducked inside the cockpit. He suffered no injuries, and the sequence made an exciting scene to fit a comedy situation in the story, where Colleen Moore is hiding in the cockpit of an airplane. When a mechanic starts the engine, she accidentally hits the throttle, starting the airplane on a wild taxi run all over the field, firing its machine guns, until it finally comes to a halt after crashing between two trees.

Airplanes and facilities at an "L"-shaped field on Cen-

tinela Boulevard between Culver City and Inglewood, operated by Bob Blair and Frank Baker, served as a base of operations in filming the dog fight scenes of the picture.[154] Howard Batt and Bob Blair flew in this part of the picture, along with several other unidentified pilots from Clover Field. Remote cameras attached to airplanes photographed several good dog fight scenes. Hand colored flames, as in "Wings," appeared in scenes of airplanes spinning down on fire. A few obvious miniatures appeared in the otherwise good dog fight scenes, spoiling the effect of reality. "Lilac Time" was released in the summer of 1928 with synchronized sound effects using the

Charles Stouffer barely missed the tree on his right as the Waco 10 passed between two trees in a eucalyptus wind break for a crash scene in "Lilac Time." Courtesy: Dick Grace

As the Waco 10 turns on its side Stouffer had to quickly duck his head inside the cockpit. Courtesy: Dick Grace

Firnatone Process,[155] and received good reviews.

Clinton E. Herberger, another future member of the Associated Motion Picture Pilots, flew a camera plane for the dog fight sequences of "Lilac Time." He was born in Kern City, California in 1902 and spent most of his childhood in Washington, Oregon and Idaho. His family moved to Los Angeles where he completed high school before enlisting in the army at the end of World War I. Released from the service in 1919, he enlisted in the Air Service and served in the Philippines for two years before passing the Flying Cadet examinations. After winning his wings, and a commission as second lieutenant in the

Army Reserve, he completed a tour of duty, and then went on a barnstorming tour. Clinton Herberger was giving flying lessons at Clover Field, and doing some theatrical acting on the side, when the flying job for "Lilac Time" came along.[156]

In the spring of 1928 Leo Nomis contracted with the Fox Film Corporation to furnish airplanes and do the flying for "The Air Circus," which was directed by Howard Hawks. The studio built a group of hangars on the south side of Clover Field as a set. The story follows two young men who leave their midwestern homes and travel to Southern California to enroll in a flying school. After a

Dick Grace crashes a Jenny at Clover Field for "Air Circus." Courtesy: Dick Grace

After Dick Grace climbed from the wreck an actor took his place and the action continues. Courtesy: Leo Stratton Nomis

crashlanding, one of the boys gives up flying, but returns to aviation when the other boy and his girlfriend unknowingly lose their landing gear on takeoff. The reluctant flyer regains his courage after taking off in another airplane to warn his companion, who safely leaves the airplane, with his girlfriend, by parachute.

The temporary Fox hangars were in better condition than some of the permanent hangars on the north side of the field, but they were dismantled as soon as the picture was completed.[157] Leo Nomis and Moye Stephens did most of the stunt flying, while Dick Grace turned a Jenny over on its nose for the crash scene. "The Air Circus" contained sound effects, a musical background, and portions of a spoken dialogue. It received good reviews when it was released in September 1928.

At this time Hollywood was turning out more aviation movies than any other story type, except for westerns, and many of the westerns contained aviation

incidents. "The Air Legion" by R.K.O. portrayed Ben Lyon as an air mail pilot who loses his courage, but eventually regains it to save the life of a comrade. Warner Brothers, "The Aviator" was a comedy in which Edward Everett Horton engages in some wild stunts while learning how to fly. Ben Lyon appears as a former Marine flyer doing movie stunt work in Columbia's "The Flying Marine." "Code Of The Air," by Bischoff Productions, tells the story of a criminal inventor who leads his gang in robbing stocks and bonds from commercial planes by use of a death ray. Hoot Gibson flew his own airplane in some of the scenes from Universal's western, "The Flying Cowboy." Al Wilson played the lead in another Universal aviation western, "The Phantom Flyer." In Universal's "The Sky Skidder," Al Wilson stars as the inventor of Economo, a secret airplane fuel that gives one thousand miles to the pint. During a trial flight to test the fuel, the flyer-inventor sees his sweetheart out for a drive with a wealthy but dishonest rival. When the car goes out of control, Al Wilson rescues the girl with a rope ladder from his airplane, just before the automobile crashes. The formula is stolen before the big demonstration flight, but the inventor retrieves it by dropping into the thief's car from an airplane by way of a rope ladder.

When news of the increase in aviation films reached Garland Lincoln, he returned to Hollywood and became the next flyer to enter the field of motion picture work.

After leaving Mercury Aviation in 1921, Garland Lincoln bought a Jenny and opened his own air field in Wilmington, south of the old Dominguez Field. He gave rides and flying lessons for a while, but this venture ended when a student destroyed the airplane. He then built two airplanes of his own design, selling one to Ernest Longbrake, and the other to the Crawford-Saunders Company in Venice. From the profits Lincoln bought another Jenny and operated from the Panorama Airport, located at Firestone Boulevard and Atlantic Avenue, in the southeast part of Los Angeles. Here he continued to give flying lessons and haul passengers on sightseeing rides.

Seeking new opportunities in aviation, Lincoln flew this Jenny to Toronto, Canada, barnstorming in small towns along the way. Continuing his barnstorming tour along the Canadian border to the west coast, he remained in Edmonton, Alberta for a while, where he was employed by a Colonel Barker to fly a geodetic survey of northern Canada. Upon completion of this project he returned to California and operated flying schools in Coalinga, San Luis Obispo and Pismo Beach.

In October 1926, Paramount Pictures had a location crew in the sand dunes near Pismo Beach, where they were filming a Foreign Legion picture, "Beau Sabreur," with Gary Cooper in the leading role. Having the only airplane in the area, Lincoln was hired to fly Gary Cooper to Hollywood on an emergency visit, and to transport small items from the studio back to the location.

Garland Lincoln returned to Los Angeles in October 1928 and worked for Frye and Richter's Aero Corporation, where he instructed and flew Fokker F-10s on a scheduled run between Los Angeles and El Paso, Texas.[158]

Several Nieuport 28s, a French World War I fighter plane used by the U.S. Army during the war, and by the U.S. Navy after the war, became available to civilians in Southern California some time in 1926.[159] Garland Lincoln obtained three of these Nieuports, and put them in flying condition in order to use them in motion picture work.

One of Lincoln's first motion picture jobs almost had a fatal ending. He recalls that incident, which took place during the filming of "The Big Hop" by Condor Pictures:

"I was flying a Wright J-5 powered Fairchild 71, called a Razorback, with two parachute jumpers for a Condor picture which starred Buck Jones and Jobyna Ralston. The motion picture was about some pilots who were trying to fly across the Pacific to the Hawaiian Islands. In the picture, the two flyers jump out in parachutes after the airplane catches fire.

"We were about two miles at sea, flying at 2500 feet with a camera ship following, and two speed boats underneath us to pick up the jumpers. To give the appearance of fire, the two jumpers dumped lamp black powder at intervals through a small opening in the bottom of the fuselage. Only one of the parachute jumpers was a professional jumper and movie stunt man, so the non-professional was to jump first, leaving the professional to continue throwing out the lamp black until he made his jump.

"After putting out several pounds of lamp black, it was time for the amateur to jump, but he pulled his rip cord before leaving the cabin. The professional jumper saw what happened and tried to push the youth through the door before his parachute became entangled. The young jumper lost his head and fought back into the cabin like a crazy man. A part of the parachute was bellying outside to make the airplane almost unmanageable, while inside a tangle of silk and whipping shrouds almost covered the two fighting jumpers. I tried to keep the airplane straight and level for the cameraman, but then a can of lamp black was overturned in the struggle.

"The inside of the airplane became as black as night. The unbreakable glass around my cockpit became coated with lamp black, which again covered the glass the instant I wiped it off. We went into a spin and I realized that our only chance was to get the pilot's window open. With my eyes full of lamp black, I fumbled around and finally stood up to kick the window out. Luckily I still had five hundred feet of altitude. Still fighting the drag of the open chute, I managed to recover, get back to land and set the airplane down with little damage in a plowed field.

"Still plenty scared, I crawled out the open pilot's window to the ground. My vision was better now, and I will never forget the sight of the two jumpers as they tumbled from the door of the cabin, enmeshed in black parachute silk and shrouds.

"We got the airplane back to my field, cleaned all the lamp black, replaced the window and completed the scene several days later with another professional jumper to replace the amateur."[160]

Howard Hughes was now almost totally involved with "Hell's Angels" and the production expanded. Seeking a cheaper and more remote location, he moved to a rented pasture in the San Fernando Valley near Van Nuys. Surrounded by agricultural fields and chicken ranches, it was located near the area that later became Metropolitan Airport, but it preceded the Van Nuys field by several months.[161] Sheds and repair shops were built to house and maintain the fleet of airplanes being collected for the picture. This location became the main base of operations for "Hell's Angels" and was named Caddo Field by Howard Hughes.

No one was able to locate a Gotha or any other kind of German bomber from World War I. With the exception of one or two in museums, they had all been destroyed by age or under the terms of the Versailles Treaty. The best available compromise was the Sikorsky S.29, a large twin-engine biplane about the same size as a World War I bomber, built in this country by Igor Sikorsky and a dedicated group of Russian immigrants. Roscoe Turner purchased this airplane in 1926 with plans for an airline between Atlanta and New York, but a lack of financial backing forced him to use the big Sikorsky for advertising. For a while he promoted cigars for the United States Cigar Company and hauled the products to various stores around the country. Turner was flying top salesmen of the Curlee Clothing Company to their sales territories when he answered Frank Tomick's telegram and agreed to lease the airplane to Hughes for the picture.[162]

Roscoe and Mrs. Turner arrived at March Field in March 1928, and were met by Frank Tomick, who came out to guide them to the Caddo Field location. Roscoe Turner was a colorful figure, justifiably proud of his flying ability, and confident of his airplane. Both he and his wife, who usually accompanied him, flew without parachutes. When it was time to take off on the last leg of his cross-country flight to Caddo Field, there was a little bit of ice in Turner's eyes as he watched Frank Tomick take a parachute from the studio car that brought him to March Field, buckle it on and climb aboard the Sikorsky. But that small blow to Turner's pride was almost forgotten during the flight over the huge Los Angeles Basin, and had completely disappeared by the time Tomick pointed out the pasture that was Caddo Field.[163]

Newspaper reporters attended a staged publicity event several days later when four Fokker D.VII's escorted the "Gotha" bomber into Caddo Field. Turner and his wife were welcomed by Howard Hughes, Gretta Nissen, James Hall, Lucien Privall, Wallace Beery, Edna May, Merna Kennedy and other members of the motion picture community.[164]

James Dunavent's important preservation of Jimmy Barton's memoirs on tape reveals some interesting details of the Sikorsky:

"After Roscoe got there we seen that the Liberty engines was run out and would have to be replaced before the ship could be flown much. I located two overhauled Liberties in San Diego, and the studio gave me a check, and I went down and bought 'em. We did the engine changes with a pair of shear legs made from heavy poles—didn't have no cranes for that then.

"It had a solid, or rather glassed-in cabin-type nose. We put a gunner's pit with a ring, and a fake pilot's cockpit behind, under the center section leading edge. It had a control wheel and yoke for realism, but all the flying was done from the pilot's cockpit aft.

"We rented the guns from Steimrich at Paramount. Otto Steimrich had the arsenal there. Didn't have no laws then like there are now. They had trouble with getting them to fire more than once until Manuel put something on them so they'd fire bursts with the blank shells. (At this point in his conversation with Jimmy Barton, James Dunavent noted that suppressors were used to give enough kick so the recoil would operate the gun.)

"Manuel, I think it was Somoza or maybe Zamora, was a whiz at anything to do with guns or explosives. He'd been in the Mexican army during the troubles they had down there, and got himself captured by the revolutionaries. They was going to shoot him, but gave him the choice of joining the revolution or getting shot. He joined, but the first chance he got, he slipped into the U.S. He'd been a lieutenant in the Mexican army—after he got in the States he enlisted in the U.S. Army. He was one of the troops detailed to help with the special effects and explosives handling at Stanley during the making of 'Wings.' After the picture was finished, he bought his way out of the army, you could do that in those days, and came to Hollywood. Some of the people he had worked with helped him to get on with one of the studios as a powder man."

In answer to James Dunavent's question about how the scene in "Hell's Angels" was made, where Ben Lyon recoils in fright as bullets chew up the rim of the gunner's cockpit, Barton replied:

"With dynamite caps. Fixed them along the edge of the cockpit rim and exploded 'em in sequence with a console. The thin copper lead wires was concealed inside the ship.

"They was a wood rim around the gun pit—the ring on which the gun was mounted was bolted to the frame. The caps was embedded in the wood rim and a metal plate shield was bolted back of the whole thing to shield Ben from any fragments of copper. Dynamite caps pack a hell of a kick—one can blow part of your hand off. We used 'em a lot—for shots where a bullet was supposed to kick up dirt or blast holes and splinters from pieces of wood, like the side of a building. The powder man sets up his board—just a plank with a whole bunch of nails stuck into it. Each one has a thin wire lead to a cap—all he does is run the other lead along the row of nails.

"The scene where the engine nacelles is hit and catches fire was done with a mockup of the nacelle. The exhaust came from a big American LaFrance fire engine, piped into the stacks. Used a wind machine to make it stream back and blow the fire.

"When we was shooting that we found out some city regulation said wherever live ammunition was used, it had to be done under the attendance of an authorized expert—a member of the police or sheriff, I think it read. The lot was in the incorporated area, so they sent down two guys from the police department to do the shooting and make sure there was no danger.

"They wasn't no good. Manuel did the shooting with a Thompson submachine gun. He showed them up when he took the gun and wrote his initials with slugs from it. Howard even had one (Thompson submachine gun) at his place. He used to shoot it in the basement until the neighbors complained. He got cited by the police for it and they made him quit."[165]

It has been said that Howard Hughes tried to rent a dirigible from the U.S. Navy for the Zeppelin sequence of the picture, but this cannot be verified. While he may have considered that possibility, he actually used miniatures for both the Zeppelin and ammunition dump sequences, which were directed by Roy Davidson. With Hughes insistence on authenticity and realism, Davidson and the people who worked under him produced miniatures that have seldom been equalled, and are almost impossible to tell from reality.

The air scenes of the Zeppelin were filmed in one of the large balloon hangars at Ross Field, the World War I army balloon school in Arcadia. The Zeppelin interiors and some of the additional miniature work was photographed at the Metropolitan Studios.

The miniatures themselves were built by Bill Butler, Lawrence Butler, and Barney Korn, with the assistance of Charles Printzlau and Bennie Zeidman. Painting of the miniatures was done by Bertram Simon. Bill Butler and Barney Korn worked together in set design and miniatures at Universal before joining Davidson for the "Hell's Angels" production. In order to comply with Howard Hughes' wish for secrecy on this part of the production, the miniatures were built in a shop behind Bill Butler's home in the Magnolia Park section of Burbank. Barney Korn, who retired from Hughes Aircraft as a design engineer several years ago, tells of his work on the miniatures for "Hell's Angels:"

"One of the primary miniatures that is of the greatest interest is the one of the dirigible. It was twenty-seven feet long and thirty inches in diameter. It was made up from little stamped duraluminum alloy girders made by the Adams Campbell Company of Los Angeles. Inside were some small balloons made by Goodyear that were supposed to float the dirigible, but after it was finished the structure was too heavy for the amount of gas we had. It was covered with Irish linen and painted with appropriate insignia and markings. This miniature had propellers that turned and a little pilot car that would drop down on a little cable controlled from inside the dirigible.
"We built several other dirigibles of the same size, but not as carefully as the first one. These were made of steel rods welded together and covered with linen. Each one was made at a different angle from the center toward the nose and tail, to simulate several stages of the dirigible breaking up in the middle. The first one was used in the final shot of the dirigible crashing to the ground.

"The next largest miniature was the one of the bomber. Its wing span was approximately eleven feet and it stood eighteen inches off the ground. It was flown over the miniature ammunition dump set, which was constructed on the Sunshine Ranch near the San Fernando water reservoir, on a piece of piano wire eleven hundred feet long. The wire passed through the miniature bomber in a piece of copper tube that ran from the nose to the tail with a ball bearing sheave at each end.
"The piano wire was fed through the bomber and hooked to the end of a pole. It was sent down the wire, from the reservoir side of the ammunition dump set, toward the gate where all of the explosions were to be. It was stopped at the other end where they had a large pole with a fulcrum that would raise the wire and decelerate the bomber. It was sent down that wire many times at different speeds and at different angles before they decided to film the flight and set off the explosions.
"We built all of the miniature trucks that were moving around the ammunition dump when it was blown up by the bomber. The object was to make the miniature trucks appear to be heavy, as the original trucks were heavy. The wheels, the frame, the radiator and hood were made from brass castings. The bodies were made of wood and covered with canvas. The trucks were pulled along the ground by small cables close to the ground so they wouldn't be picked up by the camera.
"Inside the miniature bomber was a clock work mechanism with a razor blade. As the hand rotated it would cut the thread and drop actual little bombs that were made by the powder man on the picture. As each little bomb hit the ground it would explode and dig quite a little hole. As this was occurring the different charges of powder were set off under the buildings and under the gate at the ammunition dump. In the picture you will notice that one of the trucks was blown up right at the gate.
"All of the buildings in the ammunition dump were made of scale-sized wood and put together with little pins so that at the time of the explosions, the timbers would break up like the real thing. There were no miniature people in there at the time of the explosion because we couldn't find any who were willing to stay.
"We worked many months on the picture, making and repairing the different models. Mr. Hughes was very critical. They had to be exact as possible, and he enjoyed inspecting each one before it was put on the set.
"The miniature airplanes that were used with liquid smoke, which simulated clouds, were made of cast aluminum and thin cast aluminum wings. The liquid smoke would eat the fabric if that was used. It would even eat your clothes. With aluminum airplanes we could use them many times.
"It was very painstaking work as we built everything by hand. They would shoot all day in the studio and we would receive a call to stay on. When they were through shooting, a studio car would bring out the broken models and we had to work all night to repair them for shooting by nine o'clock the next morning. We slept all day because the same thing would happen the next night.

"One of the shots in the picture shows two aeroplanes crashing head on. As they hit an explosion occurs and there is a fire at that point. The method of getting that shot was to suspend two aeroplane models from one of the catwalks in the studio on pieces of wire thirty feet long. When they were at static rest on the long pieces of wire, they would just rest with the noses touching each other. Inside each of these aeroplanes was some explosives with contact arms out front. When they were ready to photograph the aeroplanes, they were pulled back away from the vision of the camera and released where they would swing down on an arc and hit head on, and they would catch fire. Since they were made of aluminum, the damage was slight, and they could be cleaned up and spray painted for the next shot."[166]

When the "Hell's Angels" Zeppelin sequence was completed, and all of the Caddo Company equipment was removed, the Fox Film Corporation rented the same balloon hangar for a Zeppelin sequence in their production, "The Sky Hawk." A miniature Zeppelin moved over an elaborate miniature set of London, and was finally shot down by a miniature airplane.

The story of "The Sky Hawk" opens where the hero is a cadet at a flying school in England. He is in love with the same girl as the commanding officer of the school, who suddenly orders the young pilot to France when he learns that the girl and his rival are planning marriage. The hero crashes just before going overseas, suffers paralysis of the legs and is accused of deliberately crashing to avoid combat service. He returns to his father's estate, near London, and with the help of a mechanic from the flying school, an airplane is assembled from parts and is armed with a machine gun, which he names The Sky Hawk. Partial use of his legs returns, and with the use of stirrups on the rudder bar, he takes off from his father's estate and shoots down the next Zeppelin that raids London. He is shot down in the fight, but the crash restores full use of his legs, and his name is cleared.

Several biplanes appeared in the English airfield set, which was photographed at Ross Field, the former army balloon school in Arcadia. Fox completed the picture and released it to the theaters five months before "Hell's Angels" was premiered.

As additional airplanes were located, reconditioned, modified and painted, the British and German squadrons at Caddo Field grew. While Hughes employed the largest number of pilots ever to work on a motion picture, they were seldom all together at one time. Only Frank Tomick, Frank Clarke and Roy Wilson worked continually on the picture from beginning to end. Others worked for various lengths of time, and the pilots from the San Francisco Bay area only worked in the dog fight scenes filmed at Oakland.

Maurice Murphy went to work for Maddux Airlines, and Leo Nomis had contracts for other pictures in addition to "The Air Circus." Howard Batt, Ross Cooke, Clement Phillips and Al Wilson had other commitments, but worked on the picture from time to time, along with Harry Crandall, Clinton Herberger, Earl Gordon, Garland Lincoln, Jack Rand, Ira Reed and Ernie Smith.

Jack Rand and Harry Crandall learned to fly at the Wilson Aero Service in Glendale, and joined the "Hell's Angels" crew through Roy Wilson.[167]

In addition to the Fokker D.VII's, S.E.5's, Thomas Morse Scouts and Travelairs, Hughes leased various open cockpit biplanes as they were needed to fill in the backgrounds of formation shots, lineups and dogfight scenes. Clinton Herberger, who was working as a test pilot for the Thunderbird Aircraft Company in Glendale, came to work at Caddo Field when the Thunderbird Company leased a pilot and an airplane to Hughes. Herberger had the enviable position of drawing a pilot's pay from Caddo Productions in addition to his regular salary from the Thunderbird Company.[168]

Strong winds swept the San Fernando Valley the day that Tave Wilson received a call from Caddo Field to deliver a leased American Eagle. With a mechanic at each wing tip, Tave Wilson taxied into the powerful head wind and took off for Caddo Field where other mechanics waited to grab his wing tips when the airplane touched down. The wind was coming in strong gusts when he arrived at the Van Nuys field a few minutes later and turned into the wind to land. As his wheels approached the ground, the airplane stopped its forward motion and hung in the blast, descending vertically. Just before touchdown the wind stopped momentarily, allowing the airplane to drop the last few feet to the ground. Howard Hughes was watching with the other pilots, and displayed his occasional sense of dry humor by remarking, "Let's hire him for stills."[169]

A thick fog blanket covered the Hollywood area on Saturday, May 26, 1928. It stopped at the Santa Monica mountains, a small range that separates the movie capitol from the San Fernando Valley. The sun was shining at Caddo Field when a group of Fokkers and Travelairs took off for the Mines Field location in Inglewood, which was also clear. The loose formation was flying at four thousand feet over Hollywood when Al Wilson heard a loud snap in the nose of his Fokker D.VII. He quickly cut the ignition of the racing engine as his propeller and hub spun off and disappeared in the thick fog below. As the airplane started to descend, Wilson turned back toward the San Fernando Valley, since it was much closer than their destination in Inglewood. But he soon realized that his angle of glide would not clear the Santa Monica Mountains. If he stayed with the airplane as it descended into the thick fog, he would be unable to guide it clear of any buildings that may lie in its path, and he would surely die in the crash. If he bailed out he would survive, but in either case he could not prevent the airplane from crashing into the city below, whether he was at the controls or not.

Al Wilson did the only thing that could logically be done under the circumstances. He bailed out for self preservation, and landed on the sloping roof of a house on Formosa Street in Hollywood, spraining his back and cutting both hands. The airplane crashed in open ground between the homes of Frank Spearman, a writer who lived at 7278 Hollywood Boulevard, and Joseph Schenck the producer. The airplane was destroyed, but no one was injured other than Wilson himself.[170]

A large German airdrome set, complete with hangars, headquarters and various auxiliary buildings, appeared on a ranch near Chatsworth in the western end of the San Fernando Valley. Cameras photographed the eighteen-plane German formation in various positions on the ground and from several different angles during a formation takeoff. Frank Tomick and Frank Clarke appeared in short speaking roles that were filmed at this location.

With an increase in the number of pilots and airplanes, the responsibility of managing such a large group in the air had to be divided. Clarke and Tomick decided between themselves that Clarke would lead the acting airplanes, and Tomick would be in charge of all camera flying.[171] With the approval of Howard Hughes and J.B. Alexander, this delegation of authority continued for the rest of the production.

The long preparation time between scenes, and the strict separation of work established by the various unions, allowed the practical joke to appear in the motion picture industry more often than anywhere else in the nation. While carpenters changed some physical part of the set, or electricians re-routed wiring, or a new camera position was selected, the other disciplines working on the picture waited. Fertile minds often devised outlandish practical jokes during these frequent pauses, and the motion picture stunt pilots probably devised more of these surprises for each other than any other group in the motion picture industry. Even Howard Hughes did not escape the attention of the pilots who flew out of Caddo Field.

After an air scene was recorded on film, the acting airplanes and camera planes taxied to an area near the long maintenance shed at Caddo Field. Since the airplanes were always parked in a loose arrangement, no one but the few pilots in on the joke noticed that for several days Frank Tomick parked the D.H.4 camera plane with the tail pointed toward the primitive out-

house that served as the men's room in this rural location. Finally, the lanky figure of Howard Hughes entered the outhouse at a time when the pilots were waiting around for the next scene. Tomick quickly climbed into the front cockpit while Frank Clarke and Jimmy Barton rushed to the huge propeller. After two swings the powerful Liberty engine roared. With the stick held tightly against his lap, Frank Tomick pushed the throttle forward until the wheels vibrated against the chocks. The dust settled after a few seconds, and a surprised and angry Howard Hughes crawled out of the overturned comfort station. He fired the entire crew of pilots, but hired them back within one hour.[172]

One day Hughes appeared at the field in a new Packard Roadster, which was considered the height of style in luxury sports cars of that day. He parked at the edge of the field near a large asparagus patch. Before the day was over, Frank Clarke and Frank Tomick paid a group of itinerant farm workers fifty cents each to urinate in the gas tank of the new Packard. Evidently no damage was done, because Hughes started the car and drove blissfully away. The roadster was still running smooth as the disappointed pilots watched it disappear down Balboa, heading for Hollywood.[173]

Howard Batt recalls another practical joke enjoyed by the pilots at the expense of Howard Hughes:

"He bought this new Waco—brought it out to Caddo Field, and we decided to play a trick on him. We'd get in a group, three or four of us, around the Waco. It was well built and safe as any other airplane, but when Howard would come toward us to talk over something about the picture, we'd say, 'Look at those wires. The size of those fittings!' We'd give him just enough, and then we'd shut up. Next day, he would hear the same thing, but we stopped talking when he got to the airplane. Finally, he got the message. One day the Waco was gone for two or three weeks. It was sent down to Douglas at Clover Field, and the next time we saw it, every fitting and wire had been made double size."[174]

The light hearted, good time, party atmosphere that surrounded the motion picture stunt pilots contrasted with the seriousness of their flying and the sincere brotherly bond that existed between them. If anyone had financial or family problems, his comrades were always ready to help. Several of the pilots drank too much, but a few hardly drank at all. Jack Rand was always smiling and clowned as much as anyone else, but at the same time he was quietly putting his younger brother through medical school.

Hughes was forced to accept the practical jokes invented by the pilots as there were no other skilled flyers available. He eventually joined the system and devised a particularly crude joke for Frank Tomick. It involved an air compressor and a buried hose that ended under the seat of the outhouse. Jimmy Barton informed Tomick of the planned trick and the chief camera pilot was able to avoid the young millionaire's retaliatory device.[175]

After a summer of waiting for clouds as a background for the dog fight scene, Hughes moved the entire crew, consisting of pilots, cameramen and maintenance personnel, to Oakland Airport where huge cumulo-nimbus cloud formations frequently appeared over the coastal hills in the San Francisco Bay area during the fall and winter months. Approximately fifteen airplanes took off from Caddo Field at the end of summer in 1928 and headed for Oakland.

Leo Nomis had other motion picture contracts at the time and was not able to accompany the group to Oakland. Howard Batt was in Chicago at this time, where his reputation for dependability and piloting skill earned him a position as executive pilot for a group of wealthy stockbrokers. The additional twenty or so pilots and airplanes, hired and leased to make up a full squadron each of German and British fighters, came from the local flyers at Oakland, Alameda and other neighboring airports.

Clement Phillips remained behind to ferry an S.E.5 to Oakland that was being reconditioned at Glendale Airport. When the airplane was finished he took off for Oakland, but just before reaching his destination, he made a forced landing in an agricultural field near Hayward. Local farmers said that he tinkered with the engine for a while and then swung the prop to start the engine by himself. Immediately after takeoff, the engine quit and he nosed in from 500 feet, dying instantly in the crash. Frank Tomick took the train to Los Angeles and bought another S.E.5, but it took him five days to fly back to Oakland because of bad weather.[176]

Hughes expected to complete the scene in two or three weeks, but the large cloud formations did not appear as had been anticipated. After a month of waiting on the weather, he instructed J.B. Alexander to cut the per diem pay being received by everyone in addition to their regular pay. The mechanics didn't object too much because most of them were bunking in the hangars at Oakland Airport. But the pilots, who were occupying every room of a hotel in Oakland, and having parties every evening, refused to fly without their allowance for food and quarters. The situation never reached the status of a strike, but the pilots stood firm and Hughes gave in to their demands.[177]

The desired cloud formations appeared in November, and for several days the roar of straining engines and the whine of bracing wires could be heard over the foothills east of San Francisco Bay. Stuart Murphy and Ira Reed collided during one sequence, and Murphy had to bail

out in his parachute. Reed's Travelair suffered only minor damage to the wing, and he was able to make a safe landing in an orchard near Hayward.

Elmer Dyer joined the camera crew and added his skill to that of Burton Steene and other aerial cameramen working under the able direction of Harry Perry.

After four months in Oakland, the dog fight scenes were completed, and the Caddo planes and pilots returned to Van Nuys. Ira Reed, Earl Gordon and Ross Cooke each had forced landings at various locations on the way back. All three airplanes were damaged beyond repair, but no one was injured.

While the Caddo Company was in Oakland, Metro Goldwyn Mayer filmed "The Flying Fleet" at the Naval Air Station in San Diego. This was the first of a series of motion pictures that used current military aviation as a plot background, and the first time the navy opened its aviation facilities to Hollywood. All of the flying was done by navy pilots and no civilian stunt flyers were involved. Flying scenes included takeoffs and landings from the carrier "U.S.S. Langley," formations of airplanes flying over ships during fleet maneuvers, and precision stunting by the navy's three-plane stunt team, the Sea Hawks. Charles Marshall, a World War I pilot turned aerial cameraman, did most of the aerial photography from a Vought 02U flown by a navy pilot.[178]

The story follows six Annapolis graduates as they train to become naval aviators. Ramon Navarro has the leading role as the best pilot in the group. He competes for the girl, Anita Page, with another flyer, Ralph Graves. Navarro has an opportunity to fly in the Trans-Pacific Flight, but he breaks disciplinary rules and the chance goes to his rival. Graves crashes at sea before reaching his destination. While flying a search plane, Navarro sights his rival clinging to a wing in the sea. Before Navarro can return for help, a fuel line breaks. He sets fire to his plane as a signal to the fleet, bails out in a parachute, and both flyers are subsequently rescued. Released in the first part of 1929 with synchronized music and sound effects, "The Flying Fleet" was well received.

With most of the "Hell's Angels" air scenes completed, and the winter rains approaching, Howard Hughes turned his attention to editing. Except for a few minor pickup scenes, the spinning down of the bomber was the only major scene yet to be completed. The original plan for that scene called for the use of a Hisso-powered Jenny with dummy engine nacelles on the lower wings. The Jenny "bomber," which would resemble the Sikorsky from a distance, was to be put into a spin, set afire, and after the pilot had bailed out, to be photographed all the way to its crash by three camera planes flying at high, medium and low altitudes.

Before this scene could be shot, the Jenny "bomber"

caught fire in the maintenance shed at Caddo Field. It was rolled out before the fire spread to the shed, but all the fabric was burned from the framework. It was assumed that a new sheet of aluminum that was leaning against a wall near the Jenny had reflected enough heat from the sun to cause the newly doped fabric on the airplane to ignite.[179]

The frame and landing gear were intact, but all fittings and wires had been warped and weakened by the heat. Rather than have it completely rebuilt for flying, Hughes decided to recover it the way it was, and use it for a crash scene only. It was subsequently taken to a dry wash near Santa Paula, set afire and pushed from a bluff just out of camera range, and photographed as it hit the ground.[180]

The Sikorsky itself would now have to be used for the air scenes of the spin, though this was not in the original agreement with Roscoe Turner.

The spinning scene continued to cause problems. After the Jenny fire, Roscoe Turner was furious when Hughes held him to a fine print clause in the agreement that transferred ownership of the Sikorsky to Caddo Productions when the lease payments equaled the appraised value of the airplane. Neither Roscoe Turner nor anyone else expected the production to last long enough for the lease payments to reach that level. According to Jimmy Barton, Hughes and Roscoe Turner engaged in a shouting match and nearly came to blows in Hughes' office at Caddo Field. After this incident, Turner left the picture and went back east to seek legal advice.[181]

In the meantime Hughes proceeded with the ill-fated spinning scene, but was unable to find a pilot willing to perform a maneuver so far beyond the design capabilities of the airplane. Two pilots on the picture, and two pilots who were brought in from the outside, were tempted by the generous bonus offered by Hughes, but changed their minds after taking the Sikorsky up to get the feel of it in the air.

Years before, movie flyers had discovered that when lamp black was released from an airplane, it floated in the air like heavy black smoke. When it was thrown out by hand, the intensity of the smoke was erratic and varied from thick to thin as each portion was dumped into the slipstream. To insure an even discharge of lamp black from the Sikorsky as it supposedly spun down on fire, Hughes insisted on a mechanical blower system.

Jimmy Barton was scheduled to work the smoke equipment during the spin. On the day before the spin, Barton went up for a test flight with one of the pilots who wanted to collect the bonus. While making his way along the cramped aisle in the cabin that was jammed with hoppers, blowers and ducts, Barton's parachute ring caught on a projecting piece of equipment. The pilot chute quickly snapped open and flew back along the passageway that ended with two steel steps up to the pilot's open cockpit behind the wings. The pilot, who sat on the left, was barely able to grab the silk before the entire chute billowed into the slipstream. If he had missed, Barton would have been dragged along the various metal projections and sharp edges that lined the narrow passageway.[182]

After several pilots tried the Sikorsky and changed their minds, Al Wilson agreed to take the job. He was confident that he could spin the big ship down several thousand feet for the cameras, and then recover for a landing.

Phil Jones, a mechanic on the picture, persuaded Jimmy Barton to let him fly in the bomber as he needed the extra money for an emergency. Being smaller than Barton, Jones could move along the aisle easier than the stocky mechanic who had first choice on the assignment.[183] Hughes agreed to the change, but Al Wilson didn't want anyone else in the airplane. A system of wires was installed for Wilson to operate the smoke equipment from the cockpit.[184] Frank Tomick realized the danger of the stunt, and since he had arranged for Jones to work on the film, he tried to persuade the young mechanic to change his mind. Tomick had worked with Al Wilson for years, and he knew that if Wilson said he was going to spin the bomber, there would be no backing out.[185] But Jones was eager to earn the bonus, and Hughes was confident that a better scene could be photographed if Wilson concentrated on flying the airplane while a second party worked the smoke equipment.

All of the preparations reached a climax on March 22, 1929. Frank Tomick, Frank Clarke, and Roy Wilson flew the camera planes which carried Harry Perry, Burton Steene and Elmer Dyer. Tomick's position was at 7,000 feet. Frank Clarke was at 4,000 feet and Roy Wilson flew at 1,000 feet to catch the final spins of the Sikorsky before it levelled off.

The Sikorsky, the three camera planes, and Hughes in his own airplane took off from Caddo Field around 3:00 p.m. and headed northeast. The bomber levelled off at 7,500 feet and the camera planes got into position. Al Wilson started the spin over what is now Whiteman Airpark in Pacoima. The Sikorsky pulled up and fell off on one wing. Wilson recovered from his first try, regained control and fell off into another spin. He seemed to recover again, as he was getting the feel of the controls in the spin, but then the big airplane went down in a tight spin. Frank Tomick saw the fabric tear away from the leading edge of the left wing, and then pieces of cowling from the left engine began to break away. Al Wilson's head ducked below the cockpit as he struggled with the controls. Tomick saw him leave the cockpit and open his parachute. The three cameramen followed the spinning bomber as Hughes and the three pilots waited anxiously for the second parachute. But Jones remained inside and the cameras continued to follow the spinning Sikorsky.[186]

Tomick strained the DeHaviland camera plane as he tried to keep up with the doomed bomber. Flying a camera ship was more than just following another airplane. The camera pilot had to understand camera angles and maintain a course broadside to the subject in order to give the cameraman a clear field of view that would exclude the wing tips, tail and any other part of the camera plane itself.

The Sikorsky continued on down until it crashed in an orange grove near the intersection of Terra Bella and Haddon streets in Pacoima. The engines penetrated the ground for several feet and the airplane was completely demolished. Phil Jones was still inside the wreckage with his unopened parachute strapped to his lifeless body.

Al Wilson came down a half mile away at Pierce and Bradley streets, and was grief stricken when informed that Phil Jones never jumped. Wilson said that when the airplane began to break up, he yelled twice to Jones through the passageway that led to the cabin.[187] Whether or not Jones heard the commands, or if he had been thrown around the cabin by the spin and knocked unconscious, or if he heard Al Wilson and was pinned inside by the centrifugal force of the spin, no one will ever know.

Al Wilson received a lot of unfair criticism from people who were not involved in the incident. Some reports say that he jumped after the first turn of the spin. But according to Frank Tomick, who was closest to the bomber at the time Wilson jumped, this is not true.

The District Attorney's office investigated the incident for possible negligent homicide charges, but they found no evidence for any neglect. Al Wilson's license was revoked for a while, but it was soon restored. The three pilots who flew with Wilson in this incident, Frank Tomick, Frank Clarke and Roy Wilson, all agreed that Al Wilson should not be blamed for the death of Phil Jones, and that he had taken the only course of action he could under the circumstances.[188]

Only the first scenes of the bomber at the beginning of its spin were used in the completed picture. Al Wilson's parachute appeared in all of the others.

The pioneer motion picture stunt pilot grieved over the death of Phil Jones, and the unfair criticism he received from some of his peers in the Southern California aviation community. Al Wilson gave up stunt flying as a result of this accident, except for an occasional appearance in his Curtiss Pusher, and went to work as an airline pilot for Maddux Air Lines.

One month after the "Hell's Angels" bomber accident, Maurice Murphy was killed in San Diego. A Maddux Air Lines Ford Tri-Motor, with Murphy as pilot and Louis Pratt as mechanic and co-pilot, was en route from Los Angeles to Phoenix, Arizona. After stopping at San Diego, the airliner took off for Phoenix and was flying at 2,000 feet over east San Diego when an army Boeing pursuit ship, flown by Lt. Howard Keefer of Rockwell Field, followed the Ford Tri-Motor at an altitude several thousand feet higher. Eyewitnesses reported that the army plane dived on the airliner, passed below it and came up abreast and to one side. The Boeing then executed a series of tight rolls, ending up below the airliner.

Keefer put the Boeing in a steep climb after his rolling exhibition. Murphy couldn't see the pursuit ship coming up from below, and Keefer misjudged his distance. The Boeing hit the Ford's wing with its own wing and continued to climb for a few seconds. Then one of the Boeing's wings came off and the pursuit ship went down out of control. Keefer jumped out but his parachute caught on some part of the airplane and rode to his death with the airplane when it hit the side of a canyon near the intersection of Wabash and Lexington avenues.

The Ford Tri-Motor continued level for a few seconds, but then it also went down out of control, turning over on its back just before it hit the ground of a plateau about 300 feet from the Boeing. Murphy, Pratt and the three passengers on board were all killed.[189]

On several previous occasions, both army and navy pursuit planes had stunted around civilian airliners in the San Diego area. Although strictly forbidden by military regulations, the pursuit pilots occasionally succumbed to the powerful temptation of practicing on a large airplane while showing off a little in the process.

Moye Stephens was flying for Maddux Air Lines at this time, and recalls an experience he had with military flyers in the San Diego area:

"Two weeks before Murphy's accident I was flying for Maddux, going down the coast just off Oceanside. I was watching a forest fire inland a little way. As we came abreast I noticed something above my line of vision. When I looked up it was an O-2 practically rubbing wings on the left hand side. He came in from behind so I didn't see him. Then when I looked out to the right, there was another one in the same position, and then he dropped back. I started going in until he overlapped the wing. I was afraid he would get into the slipstream. I wasn't too sure of what would happen, but I was afraid of what might happen. But, fortunately, it didn't. They stayed in formation until I started very carefully letting down, throttling back and nosing down very gently, so as not to startle anybody, and went in and landed.

"But Doc Whitney, what a character he was. He started life as a cow puncher and somehow fell heir to a cracked up pusher back before World War I. He rebuilt it and taught himself to fly. When I came back and reported this O-2 incident, he got out the old hog leg that he had packed when he was a cow puncher, a .45-caliber single-action peacemaker with a four and five-eighths inch barrel—and he started packing that thing in the airplane. He was fifty-five years old for about ten years before TWA retired him."

Hughes completed "Hell's Angels" and released it for a preview. But with sound pictures becoming more popular, another silent film received less than a warm reception from the audience. The young millionaire had no choice but to do it over in sound.

The dramatic scenes had to be scrapped because of Greta Nissen's accent. Hughes selected an unknown actress, Jean Harlow, for the female lead, and the dramatic scenes were re-shot in sound. Some of the non-speaking dramatic scenes were retained in their original form. As a result, these original silent scenes, which were filmed at sixteen frames per second, appeared faster than normal when projected at the sound speed of twenty-four frames per second.

The Zeppelin interior scenes were also left at silent speed. Sound was achieved through the efforts of Joseph Moncure March and a German translator, Julius Schroeder, who spent many hours going over the scenes to write dialogue in German that would fit the lip movements of the actors and tie into the action being portrayed.[190]

The air scenes were all salvaged, but airplanes had to go back in the air to record all types of engine sounds, whining wires and machine gun fire. Crews went to Muroc Dry Lake, now Edwards Air Force Base, and to remote airports at Fullerton and Santa Ana, California. Sound men captured a variety of sound effects as airplanes took off, landed, dived, spun, and did every kind of possible maneuver in order to obtain all of the different sounds necessary for the action portrayed on the screen.

Howard Hughes could be unreasonable at times, as Frank Tomick discovered at Fullerton Airport. Tomick flew a Travelair with loosened wires to exaggerate the sounds of an airplane spinning down. At several thousand feet above the green carpet of orange groves that covered most of Orange County in those days, Tomick put the biplane into a spin with his throttle pushed forward. The motion picture stunt pilots always made a spin with power on in order to have precise control at the moment of recovery.[191] Tomick levelled off several hundred feet above the sound truck and climbed back to his original altitude. After repeating the spin five times in order to get at least one good sound track, Tomick came in and landed. When the tracks were played back for Hughes, a meadowlark could be heard singing in the background on each sound track. Hughes chastised Tomick, who was several thousand feet in the air at the time, for spending all that time with a meadowlark in the vicinity.[192]

The worst tragedy ever to hit the motion picture industry took place in the air on January 2, 1930. The Fox Film Corporation was making the final scenes for "Such Men Are Dangerous." The picture was not an aviation film, but the story was based on the death of Capt. Alfred Lowenstein, a Belgian millionaire who disappeared from his airplane over the English Channel in 1928.

The scene plan called for three airplanes, one with a parachute jumper and two with cameras, to take off from Clover Field and rendezvous three miles at sea off Point San Vicente. At that point the camera planes would spread apart while the plane with the jumper flew between them. When the jumper bailed out, the cameras would record the jump and descent from different angles. A speed boat cruised in the sea below, with another camera aboard to record the jump from sea level, and to pick up the jumper after he descended into the water.

The three airplanes took off just before 4:00 p.m. as the winter sun was approaching the horizon. In the lead was a Lockheed high-wing monoplane painted bright orange to contrast with the blue sky and sea in order to show up clearly on the black and white film. In addition to pilot Roscoe Turner, the Lockheed carried Jacob Tribdwasser, the parachute jumper, Fred White, a representative from the parachute company, and Fred Osborne. The other two planes were identical Stinson "Detroiters," leased from Tanner Air Tours, and flown by Ross Cooke and Halleck Rouse. Kenneth Hawks, who was acting as director and was brother of Howard Hawks and husband of actress Mary Astor, flew in one plane. Max Gold, the assistant director on the film, rode in the other Stinson. Cameraman George Eastman, assistant cameraman Ben Frankel, and prop man Tom Harris, rode in one of the Stinsons, while the other cameraman, Conrad Wells, his assistant Otto Jordan, and prop man Harry Johannes rode in the other Tanner airplane. Newspaper accounts don't say which group rode with which pilot, but each camera plane carried five men, and the doors were removed to give the cameramen more freedom of action.

When they reached the rendezvous point, Turner, in the faster airplane, was ahead while the two camera planes, cruising one above the other, headed directly into the brilliant sun. Hoot Gibson, the cowboy star and a flyer in his own right, had planned to fly with Turner to watch the stunt, but at the last minute a representative of the parachute company decided to ride with the jumper. The cowboy actor drove to the coast to watch the action from his car. Gibson, the men in the speed boat, and the people who had gathered along the shore to watch, saw the two camera planes point their noses down slightly, and then something happened.

Perhaps the sun affected the vision of one or both of the pilots. The higher airplane banked slightly to the right, and the one below suddenly swerved upward and to the left. They were about 3,000 feet high when their wing tips touched, drew apart and then touched again. When the second contact was made, one plane pivoted on its wing tip and collided with the other, almost nose to nose. A burst of flame suddenly consumed both Stinsons as two twisting bodies fell or jumped from the fireball. Ten men were already dead as the two burning airplanes struck the water and sank in forty fathoms of the sea.

Roscoe Turner was so overcome with grief that he was barely able to land at Clover Field, and had to be helped from his airplane. He had seen three close friends—Kenneth Hawks, Ross Cooke and Hal Rouse—plunge to their deaths along with seven other men. That same morning, Turner and Cooke flew two airplanes over the route in a dry run with Howard Hawks, the director, who was aboard Turner's Lockheed. Just before takeoff time that afternoon, Howard Hawks received a call from the studio and had to return to the Fox headquarters on Sunset Boulevard. His brother, Kenneth, took his place as director. Divers spent several days searching for the bodies.[193]

Air traffic increased at Glendale Airport and it became the Grand Central Air Terminal. Motion picture companies could no longer work without interruption, and were particularly limited when recording sound. Roy and Tave Wilson moved to a secluded spot on the line between Burbank and North Hollywood, and opened their own airport. With nothing but farms and chicken ranches in the area, they established the Wilson Airport at the intersection of Vineland Avenue and Sherman Way. This was the only airport ever licensed exclusively for motion picture work, and was ideal for the motion picture companies. They were free to build sets, crash airplanes and set off fires and explosions, which was increasingly difficult to do at airports handling commercial traffic.

For a while the studios made good use of this isolated location, but unknown to the Wilsons, plans had already been made for a major airport less than one mile to the east of Wilson Airport.[194]

Howard Hughes found himself in a minor dilemma while completing the final scenes of "Hell's Angels." He was anxious to finish the picture, but he also enjoyed his association with the stunt pilots and hated to see the flying activity come to an end. Hughes told the pilots, on several different occasions, that this would be the last day of work. But before the day was over, he changed

his mind and told everyone to come back the next day, even though there was nothing left to do.[195]

Two weeks before Hughes issued his last final notice, Frank Tomick accepted an offer of more money from Howard Hawks, who was directing "Dawn Patrol" for First National. Even though he would have been laid off with everyone else two weeks later, Hughes never forgave Tomick for what he considered to be a breach of loyalty, and retaliated by minimizing Frank Tomick's name on the "Hell's Angels" credits.[196]

Paramount was making "Young Eagles" at this time, another World War I air film directed by William Wellman, which starred "Buddy" Rogers, Jean Arthur and Paul Lukas. Leo Nomis, who had already signed a contract as the aviation director on "Dawn Patrol," worked with Wellman on the aviation part of "Young Eagles," and was able to complete his work before the air action of "Dawn Patrol" was ready for filming.

Paramount hired Frank Clarke and Earl Robinson to fly with Nomis in the picture, and engaged Dick Grace for two crash scenes. The air scenes were a minor part of the picture and came primarily from "Wings." The same Spad used in "Now We're In The Air" appeared in ground scenes along with a Thomas Morse Scout and

Dick Grace at Metropolitan Airport before making the crash that appeared in "Young Eagles" and later in "Eagle And The Hawk." Courtesy: Dick Grace

Dick Grace crashing the Allied plane for "Young Eagles." Courtesy: Dick Grace

Actors and pilots pose by Dick Grace's crash for "Young Eagles." From the left: Frank Clarke, Buddy Rogers, Dick Grace, Paul Lukas, Leo Nomis and Earl Robinson. Courtesy: Dick Grace

three large biplanes that appear to be Orencos. Appearing in a minor German air field scene were four unidentified biplanes with false cowlings to resemble Curtiss P-1s and thus tie into the leftover "Wings" scenes in which Curtiss P-1s served as German airplanes.

"Young Eagles" was based on two magazine stories by Elliott White Springs who was a well known ace from World War I. "Buddy" Rogers plays an American aviator who falls in love with Jean Arthur while on leave in Paris. In a later air battle, Rogers shoots down and captures a leading German aviator, Paul Lukas. Rogers takes Lukas to American Intelligence Headquarters in Paris for interrogation, but Jean Arthur drugs Rogers and steals his uniform to help the German flyer escape. Shaken by the realization that he has been duped by a German spy, Rogers returns to combat. In another air battle he is shot down by none other than Paul Lukas, who is wounded in the fight. The sympathetic German aviator lands and takes Rogers to an American hospital where he assures Rogers of the girl's loyalty, who turns out to be an American double agent posing as a German spy.

Several cameras photographed the Allied plane crash from hidden locations along a stream near Thousand

Oaks, California, that has since been covered by Lake Sherwood. Grace flew an old American Eagle painted with U.S. insignia, while Leo Nomis, as the German aviator, pursued him in a J-5 Waco Taperwing. Nomis was about fifty feet behind Grace and ten or fifteen feet above the ground when the American-marked airplane hit the shallow streambed at eighty miles per hour. Grace distributed the impact forces between the landing gear, wing tip and nose. The tail went up and the fuselage turned on its own axis, smashing the wings into a shapeless mass of fabric, wood and wires. The totally destroyed airplane ended up on the opposite bank of the stream with the fuselage upside down and wrapped in what was left of the wings. Leo Nomis, a master stunt flyer, turned and swooped over his victim, clearing the steaming wreckage by no more than four feet. Elmer Dyer, who was operating the camera closest to the wreck, was relieved to see Dick Grace kick the rudder as a signal to the rescue crew that he was not injured. The force of the impact knocked the shoes from Grace's feet, and he said years later in retrospect that this was the most violent crash he ever made.

The scene where Paul Lukas is shot down was made at the edge of Metropolitan Airport in Van Nuys. In what appears to be an American Eagle, painted with German markings, Grace hit the ground with his wheels and nose, bounced back into the air as the airplane continued forward and over on its back, and then traveled approximately one hundred feet—upside down and tail first—before coming to rest in an upside down position. This particular scene was used three years later in "The Eagle And The Hawk."

"Young Eagles" was released in the first part of 1930, but Wellman was unhappy with the final editing of the film, and asked for a release from his contract with Paramount, which was granted.

In the meantime Columbia Pictures released "Flight," a story of the flying Marines. The aerial scenes consisted primarily of Naval and Marine airplanes photographed by Elmer Dyer and Paul Perry at the Naval Air Station in San Diego. In the story, Jack Holt portrays a veteran Marine flyer who befriends Ralph Graves, a former college football player who joins the Marines to become a flyer. Failing to win his wings as the result of a training accident, Graves becomes a mechanic for Jack Holt as the Marines are ordered to Nicaragua. Graves falls in love with Lila Lee, but backs off when he discovers that Jack Holt is after the same girl. When Holt asks Graves to propose for him, the girl reveals her true love for Graves. After a fight between the former friends, Graves is transferred, but is then lost in the jungle. Jack Holt flies to his rescue, but is injured in the attempt and cannot fly back. Graves flies the airplane out, wins his wings in the pro-

cess and all is forgiven.

Leo Nomis and Frank Tomick started work on "Dawn Patrol" as soon as the flying work on "Young Eagles" was completed. The first air scenes were filmed in the Newhall-Saugus area where First National built a German airfield set at the edge of Pico Canyon, near the site where Dick Kerwood was killed. A conglomeration of aircraft types, including two German Pfalz D.XIIs,[197] were leased from various owners, painted with what the art department regarded as appropriate German insignia, and lined up in front of the hangars.

The plot for "Dawn Patrol" came from the John Monk Saunders story, "The Flight Commander." The main theme deals with the conflicts endured by the squadron commander who is forced to send inexperienced flyers to their death in combat. The setting is a squadron of the Royal Flying Corps in France about the middle of the war. Neil Hamilton is the troubled C.O., and Richard Barthelmess and Douglas Fairbanks Jr. are his best pilots. When the leading German ace, von Richter, moves into the area, Barthelmess and Fairbanks raid the airdrome in defiance of the C.O.'s orders. When the C.O. is transferred to Wing, Barthelmess finds

Howard Hawks, Leo Nomis and Hal Wallis, the producer, discuss the aspects of a scene for "Dawn Patrol" at the Pico Canyon location near Saugus. Courtesy: Leo Stratton Nomis

A Stearman camera plane, rented from Roy Minor who was the Stearman distributor at Union Air Terminal in Burbank, as it was used in "Dawn Patrol." The camera was mounted for this camera plane to fly in front of the Speedwing Travelair flown by Leo Nomis, and photograph bomb explosions on the ground as Nomis climbed above the German airfield supposedly under attack. Courtesy: Frank Tomick

Earl Robinson, Leo Nomis, Frank Tomick and Ira Reed by a Speedwing Travelair at the German airfield location near Saugus, during the filming of "Dawn Patrol." Courtesy: Leo Stratton Nomis

Richard Barthelmess, Rupert McAllister and Douglas Fairbanks Jr. after McAllister pancaked this Thomas Morse Scout for a scene in "Dawn Patrol." Warner Brothers technicians meticulously placed another Thomas Morse in this identical position for closeup shots of Errol Flynn in the 1938 remake of "Dawn Patrol." Courtesy: Howard Batt

A lull in the shooting of "Dawn Patrol" at the Triunfo location. Howard Hawks stands in the center with coat and hat. Courtesy: Jimmy Barton

Four of the airplanes furnished for "Dawn Patrol" by the Wilson Aero Service are photographed from the top of a hangar at the Wilson Airport. Courtesy: Tave Wilson

himself in the frustrating position of squadron commander. His friendship with Fairbanks is broken when Fairbanks' younger brother joins the squadron, and Barthelmess is forced to send the inexperienced flyer to his death. When a one-plane mission is ordered to bomb a munition depot deep in the German lines, Fairbanks volunteers. Barthelmess gets him drunk the night before and flies the suicide mission himself. The picture ends with Fairbanks now in the position of squadron C.O. welcoming the next group of inexperienced replacement pilots.

Explosive charges were placed on the field, in some of the buildings, and under one of the airplanes for the series of scenes in the story where the two British pilots bomb and strafe the field of the feared von Richter. Buried wires ran from each charge to a control panel where the powder man would set off the explosives to simulate bombs dropped by the raiding airplanes. Leo Nomis and Earl Robinson flew the two Speedwing Travelairs for the air raid sequence on the German airfield.

After planning the action with Howard Hawks and the powder man, the two flyers made several passes over the field for the cameras. Then they roared in at 250 miles per hour about 30 feet above the hangars and airplanes, one of which was set to explode after they passed over. Leo Nomis led the attack with Robinson right behind and to one side. The powder man detonated the German

airplane immediately after Nomis passed over, and from a widely publicized still photograph of this incident, it appears that Robinson met the full blast of the explosion as he followed Nomis. According to an article written by Robinson, debris from the ground and pieces of the demolished airplane damaged his Travelair.[198]

Other scenes of the airdrome attack included the destruction of buildings, the burning of a German airplane that tries to take off in pursuit of the attackers, and a brief but spectacular head-on shot of the Travelair flown by Leo Nomis, climbing steeply above an explosion on the field below.

Roy Wilson, Ira Reed, Garland Lincoln and Roscoe Turner also worked in the picture, but Leo Nomis and Frank Tomick did most of the flying. Jimmy Barton worked as a mechanic on "Dawn Patrol" and takes us behind the scenes to describe some of the devices used in making this part of the film:

"First thing the location crew did was to lay out the action diagrams for the scenes, working from the shooting script. Then the charges were laid. For the bomb blasts we mainly used regular blasting powder—easier to handle and not as dangerous as dynamite—but you got to be careful about any sparks or metal around it. Dynamite has to be kept cool or it'll sweat beads of pure nitro when it starts to get old. Then it's touchy as hell.

"They dug holes like inverted funnels—bigger at the

bottom than the top—powder charge on the bottom and lamp black on top. It made a nice high blast—everything went up straight. When things had to be blowed apart, we used dynamite.

"One time we used three or four sticks of 60% dynamite inside a fuselage. You'd think it would blow the whole thing apart, but all it did was to peel the fabric off and left the bare frame sitting there. We found out we had to box it in some way so's it was confined, then the whole thing would go.

"The powder man had to be on his toes. He was real busy following the action and the script at the same time. The console was all labeled for each take, and all charges was numbered. It took two days to set up the charges and stuff for the first day's shooting.

"The powder crew laid charges for the bomb bursts and wired the string of dynamite caps for the machine gun strafing runs. The long shots were filmed first, before we wrecked any planes. These showed the ships coming in for the first pass at the field. They shot this several times and then switched camera set ups down behind and among the airplanes to get shots of the first powder charges doing off and guys running from machine gun strafing.

"The director broke the action down into sections, using two or three camera set ups on each so's to get different angles. Each of the bit players in these scenes was coached on just where to go and how fast, and how to go about it. Some of them had to count to themselves as they went so they would be just clear of the cap strings when they was touched off—like the bullets had just missed 'em. Some had to wave their arms and yell. Others just tucked their heads down and ran like hell.

"The ships blown up and burned on the field were old Standards and a couple—it might have been three Boeing CW's we got from Waldo Waterman, who had bought 'em to start an airline flying up to Big Bear. They had Hall-Scott engines in 'em. The Pfalzes was gotten from one of the studio back lots where they had set for some time.

"We wrecked three of these—two Standards and one of the Boeings—off the wrecking track in the airfield attack scenes. You could tell the Boeing in the film by the raked ailerons—wider at the tip than at the inboard end.

"I think they had three cameras on each wreck scene, so there was plenty of footage shot to allow the cutter to match the camera angles. They always shot a lot more film than they needed on each set up—use the best for the particular scene—and squirrel the rest away in the vault. This gave them plenty of stock footage which they could sell for clips to the other studios or use in their own films as needed.

"One Standard we let get up about twenty feet and then dumped it in on the nose. The old Boeing had been pretty well sawed through in spots to make sure it would come to pieces. It didn't get as far as we intended before it busted, but the shots was usable.

"The best one was the Standard we rigged to come off the track, pull up into a full stall as it started to burn, then fall off on one wing into the ground. On this one the stick was lashed so it would fly off—then when it had got off the track into the air, a cable at the end of the track pulled a pin which released the stick and set off the fire squibs. We had put in a couple of loops of

shock cord to pull the stick hard back when the pins was released, so it stalled and hung there with the fire busting out of the fuselage, then fell off on a wing into the ground. It worked real good.

"That pass made by Robby Robinson wasn't nearly as close as it looked. Robby claimed the debris hit his ship, but I looked it over and couldn't see anything that wasn't there before. He got rather hot about it anytime it was discussed—said it was the powder man's fault. He left before the picture was finished."[199]

In the story of "Dawn Patrol," the two British airplanes head for their home field after the attack, but one is forced to crash land behind the German lines after being hit by anti-aircraft gun fire. The other pilot lands nearby and takes off with his companion sitting on the bottom wing and clutching the center section struts. This airplane is also then hit by ground fire and crash lands in no-man's-land, turning over on its back and dumping the two flyers in a trench where they are rescued by French infantrymen.

Rupert McAllister made a pancake landing in a Thomas Morse Scout at the edge of the air field set for the first crash landing. This pilot was on the West Coast only a short time and was killed a short time later in the east, while demonstrating a Bach tri-motor.[200]

The scene where Douglas Fairbanks, Jr. lands to pick up Barthelmess was made with one of Garland Lincoln's Nieuports. Lincoln contracted with First National to furnish three Nieuports and one Swallow as part of the British squadron.[201] In a closeup of this incident, Barthelmess sat on the bottom wing of the Nieuport until Lincoln taxied out of the picture. The take-off portion of this rescue was made with Lincoln's Swallow leaving the ground instead of the Nieuport, with the silhouette of a figure painted on the side of the fuselage at the bottom wing root.

The second crash landing, where the airplane turns over in front of the French trenches, was also made at one edge of the German air field set in Pico Canyon. The camera was placed at ground level, looking through a small area of trenches and barbed wire. A long track, consisting of three wooden troughs to guide the two wheels and tail skid, ran in front of the trenches across from the camera position. The Thomas Morse that McAllister pancaked for the first crash landing of this series was repaired and a long tail skid was added to elevate the tail and keep the fuselage level with the ground. With its engine running, and a dummy in the cockpit, the Thomas Morse roared down the track. Blocks had been placed at the end to cause the airplane to turn over on its back. The blocks failed to stop the little fighter, and it continued to taxi along the ground, turned 180 degrees and headed back toward its starting point. With larger blocks and a lesser power setting, the drone

"Dawn Patrol" pilots and ground crew, who are working as extras, at the German airfield location near Saugus. Roscoe Turner and Frank Tomick are standing at the left. Roy Wilson in helmet and goggles is seated on the sand bags. Next to him in German officer's uniform is Ira Reed. Leo Nomis sits in the center with helmet and goggles. Rupert McAllister is in the white sweater and Jimmy Barton is seated on the ground in front of Leo Nomis. Courtesy: Frank Tomick

airplane performed according to plan in a later attempt, and turned over in front of the camera position.

Two weeks later the "Dawn Patrol" crew moved to Triunfo, near Thousand Oaks, where a British air field set had been built on the Russell Brothers Ranch. The British lineup consisted of the two Speedwing Travelairs, two Thomas Morse Scouts owned by First National, two Orencos leased from the Wilson Aero Service, and Garland Lincoln's Swallow and three Nieuport 28s. Takeoffs, landings, taxi scenes, and all of the exterior ground scenes of the British air field were shot at this location.

Garland Lincoln, now operating from a fixed base at Metropolitan Airport, noted an accident in his log book on March 24, 1930. While taxiing one of the Nieuports at the Triunfo location he sank a wheel in a gopher hole causing the ship to end up on its nose with a broken propeller.

Four days later Lincoln took off in one of the Nieuports to fly it back to his hangar at Metropolitan Airport for the purpose of some modification work. Soon after

heading for Van Nuys the rotary engine began to misfire. Several minutes later a small explosion shook the wooden frame of the little fighter plane. Fire began to creep out of the floor boards and scorch the bottom of Lincoln's coveralls. He could have bailed out in his parachute, but Lincoln did not want to lose the airplane. Recalling a new fire station that had been built in Reseda, he side slipped back and forth in an effort to extinguish the fire. The fire station soon came into view and he landed in a wide alley behind where there was room between the few buildings in the sparsely settled area. By the time he beat out the flames in the legs of his coveralls, the fuel that had collected in the engine cowling had burned itself out. The stunt pilot expected the firemen to see him come in smoking and meet the airplane with all kinds of equipment. But since fires seldom come to fire stations no one appeared. Lincoln ran into the station and announced that his airplane was behind the station with a few sparks and hot spots in the cowling. Several surprised firemen rushed out with extinguishers and smothered the remaining embers. A thankful Garland

Lincoln dismantled the Nieuport and trucked it to his hangar where he made the necessary repairs before flying it back to the Triunfo location.[202]

While the final scenes of "Dawn Patrol" were being edited, Howard Hughes released the sound version of "Hell's Angels." At this time Hollywood, California, was the glamorous center of the giant motion picture industry, and one of the cleanest and most charming of small cities. Movie stars ranked a little lower than celestial beings and fully lived their parts as regal creatures with an image of magnificent splendor. One could join the well-groomed strollers along Hollywood Boulevard any evening and recognize familiar faces that had been seen many time on the screen in supporting or character roles. Regardless of one's level of sophistication, it was always a thrill to see a major star pass in a luxurious automobile, enter a theater, or leave the lobby of the rambling Hollywood Hotel. If you had been there on the particular night of May 27, 1930, you would have seen Hollywood in all its glory during the most spectacular motion picture premier ever to take place anywhere in the world.

The main part of Hollywood Boulevard, which extends from its intersection with Vine Street for more than a mile to the west, where it crosses LaBrea Avenue, was open for west-bound vehicles only. The plan was to have four lanes of traffic in one direction so that theater patrons would have plenty of time to make the traditional drive along the famous boulevard on their way to Grauman's cathedral of the motion picture industry, the Chinese Theater. But no one expected the massive crowd that almost created the first case of urban paralysis—"gridlock."

Hissing studio arc lights, stationed every few yards along both sides of Hollywood Boulevard all the way from Vine Street to LaBrea, stroked the darkening sky

Garland Lincoln ran into a gopher hole with one of his modified Nieuport 28's during the filming of "Dawn Patrol" at the Triunfo location. Courtesy: Garland Lincoln

The mechanics and technical workers on "Dawn Patrol" pose in front of a Nieuport 28 at the Triunfo location. Jimmy Barton is in the center of the picture. Harry Reynolds stands in front of the outer wing "N" strut, and Manuel Zamora, the explosives expert, is on the end. Courtesy: Jimmy Barton

with their powerful beams. Clusters of multi-colored search lights fanned out from positions in the hills just north of Hollywood Boulevard to further illuminate the sky and the banners, flags, and huge airplane cutouts that decorated the famous street.

As the crowd thickened and the area became choked with automobiles, the curious spectators turned their faces upward to behold a sight that came straight from the First World War. A tight formation of low-flying, open-cockpit biplanes with ominous Maltese crosses on their wings droned along the boulevard.

Showtime at the theater was scheduled for 8:15, but the masses of spectators were so dense along both sides of the street that they eventually spilled over the curbs into the street itself, limiting traffic to only one lane in the vicinity of the Chinese Theater. One reporter noted that it took his car one hour to travel only four blocks.

It was well after 10 p.m. before all the seats were filled and "Hell's Angels" was presented to the public. The critics did not compliment the dramatic portion of the film, but everyone agreed that the air scenes were without equal and worthy of all Hollywood superlatives. They remain as the classic of airplane scenes, and despite the technical errors of the picture, the flying scenes of "Hell's Angels" have yet to be surpassed.

The story contrasts two American brothers, played by Ben Lyon and James Hall, who are attending Oxford. On a pre-war vacation trip to Munich with a German fellow student, Ben Lyon as the irresponsible brother finds himself challenged to a duel with a German nobleman over the affections of the latter's wife. Lyon immediately departs for England, leaving the serious-minded brother, James Hall, to uphold the family honor by facing the duel in which he is slightly wounded in the arm.

When all three students are back at Oxford, the German boy receives a notice from his War Department, and he reluctantly returns to Germany for mobilization with his regiment. The brothers join the Royal Flying Corps, though Ben Lyon is opposed to the idea. After winning their wings Ben Lyon is drawn into a one-night love affair by his brother's fun-loving girlfriend, Jean Harlow. The unsuspecting James Hall rebuffs his brother's warning that beautiful Jean may not be as innocent as he imagines her to be.

The German student shows up in the crew of a Zeppelin that is bombing London. Lowered in an observation car below the clouds to direct the bombing, and torn between duty and his love of England, he causes the bombs to be dropped into a lake. In an effort to gain altitude after being pursued by British planes, the Zeppelin commander orders all expendable equipment to be thrown overboard. When British planes continued to gain on the airship, and the commander is informed that the reeling in of the observation car will require ten more minutes, he cuts the cable. Finally, several members of the crew volunteer to jump overboard to lighten the load of the fleeing Zeppelin. The attacking planes are unable to down the dirigible, but with jammed machine guns one pilot climbs above and dives his airplane into the ship, setting it afire.

The brothers are assigned to combat duty in France and Ben Lyon is accused of cowardice by his squadron mates. When volunteers are requested to fly a captured German bomber deep in the enemy lines as the only way to bomb an important ammunition dump, Ben Lyon steps forward in an effort to prove his courage. He is joined by his brother and they are given leave until takeoff time at dawn. While visiting the local bistros, they meet canteen worker Jean Harlow who reveals her true character in a drunken stupor with her current lover, an artillery officer.

Flying dominates almost the entire second half of the picture as the brothers take off in the captured German bomber. After they successfully bomb the ammunition dump, a squadron of German fighter planes tries to shoot them down as they flee for the Allied lines. A squadron of British fighters comes to the rescue and a gigantic dog fight develops. But before they reach the lines the German leader, supposedly von Richthofen, brings them down. Questioned by a German general who turns out to be the officer who challenged Ben Lyon to the pre-war duel in Munich, the brothers refuse to reveal plans for the imminent Allied offensive. Faced with execution by a firing squad as spies, Ben Lyon weakens when they are returned to their prison cell and is ready to talk. As the stronger brother, James Hall per-

Garland Lincoln's three modified Nieuport 28's at the Triunfo location for "Dawn Patrol." Courtesy: Garland Lincoln

suades Ben Lyon to let him do the talking. James Hall tells the general he will talk only on the condition that he is allowed to shoot his companion, whom he supposedly hates, to prevent any post-war knowledge of Hall's cooperation with the enemy. With a Luger and one bullet, Hall is returned to the cell. When Ben Lyon can't be persuaded to remain silent, Hall shoots his brother to keep the battle plans secret. As James Hall is then executed by a firing squad, the British troops go over the top and rout the enemy as "The End" is superimposed over the battlefield scene.

The German government regarded "Hell's Angels" as an offense to the nation and lodged protests through its embassies when the film was released in Europe.[203]

"Dawn Patrol" received better reviews when it reached the theaters several weeks later, even though the flying action, while excellent, was not as spectacular as the flying scenes of "Hell's Angels." Howard Hughes resented the competition from "Dawn Patrol" and filed a suit in New York, claiming that "Dawn Patrol" was stolen from the script of "Hell's Angels." He demanded that it be withdrawn from circulation. Gainsborough Pictures of Great Britain filed a separate suit against First National and Warner Brothers[204] claiming that portions of their play, "Journey's End," currently being filmed at Universal, was also used in "Dawn Patrol." After viewing all three films, a judge ruled that each had drawn from similar events of the war and that no plagiarism had been committed.[205] "Dawn Patrol" continued its run.

When Warner Brothers-First National started work on "Dawn Patrol" the studio heads tried to avoid any similarities with "Hell's Angels." As the director, Howard Hawks was told to check the script with the pilots and mechanics who had worked on "Hell's Angels." In his tape-recorded interview with James Dunavent, Jimmy Barton recalls that situation:

"Howard Hawks was a good man to work for. He'd been in the Air Service in the war and knew what he wanted. One time, when we first started filming, he come to me and asked me to tell him if anything in the script came up that could be thought of as anything in 'Hell's Angels.' Seems like Hughes had got wind of things and tried to hire all the pilots back, saying he wanted retakes made of some of the air scenes. None of them would go, so he tried to get an injunction against First National claiming 'Dawn Patrol' was copied after 'Hell's Angels.' "

Leo Nomis and Frank Tomick in Travelair "Wichita Fokkers" lead two other pilots in a takeoff from the Saugus location for "Dawn Patrol." Courtesy: Frank Tomick

CHAPTER FOUR
THE ASSOCIATED MOTION PICTURE PILOTS

Night shooting for a scene in one of the "Tailspin Tommy" pictures. Courtesy: Jimmy Barton

MOTION PICTURE STUNT flying became a widely recognized profession after the release of "Hell's Angels" and "Dawn Patrol." The stunt and camera pilots, who were already well known in aviation and motion picture circles, now came to the attention of the general public. Newspapers, periodicals and movie fan magazines noted the existence of this special group of flyers.

Depending upon mutual skill and experience, and often placing their lives in each other's hands, the motion picture stunt pilots drew closer together into a brotherly relationship. If a man faced family or financial problems, he could depend upon help from his flying comrades. When one pilot was awarded a contract from the studios, he always shared the work with his fellow flyers. Through years of competition with each other and others flyers, a fair market value of compensation from the studios had been established. A gentleman's agreement among the pilots kept this pay scale intact, and with the current flood of aviation movies, the motion picture stunt pilots enjoyed a comfortable living.

Frank Clarke, Roy Wilson and Frank Tomick became well known in the motion picture capital because of their minor acting roles in "Hell's Angels." They could occasionally be seen among the motion picture people who traditionally strolled, or cruised their automobiles along Hollywood Boulevard in the evenings. Tave Wilson recalls a minor incident of that time as it was related to him by his brother, Roy:

"Roy, Tomick and Clarke were riding along Hollywood Boulevard one night with Roscoe Turner in this old Packard touring car he had. Turner had on that trick uniform we used to call his circus uniform. He had wings on his sleeves, wings on his pockets, and wings on his collar. The car had wings on the radiator cap, wings on the hub caps, and wings on the doors. They were stopped at Hollywood and Vine by a new policemen when they ran a red light or something, and the regular officer wasn't there or he would have known them. But this new man put his foot on the running board to write a ticket, and he looked at the wings all over the place. He looked at Turner and said, 'What are all these hawk wings for?' Turner said in his soft southern drawl—he was from Georgia or South Carolina, some where down there—'We're aviators, sir.' Clarke was sitting in the back seat and he said, 'Oh no!', kidding Turner, 'He's the aviator. We're just pilots.' From that day on we called him Hawk Wings Turner. We were always kidding each other. But Turner was a cracker jack pilot. When he was flying that Sikorsky in 'Hell's Angels,' and they were coming at him from all sides, they didn't scare him one bit. He just held her in there and didn't budge one inch."[206]

With the cooperation of the U.S. Navy, Columbia made "Dirigible" in 1930, a very realistic film that featured the giant rigid airship "Los Angeles." While some miniatures were utilized for a crash scene, much of the air action was photographed at the Navy's Lighter Than Air Base in Lakehurst, New Jersey.

The basic plot for the story, which was influenced by Admiral Byrd's recent flight to the South Pole, is a rivalry between airplanes and dirigibles in the Naval Air Service. Jack Holt is the lieutenant commander who favors the dirigible, while Ralph Graves is a sometimes foolhardy lieutenant who champions the airplane. When Graves agrees to accompany Holt on an expedition to the South Pole, Fay Wray, as Graves' wife, secretly appeals to Jack Holt who removes Graves from the list. When confronted by the angry airplane pilot, Holt is forced to say that Graves was dropped because of his reckless reputation, rather than reveal the intervention of the flyer's wife.

The expedition boards the dirigible and leaves for the South Pole, but a storm on the way destroys the air ship. The crew and expedition members are rescued, and Graves receives an opportunity to show what an airplane can do when the expedition leader agrees to fly with him on the next attempt. The flight to the South Pole is a success, but the airplane noses over on landing in the snow.

The dirigible redeems itself when Jack Holt successfully flies another air ship to the Antarctic where the two survivors of the airplane crash are located and eventually rescued.

As cinematographer on the picture, Joseph Walker took charge of the ground scenes and interiors of the "Los Angeles." Elmer Dyer photographed all of the exterior air scenes and did much of his work sitting astride the motor gondola of a navy blimp, secured only by straps and ropes.

One incident in the picture required scenes of a naval airplane attaching itself to a trapeze-like framework anchored to the bottom of the dirigible. While Elmer Dyer photographed the exterior action from a blimp flying alongside the "Los Angeles," Walker had a cameraman in one of the dirigible's motor gondolas, a remote operated camera on the airplane, and spread-eagled himself among the aluminum girders above the opening in the bottom of the air ship with a hand-held camera.

Docking the airplane to the dirigible required special skill by the navy pilot. He had to approach the hook on the trapeze framework by a circuitous route around the aft engine gondola while throttling down to the airplane's minimum flying speed in order to keep pace with the slow-moving dirigible.[207]

Columbia built an Antarctic snowfield set at the old Arcadia Balloon School for that part of the story where the airplane crashes at the South Pole and parachute jumpers from the dirigible come to the rescue. Elmer

Dyer had already photographed closeup scenes of navy jumpers parachuting from the "Los Angeles" over Lakehurst. Scenes now had to be made showing jumpers landing in the snow at the South Pole. Roy and Tave Wilson signed a contract with Columbia to drop two jumpers on the set for that part of the picture.

The Wilson brothers, each in a Travelair with a jumper on the wing, flew to the set from the Wilson Airport. As they approached the artificial snowfield, they dropped to one hundred feet altitude, so the jumpers would be sure of landing on the small target. The jumpers popped their chutes while still on the wings and were pulled off horizontally. By the time their bodies swung pendulum fashion into a vertical position below the canopies, they were only twenty-five feet above the simulated snow. Both jumpers landed well into the set, but it happened so fast that the cameramen missed the shot and it had to be repeated.

A large group of spectators gathered at the set one evening while wind machines blew painted cornflakes all over the area to simulate a snowstorm. The spectators that were downwind from the action began to scratch under their clothing and soon returned to their homes. The actors and technicians on the set had the same problem and the entire production had to be shut down for several hours. The uncooked cornflakes had been in storage for some time and had become infested with small weevils. Shooting was resumed after everyone changed clothes and the cornflakes were sprayed with a disinfectant.[208]

Jimmy Barton recalls making that part of the picture where the airplane crashes in the snow:

"They shot some scenes with a Fokker model for intercutting with the location scenes. The special effects department made up a snow and ice landscape miniature set where they shot footage using both the Fokker model and a seven or eight foot scale dirigible—things they couldn't get on location or from stock footage.

"The studio leased an F-10 Fokker Trimotor from Western Air Express for the full scale live action shots. It had to be on skis, and the studio prop department built us up a set from sketches we give 'em. They wouldn't work at all—weren't heavy enough to take the weight of the airplane when we put 'em on to use it. We built another pair that looked better and would take the gaff. Used real heavy wide runners and a hefty steel tube spider with axle bushings welded in.

"The grip crew had laid a set of troughs down the length of the set before the flakes was spread down. When the time come to film the take off, they sent the crew out to scoop flakes out of the trough and sweep 'em clean before they put on a good coat of grease.

"The F-10 Fokker had been trucked over on a big lowboy trailer from Alhambra Airport where Western Air Express had their main base. I don't remember if the wing was taken off or not. I would think they had to, because it was several miles and some of the area

was built up, with telephone poles along the route. It had the wing on it when I first saw it. Anyway, it was brought up to where the track started. We took off the wheels after jacking it up, and put on the skis, then manhandled it onto the track using sheets of greased heavy plywood and planks under the skis. It had been stored at Alhambra for some time, and it took quite a while to get two of the engines running.

"The track wasn't too long, but the pilot, a Western Air Express fellow named Pat Patterson, managed to get the tail up on one of the two runs they made. I think they used three camera set ups in order to cover the sequence—one for long shot, one for medium closeup, and one almost head on. They shot it slow, at silent speed on the cameras, then when it was edited and run at sound speed, it would look like the ship was going a lot faster. Any time they did any shooting during the day, they put a dark red filter over the lens to give 'em almost a night effect. It was near blinding white with those fake snow cornflakes under the sun. They actually shot a lot of it at night to get the low light angle they needed. They was a full moon and a set of big sun arc lights which they cut in to cast long low shadows. On a couple of scenes they dropped flares. I wasn't on the location most of that time, so I didn't see what they did then—worked days on the equipment and set ups they needed.

"The crash was done on the set, out at location. We got an old Fokker F-7 Trimotor that had been wrecked and fixed it up to look like the bigger F-10. It had sat around the hangars at Alhambra or Vail Field—one wing was smashed and the engines taken out. First thing we had to do was rebuild the wing to make it look like it was complete. Since they was not going to make it fly, there was no use in rebuilding it like it was—with the box spar and different size ribs like they used in Fokker wings. What we did was get a big heavy timber—solid—and set it into the busted spar root with bolts, then nailed pieces of plywood on it to give it the tapered shape. The outside skin was plywood, nailed down to the rough structure. It looked pretty good when it was all done, if you didn't look too close. All it was going to be used for was the long shots and wreck scene. They shot all of the closeups and ground action with the F-10.

"Couldn't get Whirlwind J-5's to mount on the nose and wing nacelles—wasn't any available. The studio didn't want to put out money for good engines to mount on such an old hulk, and used Whirlwinds were being picked up as quick as they was offered, by people with Travelair 2000's that wanted to replace their OX engines with J-5's. The Department of Commerce had just authorized a regulation that you could substitute J-5's in an OX 2000 airframe provided you beefed up parts of the forward fuselage to comply with the factory standards they come up with.

"Well, anyway, we got three old LeRhone rotaries and put 'em on in place of the original engines. The cylinders looked too skimpy—you could tell right off they wasn't right. We finally took oil cans and put 'em on over the tops of the LeRhone cylinders, and wrapped heavy wires around them to make it look like cooling fins. Put small blocks on the ends for valve gear covers, and pieces of broom sticks for the push rods. Painted up, they was a good imitation and worked well

Paul Mantz flies through a hangar at Bishop Airport for a scene at Universal's "Air Mail." Courtesy: Jerry Phillips

The elaborate arctic set constructed by Columbia at the Ross Field Balloon School in Arcadia for "Dirigible."
Courtesy: Tave Wilson

Harry Perry with an unidentified pilot in a Travelair with a modified tail. Courtesy: Harry Perry

Frank Clarke and an unidentified pilot (to his left) buzz the camera at Metropolitan Airport for "Sky Devils." Courtesy: Tave Wilson

on camera.

"We pulled it over with a cable for the nose over. This was a way we could make it look real, and still control the way it would go. We had shot the take off going one way, and the director decided that to shoot from the opposite direction would give the idea that they was two separate scenes better, so all of the crash scenes with the old F-7 was done moving from right to left along the back drop. It was high enough to screen out most of the background, except where the tail would rear up into the sky as it went over. The laboratory would take care of that with what they called a travelling matte, blanking out anything above the backdrop and printing in the snow covered mountains and skyline like it was in Antarctica. I think they shot the miniature set to get footage for that.

"The camera crews shot extra footage of the ship as the cable pulled it along the track once to set the pace for the camera crews, and check the towing bridles.

"They had fixed a bridle to the landing gear that was attached to posts off camera back at the start of the track. Another one on a winch at the crane pulled the ship along the track—both of 'em was spring loaded with shock cord lengths. The cable on the winch had a load trip to release it once the back cable had reached its limit, at the place where the Fokker was to upset. A third cable run from the boom of a big crane to the aft fuselage just ahead of the tail. The crane operator kept it from getting slack as the ship came along the track, pulled by the winch at the crane. It had to be kept taut, but not too taut so's it wouldn't lift the tail until the ship was snubbed and the forward towing bridle let go.

Then the crane man would cut in his reel clutch and lift the boom arm to pull the tail up and over. We tried it once in a slowed up dry run and it worked good. Naturally we didn't take it all the way through—just to where the tail started to lift up.

"On the take they ran the cameras slow so it would look faster at projection speed. It worked just like we had intended up to the point where the Fokker was on its nose, then the rebuilt wing that had the heavy timber in it caused it to fall over cock-eyed—too much weight on that side. I had worried some about that when we was setting up. I told the director and he moved one of the camera positions back about twenty feet. Good thing he did—the tail come over sideways and smacked right down on the spot he'd originally picked. It would've wrecked the camera and maybe hurt someone.

"When the ship went over on its back, they cut the cameras and the actors got in and then come scrambling out in the next take, when we lit off the squibs that set it on fire. Couple of days before, they sprayed the corn flakes with a stiff borax solution and let 'em dry. Made 'em fireproof—leastways enough so for the take."[209]

In August 1931 the Fox Film Corporation leased Garland Lincoln's three Nieuports, bearing Department of Commerce license numbers 75W, 10415 and 2539, for the air scenes of "Heartbreak."

The main theme of the picture is a love story with the air war between Italy and Austria-Hungary as a background. The story opens in Vienna before the U.S. enters World War I. Charles Farrell, an attache at the U.S. Embassy, falls in love with Madge Evans, a beautiful Austrian countess. When America enters the war, Farrell joins the Air Service and is eventually sent to the Italian front. Hearing that the famous and ruthless Austrian ace, Count Molke, is over the Italian lines, Farrell takes off to do battle. The only air action in the picture takes place as Farrell eventually shoots down the Austrian plane. When he lands nearby in an attempt to rescue his opponent from the burning wreckage, he discovers that his dead victim is the brother of his Austrian sweetheart, who had borrowed the plane of Count Molke. The countess is unaware of the identity of the flyer who killed her brother, but Farrell is so distressed that he refuses to fly any further combat missions. One day he steals an airplane and flies into Austria where he secretly lands and sees the countess to explain what happened. When he returns to his field he is court martialed and spends the rest of the war in prison. The story ends happily when he is released after the Armistice and is eventually forgiven by the countess.

Nieuports 10415 and 2539 did no flying and appeared only in ground scenes. Critics commented favorably on the brief but excellent air scenes in which Lincoln, flying 75W as the American pilot, dog fights with Frank Clarke flying a Travelair as the Austrian, over the Italian Alps.

Actually, they were the San Gabriel Mountains east of Los Angeles Basin still capped with snow from the previous winter.[210]

Metro Goldwyn Mayer returned to the navy for its next aviation film, "Helldivers." In the story Wallace Beery and Clark Gable portray two rival aerial gunners in the Naval Air Service assigned to the aircraft carrier, "U.S.S. Saratoga." Competition over girls and aerial gunnery ability results in a fight and feud between the two chief petty officers. During fleet maneuvers Clark Gable parachutes from an airplane that breaks up during a dive bombing run. He is injured when he comes down on a rocky island, but the chute is spotted by Beery and his pilot. They land on a sandy beach to rescue Gable, but Beery's pilot sustains an injury that prevents him from flying out. Beery loads both injured men aboard the Curtiss Helldiver and is able to take off. Returning to the carrier in a heavy fog, he crashes on the flight deck. Clark Gable and the pilot survive, but Wallace Beery dies in the crash, and the picture ends as he is buried at sea.

Except for a few obvious miniatures, all of the flying action was done by navy pilots and photographed by Charles Marshall. Shots of Curtiss Helldiver formations and takeoffs and landings on the "Saratoga" were made on locations in San Diego, Guantanamo Bay, Panama and over the Carribean Sea. Portions of scenes showing the airplane's arrestor hooks and cables stretched across the flight deck were blacked out by military censors as this method of landing on a carrier was new at the time.

Marshall made fifteen bombing dives in a Curtiss Helldiver to obtain shots of other Helldivers making their bombing runs.[211] One scene showed the dirigible "Los Angeles" mooring to the deck of the "Saratoga" while on fleet maneuvers at sea. "Helldivers" received good reviews and was one of the better aviation movies of the early 1930s.

Sometime in 1931, R.K.O. started work on "The Balloon Buster," a story based on the life and amazing war record of Lt. Frank Luke. The studio purchased two World War I British fighters, S.E.5s, from the Skywriting Corporation of America. Wally Timm reconditioned the airplanes at Metropolitan Airport, but after months of revising and rewriting the script, "The Balloon Buster" was finally abandoned.[212]

The colorful story of Frank Luke never reached the screen, but another motion picture stunt pilot settled in Hollywood as a result of the attempt.

Oliver C. "Boots" LeBoutillier was born in Montclair, New Jersey, in 1881 and learned to fly in 1916. He joined the Canadian Army in 1917, entered flight training and was soon a fighter pilot in the Royal Air Force. He served in No. 209 Squadron and was a participant in the famous dog fight on April 21, 1918, in which Baron Manfred von

One of Garland Lincoln's Nieuport 28's on its way to the Triunfo location for the Fox picture, "Heartbreak." Courtesy: Garland Lincoln

Elmer Dyer with a pilot-operated remote camera mount he installed on a Waco at the Triunfo location for "Aces of Aces." The camera was positioned to shoot past and show part of the Waco's tail as it photographed a Travelair "Wichita Fokker" in close pursuit firing its machine gun. Courtesy: Stacy McCullough

Richthofen was killed. After barnstorming in the northeast he made an unsuccessful attempt to fly the Atlantic in 1927. He then joined the Skywriting Corporation of America and wrote Lucky Strike and other advertising slogans in the skies above cities all over the United States. He was sky writing in Los Angeles when R.K.O. purchased the two S.E.5s. After meeting Howard Batt and other motion picture stunt pilots at Clover Field, he was able to obtain studio flying jobs from time to time.

Paul Mantz arrived in Southern California at about this same time. He rented hangar space at the new United Airport in Burbank, a large commercial field next to the small Wilson Airport, operated by United Air Lines. In addition to being the Pacific Coast distributor for Consolidated Fleet Airplanes, Paul Mantz established a charter flying service, and gave flying lessons and sightseeing rides.

Born Albert Paul Mantz in Alameda, California, on August 2, 1903, his family moved to Redwood City, California, when his father accepted a position as principal of the elementary school. After seeing Lincoln Beachey perform at the Panama Pacific Exposition in

1915, twelve-year-old Paul Mantz was also attracted to the profession of aviation. Upon completing his high school education, he went to work for the Pacific Gas and Electric Co., and took flying lessons at the Redwood City Airport.[213]

The professional aviation career of Paul Mantz began in 1927 when he was accepted for the U.S. Army Flying Cadet Training Program. His biography, "Hollywood Pilot" by Don Dwiggins, gives a detailed account of his early life and covers the situation in regard to the academic record from Stanford University which was submitted to the Flying Cadet Examining Board.

Mantz went to March Field for flight training where he demonstrated his outstanding ability as a pilot. But he failed, according to "Hollywood Pilot," to complete the training program as he was discharged by the Cadet Disciplinary Board for buzzing a train.[214]

Fearless and undaunted by the setback, he returned to the San Francisco area where he became the local distributor for Consolidated Fleet Airplanes. Palo Alto was his first base of operations, and it was here that he established a world record on July 6, 1930, by performing forty-six consecutive outside loops.[215] With a larger aviation potential in Southern California, he moved to Burbank the following year.

The air war of 1914-1918 continued to serve as a background for aviation films in the early 1930s, though the air action was almost always relegated to minor scenes. "Body And Soul," by the Fox Film Corporation, contained several effective flying episodes, but the major emphasis was on dramatic situations between the characters. The story revolves around three American flyers, played by Charles Farrell, Humphrey Bogart and Donald Dillaway, who are attached to a British squadron. Humphrey Bogart is killed while trying to bring down an enemy observation balloon, but Charles Farrell succeeds in the mission and allows the credit to go to his dead companion. Farrell then looks up Bogart's girl friend, Elissa Landi, to break the news. They soon become romantically involved, but she is suspected of passing information to the enemy when a situation results in the death of Dillaway. Chief among her accusers is Myrna Loy, in a minor role. Elissa Landi is eventually cleared of the charges and the film closes with a happy ending.

R.K.O. released "Born To Love" in April 1931 with Constance Bennett and Joel McCrea in the leading roles. The story takes place in war-time London where McCrea, as an American flyer on leave, meets hospital worker, Constance Bennett, during an air raid. They fall in love and live together during the remaining days of his leave, planning to marry when the war is over. Soon after he returns to his squadron, Joel McCrea is shot down behind the German lines and is assumed dead. Constance Bennett has a baby and is befriended by a wounded British officer in the hospital. He marries her after the war and raises the child as his own. The missing aviator reappears and a triangle situation develops. McCrea and Bennett are eventually reunited and marry, though the child stays with the British officer.

"The Last Flight," by First National Pictures, opens with a few flashes of air battle from "Dawn Patrol," but that is the end of the flying action. The rest of the picture deals with the post-war lives of four American aviators who suffer various physical and psychological effects as a result of their combat flying during the war.

First National also released "Men Of The Sky," a musical comedy about espionage activities in France. At least one still photograph from this picture shows a pilot helping his wounded observer from the bullet-riddled rear cockpit of an airplane. How much flying action, if any, appeared in the film is unknown.

"The Sky Raiders," by Columbia, contained stock aviation scenes from other films. Lloyd Hughes and Marceline Day play the leading roles in the story that deals with air pirates who capture commercial airplanes transporting large sums of money. Hughes, as a pilot, resorts to the bottle and loses his sweetheart after he is responsible for a crash in which her brother is killed. Eventually he reforms from alcoholism, joins the pirates to uncover their operations, and is forgiven by the girl.

"The Sky Spider" was released to the theaters by Action Pictures in August 1931. Similar to the melodramatic plots of the early serials, the story revolves around criminals who rob the U.S. Air Mail. According to contemporary reviews, the picture contained deficiencies in dialogue and acting, and contained several questionable feats such as the precise dropping of a stick of dynamite on a mountain cabin from an airplane several thousand feet in the air.

"Air Eagles," by Big Productions, reached the theaters toward the end of 1931. The story is a post-war love triangle situation involving two buddies, a German and American flyer who formerly fought against each other, but are now performing air duels for a traveling carnival, and their competitive love for one of the carnival girls. When the carnival fails, the trio lives in the American flyer's home where his younger brother, also a flyer, falls for the girl. Desperate for money, the German boy tries to persuade the younger brother to rob the payroll he flies. When the kid brother refuses, the German flyer tries to bring him down. The older brother discovers the plan and takes off to protect his brother. A lengthy air fight takes place in which the two former comrades are killed. The girl confesses her love for the surviving younger brother for a bittersweet ending.

Despite the proximity of the busy United Airport, the Wilson Airport thrived as the center of aviation movies and served as a gathering place for the motion picture stunt pilots when they were not working. Idle time was passed by tinkering with their airplanes, pitching horse shoes, devising practical jokes, and inventing new ways to compete with each other.

One of their games was related to the puddles of water that lingered on the field for a day or two after each winter rain. A large puddle near the center of the field was selected as a mark, and each competing pilot put five dollars in a pool. Using the same airplane, the competitors climbed to a prescribed altitude, cut the engine and tried to hit the selected puddle with the airplane's landing gear. Frank Tomick won most of these pools and carried the nickname "Deadstick" for a while.[216]

Tave Wilson recalls some of the events that took place at the Wilson Airport during the early 1930s:

"A fellow came out to the field who had been up in Alaska, and he wanted to rent the little restaurant we had there, and stay at the old farm house that went with the property. I told him about our work at the field, and that we didn't have any lights so there was no night flying, and nothing went on at night unless they happened to be shooting a picture some night. That sounded all right to him and he moved in.

"When I came out the next morning; that old man had everything packed and he was ready to move out. I noticed tire tracks all around the hash house and up and down the field. I wondered what was going on, and when I pieced the story together this is what happened.

"The fellow we leased the land from got half shot and came out there trying to get some gas from one of our pumps. The mechanic who slept there as a guard fired a rifle shot in the air which scared this guy. He banged his car into one of the apricot trees right in front of the house where the old man was sleeping. He heard all this glass crashing and lights were shining right in the room where he was sleeping. Well, the drunk got untangled and left, but it scared the daylight out of the old man.

"A few hours later some guy who had rented an airplane on the other side of town tried to land at our field. He didn't have any lights on the airplane, and he knew that if he landed at United next door, which was all lit up, he'd be in trouble with the authorities because he was flying without lights. So he thought he'd sneak into our field and land. Well, he came in and overshot the field and knocked out all the wires down at the other end, at the railroad tracks, which knocked out all the block signals on the railroad. The airplane cracked up on the other side of the railroad tracks and there was a freight train at Vineland. He was sitting there blowing his whistle. He couldn't go anywhere, and there was a passenger train on the other side of Hollywood Way blowing his whistle. He couldn't get out this way because the block signals were all against him. And both cross streets, Hollywood Way and Vineland, were blocked by the trains. The fire department from

North Hollywood was trying to get over here to the crash, and the police department was driving into our airport trying to find the airplane, which was across the railroad tracks from our field. With sirens going, red lights flashing, and train whistles blowing, that old man didn't know what was going on. After everything quieted down, the C.A.A. drove into the field about four o'clock in the morning and the mechanic fired another shot in the air.

"Over at United, Boeing had just put new Hornet engines in their mail planes. About five o'clock Harry Crandall took off in one of these Boeings with a Hornet. He was taking off on the cross wind runway over our airport and right across the house with the old man in there. He noticed the lights in the shack and thought we were shooting something, so he flattened the prop out to take a look and came across there with a full load. You can imagine the sound of that Boeing airplane with a Hornet in it, revving up for all she had. It just about took the shingles off the shack.

"About six o'clock Al Gilhausen was coming in from the other way. He also had a Boeing with a Hornet in it. He saw the lights and he came over to take a look and just about took off the rest of the shingles.

"When I got out there that old man was just about crazy. He said he wouldn't stay in this place if we gave him free rent. He said it was worse than an earthquake and a tornado at the same time.

"There were always cameramen who wanted to be aerial cameramen because it paid more. We used to pull a trick on new cameramen that we called 'split shots.' We had a new cameraman once and we fixed it up with the director to get some 'split shots' while flying from our field over to the location. That was when Frank Clarke and Roy would fly wing to wing and come right to my camera ship head on. About the time you thought they'd come through the ship, they'd split. One would go over the top and one underneath. That poor cameraman in the back was looking through his finder and all he could see was propeller hubs. It was too late to jump and he ducked in the cockpit waiting for the crash. After we landed at the location, this new cameraman jumped out and said he would never fly again.

"Roy and Clarke would come over, look at the camera ship and find a little scratch that was already there and say, 'We just nicked the wing tip a little bit. It didn't do any real harm.' And I'd say, 'You remember the last time you were doing spins around my ship and you knocked the navigation light off? I don't mind you scratching the wing tip a little, but I don't want you knocking any more lights off.'

"The old time cameramen like Harry Perry or Elmer Dyer would stand there with a sober face and say, 'You shouldn't squawk too much, all they did was scratch the wing tip.' By the time we got through with that cameraman, he didn't want any part of it.

"Sometimes they'd do it from the side, the same trick. Roy and Clarke pulled that on Roscoe Turner in his Sikorsky when he first came out here. He swore that one of them came over and then in between the wing and the stabilizer.

"Frank Clarke wrote an article once for the Saturday Evening Post, or one of those magazines. Tomick was sitting in our restaurant reading this article when Clarke came in. Tomick was counting, '142, 143, 144.'

Clarke said, 'What the hell you counting, Swede?' Tomick said, 'I'm just counting the number of times you said I.'

"They'd get in an argument, kidding each other—Tomick talked broken you know, and Clarke was part Indian and proud of it. Tomick would say, 'Yeah, the first time I saw you Clarke, you were walking down Hollywood Boulevard wrapped in a blanket gnawing on a bone.' And Clarke would say, 'Yeah, and you damned foreigners came over here and cut down all the trees and wrecked the place.' They were just like two brothers. If you found one you could find the other. If they weren't together, one could always tell you where the other one was.

"Frank Clarke was a man's man. He didn't talk too much, never had much to say, but when he did, he'd come right to the point.

"Frank Tomick was a very genial sort of fellow. He liked to drink pretty well, but when he had two or three drinks and brought an airplane in, oh boy, he was very meticulous with it. It was absolutely a perfect three point landing. I could always tell when he had a drink or two.

"Then he'd come in and squawk about the field, just kidding, you know. He always called me the Scotchman. He'd say, 'You Scotchman, when are you going to spend some money and drag this field. It's full of gopher holes.' I said, 'There's nothing wrong with this field. You've just got a couple of gallons of gin in there, and you're afraid they'll bump together and break.' He was a heck of a good pilot. Some guys would say, 'Well, he's about half shot.' I'd say, 'Listen, he can fly better with two or three drinks under his belt than you and I could cold sober.' He was a very conservative pilot.

"I'll never forget one time Tomick and I were working on a picture with Roy and Clarke. We both had Standards for camera ships and they had J-5 Travelairs. Roy and Clarke were out doing monkey shines, chasing each other and going clear back into the mountains. That was up on that location where they had the German airfield in "Dawn Patrol." They wanted to go back in there with their J-5's, and we only had Hissos in the Standards. Tomick said, 'What! You think I go back in there. I'm no damn fool. Get back in there and that thing crack up. Take me four days to ride out on jackass!'

"I did most of the camera flying in a Stearman that we fixed up for camera work. I took out the 220 J-4 and put in a J-5, but I was disappointed when it took just as long a run to take off. Then a prop man installed a wide blade propeller, and I enlarged the fin and rudder. It was the best camera ship around. I could set the nose up and give it a little rudder and it would mush along a railroad track in perfect position for the cameraman to follow a train or action along a road. Howard Batt said it was the sweetest ship to fly that he ever flew, and Frank Clarke couldn't keep his hands off of it. He always wanted to fly it when he came over to our field.

"One time we had a fellow come out here from back east, a newsreel cameraman who wanted to get a close shot of a parachute jumper. We asked him how close do you want it, and he said as close as you can get. We said okay, and I told him to put a wide angle lens on it. He said, 'How long is it going to take?', and we said,

About a half hour.' Then he said, 'How much is it going to cost?', and I said, '$50.00 for each ship, $50.00 for each pilot, and $50.00 for the jumper.' He couldn't believe that he could get all of that in thirty minutes.

"I took off, and Roy took off with the jumper, and we got our altitude. Roy pulled his ship right on in, with his aileron right over the top of the cameraman, and there the jumper was, on the wing about ten feet away, as close as you can get without the prop cutting into the wing. The cameraman pressed his button and the jumper let go of the wing. Roy pulled out of the way, and I slid in there with the camera ship and slapped it into a vertical bank, and trailed him right down to the ground. He got a shot of the guy landing on the ground—the chute falling all over him, and we came on in and landed in less than thirty minutes.

"The cameraman said, 'I don't believe it. All I had to do was press the button. I didn't even have to pan the camera. I've been flying with these fellows back east and it takes them two hours just to get in position.'

"About two weeks later he came by and told us he got a $250.00 bonus for the best shot of the week.

"Carl Laemmle, Jr. got sick on location in the Petrified Forest and the studio called up to send his private doctor. My brother used the Waco Taperwing, which was the fastest job we had. We put a parachute on the doctor, and he wanted to know why he had to wear a parachute. Roy said, 'That's rough country, nothing but rocks and trees. Even the crows wear parachutes when they fly across that country.'

"The studio called up about getting insurance on him, and they had an awful time getting the insurance company to insure him with a parachute. This same doctor had to fly up to San Francisco the next week. In those days, when the airlines were just starting, if you demanded a parachute you could get one. Well, he went to the airline and asked for a parachute. They tried to discourage him, but he insisted. He said, 'Even the crows wear parachutes when they fly over the mountains.'

"Why all the fuss about insurance on a guy with a parachute? I called up the insurance company and they finally gave me the low down. He said that in the airlines, if they crack up we just pay off so much a dead person. But if a guy bails out in a parachute and lands in a bunch of rocks and messes up his spine, that might cost a lot more. We'd much rather pay off on the deceased than to get mixed up in the other deal. Just a matter of statistics."[217]

In 1931 the Metropolitan Airport in Van Nuys began to compete with the Wilson Airport as a center of aviation movies. Garland Lincoln increased his small fleet of movie airplanes, and Howard Hughes moved the fourteen airplanes that remained after Caddo Field was abandoned to Metropolitan Airport.[218]

Using leftover scenes from "Hell's Angels," Hughes made two more aviation movies, using Metropolitan Airport as a base of operations. "Cock Of The Air" and "Sky Devils" were both comedies and required a few additional air scenes, but most of the air action for both pictures came from scenes left over from "Hell's Angels."

Garland Lincoln's D.H.9 painted up for the Paramount picture "Eagle and the Hawk." Courtesy: Garland Lincoln

A Curtiss JN-4 is undergoing an engine change and major modifications in one of the hangars at the Wilson Airport. Courtesy: Tave Wilson

Looking east toward the Verdugo Mountains and the early Union air terminal in Burbank. The Wilson Airport is in the foreground. Courtesy: Tave Wilson

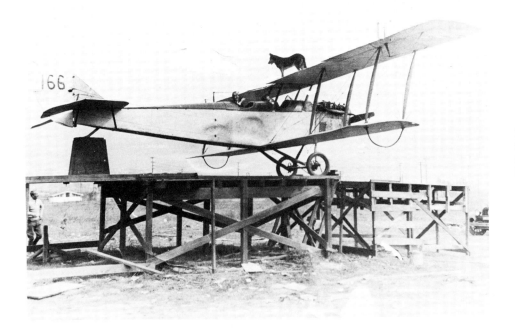

The original Rin Tin Tin atop a Jenny on the parallel at the Wilson Airport. Courtesy: Tave Wilson

Hughes recovered some of his investment by selling these excess "Hell's Angels" scenes to other studios, where they appeared in at least six subsequent movies.

In "Cock Of The Air" Billie Dove plays a French actress who is sent to Italy because her amorous influence on many high-ranking Allied officers is affecting the war effort. Here she meets a playboy American flyer, Chester Morris, who flies her back to Paris when she yearns for a champagne cocktail at a certain bar. After a minimum of flying and various romantic encounters, boy gets girl at the end of the picture.

"Sky Devils" contained more flying than "Cock Of

The Air," but not nearly as much as "Hell's Angels." The story opens at Coney Island where Spencer Tracy and George Cooper are life guards who cannot swim. Drafted into the army, they arrive in France as privates in the Air Service. William Boyd is their tough sergeant, and Ann Dvorak is an entertainer who wants to see some of the war after completing her dancing act for the troops. Hughes utilized the comedy flight-training sequence originally made at March Field for "Hell's Angels" in which Cooper goes up on a solo training flight believing that his instructor is in the rear cockpit. After Tracy and Boyd are thrown in the guardhouse for being a.w.o.l., and the girl is locked up as a spy suspect, the trio escapes and heads for Switzerland in a stolen bombing plane. The "Hell's Angels" scenes appear when they accidentally bomb an enemy ammunition dump, and German fighter planes try to bring them down. Frank Clarke appears in a brief scene where, as von Bruen, the German leader, he barks an order and enters a Fokker D.VII for the squadron takeoff.

Jimmy Barton explains a scene in "Sky Devils" where William Boyd is thrown to the ground while trying to crank an S.E.5 propeller:

"We rigged up an S.E. with dummy cylinder banks and a long shaft running through the fuselage—had a crank on the back end—the front was a prop shaft. Boyd gets on the prop to show how it's spun, and the crew on the back crank gives it a big heave. Actually, it wasn't right, though. He got thrown in the direction of rotation, not by the engine kicking back off compression, which is the only way he might get picked up off the ground and slung. Either way he'd get whacked by the prop blade, but it made a good scene."[219]

As the last scenes of "Sky Devils" were being shot at Metropolitan Airport, a construction crew from R.K.O. finished the sets to be used in "The Lost Squadron," a story of movie stunt flyers written by Dick Grace. The studio contracted with Garland Lincoln for the use of his three Nieuports, and a Stearman camera plane bearing Department of Commerce number NC6440. By now Lincoln had shortened the wings of the Nieuports and wide fabric-covered balsa wood "I" struts replaced the normal outer wing struts. Lincoln said this was done to increase their speed. Only one of the Nieuports flew in the picture, when Lincoln made several low passes over the war-torn village set at the edge of Metropolitan Airport. Frank Clarke, Leo Nomis, Dick Grace and Art Goebel appeared as flyers in the picture, and did some of the stunt flying. A World War I Bristol Fighter of unknown origin and ownership appeared in a brief scene, painted with German crosses, but this seems to be the only time this airplane was ever used in motion picture work.

R.K.O. carpenters also built a high trestle structure for a scene in which an airplane is supposed to crash in the streets of a shell-torn village. With its engine running, and a dummy in the cockpit, a Thomas Morse Scout went down the track along the top of this structure, just out of camera range. Instead of continuing into the street below with its nose down, the airplane turned nose up as it reached the end of the track, and stalled. It fell to one side and crashed into the roof of a building in the set. Instead of repeating the scene, the director decided to add some spectacle and have the airplane catch fire after it hit the building. Being only partially damaged, the Thomas Morse was removed and replaced with a mock-up before the fire was set.

Tave Wilson's Stearman camera plane at the Wilson Airport. Roy Wilson is in the front seat. Courtesy: Tave Wilson

One of Garland Lincoln's modified Nieuport 28's at the Metropolitan Airport, Van Nuys. Courtesy: Garland Lincoln

Garland and Pauline Lincoln, and a Union Oil Co. representative with Garland Lincoln's movie airplanes at Metropolitan Airport, Van Nuys. Courtesy: Garland Lincoln

The fourteen airplanes owned by Caddo Productions still included two S.E.5's when they were lined up for a scene in "Sky Devils." The Nieuport 28 was rented from Garland Lincoln. Courtesy: Jimmy Barton

The basic plot for "Lost Squadron" involves Hollywood stunt flyers with a film director who is an evil genius. Richard Dix, Joel McCrea, and Robert Armstrong play three World War I flyers who return home to various disappointments after the war. Richard Dix discovers that his sweetheart has married another man. Joel McCrea does not like the menial job he is given by his old employer, and Robert Armstrong's business partner has disappeared with all the funds. Armstrong moves to Hollywood where he becomes a successful stunt pilot. Dix and McCrea follow their comrade to the movie capital, and all three are hired by Erich von Stroheim, the egotistical director who stresses realism in his films. Richard Dix soon discovers that the great director is also the man who married his sweetheart. In an effort to eliminate his rival, and obtain added realism for a crash scene, von Stroheim places acid on the control wires of the airplane Dix is scheduled to fly. Robert Armstrong flies the airplane instead, and is killed in the resulting crash. The deed is eventually discovered and the director is killed in the end.

"The Lost Squadron" received good reviews, but Eric von Stroheim's portrayal of the cruel German director almost caused an international incident. The German consul from San Francisco called on von Stroheim to personally deliver an official protest from the German government.[220]

In addition to being the West Coast distributor for Fairchild airplanes, J.B. Alexander continued to act as an aviation coordinator for the motion picture work of Howard Hughes. The Caddo Company airplanes stayed in Alexander's hangar at Metropolitan Airport, where they were leased to other film studios from time to time. But after several months and only a few rentals, Hughes sold the various biplanes to different owners.

Universal made a twelve-chapter serial in 1932 titled "The Air Mail Mystery." Frank Clarke, Roy Wilson and Frank Tomick did most of the flying from the Wilson Airport as a base of operations. Much of the air action, which involved airplanes and automobiles, was filmed in dry lake locations on the Mojave Desert. The story revolves around the Black Hawk's attempts to steal a gold mine operated by Air Mail pilot James Flavin, and the brother of his girl friend, Al Wilson. The Black Hawk, with a secret catapult device to launch his airplane, is able to harass the mining operation and kidnap Al Wilson, who escapes and is recaptured in several subsequent chapters.

Since Al Wilson had retired from stunt flying at this time, he was probably not involved in any of the actual flying in the serial. Wing walking and aerial transfers, so ably accomplished by Al Wilson and others during the 1920s, disappeared from movie screens during the 1930s.

The faster Travelairs, Wacos and Stearmans were now favored by pilots and producers, and the Curtiss Jenny was relegated to the junk pile. Where the Jenny, with its slow speed, double strut bays, and numerous wires, allowed stunt men to scramble all over the wings, the later model biplanes with only a single bay of struts placed the stunt man too close to the propeller in a more powerful slipstream.

Mascot's serial, "Shadow Of The Eagle," also came out in 1932. Based on the currently popular advertising medium of sky writing, it starred John Wayne as a sky writing pilot. The twelve chapters consist of many thrill and spill incidents connected with attempts to capture a criminal who sends mysterious death threats to the officers of a corporation by sky writing. The Wilson Airport served as a set and as a base of operations, though the air action was minimal.

The number of aviation movies, along with all other types of productions, declined when the effects of the 1929 stock market crash reached Hollywood. In an effort to gain motion picture contracts, flyers who had never worked in a picture competed with and underbid the experienced motion picture stunt pilots. Sometimes they signed a contract knowing that they would make little or no profit. They reasoned that even a loss on one or two jobs would be worth the privilege of "getting their foot in the door."

Foremost among the new competitors was Paul Mantz, who resolved to expand his operations into motion picture work. With a contract from Mascot for a flying sequence in the non-aviation serial, "The Galloping Ghost," Paul Mantz began his career as the most famous of the motion picture stunt pilots.

After years of competitive bidding between those flyers doing motion picture work, a standard set of fees emerged, which represented a fair market value for the risks undertaken and the services furnished to the studios. The fees were not exorbitant and had not been arbitrarily set by any conspiracy or governmental agency. They were a function of the open market in a free enterprise economic system. All of the pilots doing motion picture work adhered to these standard fees and shared the work with each other, even though they bid against each other in obtaining the contracts. According to Tave Wilson:

"We all worked together. If Roy and I got a picture, and it was a war picture, we'd get a hold of Garland Lincoln—he had three Nieuports. We shared the work that way. It was the same with Howard Batt. The last picture I worked with Howard—Frank Clarke used his Speedwing Travelair to do the stunts. He had his own Speedwing, and we made arrangements with Howard for his Trimotor, which was supposed to be the airliner. We never did any chiseling."

While any pilot had every right to compete for motion picture work, the experienced stunt pilots resented a threat to their income, and their feelings toward Paul Mantz were less than amiable.[221]

While Mantz himself was a skilled and fearless flyer who was capable of executing dangerous stunts, the situation eventually reached the point where inexperienced and even incompetent pilots were attempting dangerous stunts for only a few dollars a day. In one case an inexperienced pilot was flying in a picture for ten dollars a day, while one of the highly skilled motion picture stunt pilots was working as an extra in the same picture for $7.50 a day, just to pay the rent and feed his family.[222]

Howard Batt recalls another aspect of the situation:

"There was six or eight of us, mostly at Clover Field, who were doing the hard flying. Directors and assistant directors had friends and relatives with airplanes, and they would give them the easy flying jobs. We thought that was unfair."[223]

While the free market and open competition is the basis for a healthy economy, the motion picture stunt pilots looked back at precarious flying assignments that resulted in more than one death. Seeing the competition from inexperienced pilots, which forced the experienced pilots to risk their lives for less and less, the motion picture stunt pilots discussed the possibilities of an organization. Union leaders from other trades and professions in the motion picture industry encouraged the flyers. When a film company hired pilots for five dollars a day, the motion picture stunt pilots decided to take action.

Florence Lowe Barnes, the granddaughter of Civil War balloonist Thaddeus Lowe and an accomplished flyer in her own right, opened her home in San Marino to the motion picture stunt pilots. She hosted a series of dinners in which the pilots planned their organization. She provided secretarial work for all of the correspondence related to the granting of a charter by state and union authorities, and provided room and board for any movie pilot who found himself temporarily without funds.

The airline pilots were organizing at the same time, and their charter was granted by the American Federation of Labor one month before the motion picture stunt pilots established their organization. As a result, the Associated Motion Picture Pilots, as an official organization, was granted a charter through the Airline Pilots Association on January 4, 1932.

The pilots were unanimous in their election of Leo Nomis as president. Frank Clarke won the vice presidential position, and Florence "Pancho" Barnes served as secretary-treasurer, though she was not a working motion picture stunt pilot at this time, and had no voice in the conduct of business. Richard Rinaldi was sergeant at arms, and the following members served on the executive and examining boards: Roy Wilson, Earl Robinson, Jack Rand, Garland Lincoln and Clinton Herberger.

The organization's bylaws barred incompetent pilots from the dangerous work, and allowed the motion picture stunt pilots themselves to have a part in the planning of flying scenes, along with final approval for all stunts.

In addition to their unlimited knowledge and skill in flying matters, they had access to any kind of airplane, and through years of experience in motion picture work, were camera-wise with a knowledge of camera angles, scene values and production problems.

"Robby" Robinson had already contracted with Paramount for the aviation work on "Sky Bride." He arranged for every member of the organization to have at least one day's work at fifty dollars a day.[224]

In the "Sky Bride" story, Richard Arlen is the overly daring star flyer of a barnstorming trio that travels from town to town thrilling the inhabitants with stunts and taking up passengers for joy rides. In a mock dog fight Arlen comes too close to his friend, who is killed in the resulting crash. The remorseful stunt flyer disappears and resolves never to fly again. As the barker for the flying circus, Jack Oakie locates Arlen and convinces him to at least work as an aircraft mechanic. Arlen boards with a lady who turns out to be the mother of the friend whose death he caused. The dead flyer's young nephew enters the story as an air-minded lad who is constantly trying out improvised parachutes. While playing around an airplane, the child is unwittingly taken aloft on the plane's landing gear. There is no one to rescue the boy but Arlen, who takes off in another airplane. After signaling the other pilot and fixing his own controls with wires, Arlen climbs to his top wing and rescues the boy. He resumes his flying career and wins the girl, Virginia Bruce.

The Associated Motion Picture Pilots suffered a tragic loss just one month after its official recognition. Leo Nomis was killed at Metropolitan Airport on February 5, 1932, while working on "Sky Bride."[225] The beloved stunt flyer complained of feeling ill the day before. He was seriously injured and nearly killed a few weeks prior to this accident when he skidded a racing car across the Ascot Raceway track for a scene in "The Crowd Roars." The racer spun around, stood on its nose and landed upside down. The other pilots were convinced that an incomplete recovery from the race track injuries was the cause of Nomis' fatal crash. Moye Stephens relates the circumstances of that tragedy as they were told to him by Earl "Chubby" Gordon, who flew in the picture:

"Almost the first thing when Leo got out of the hospital, he went to work on 'Sky Bride.' At what is now Van Nuys, Metropolitan it was, he was supposed to spin down over the railroad tracks, and land toward the camera on a north-south heading. They set up the camera and they wanted him to spin, come down over the railroad tracks, come out of the spin and land, and stop rolling right in front of the camera. So Leo did as he was directed, but at the last minute he still had so much speed that he couldn't stop and had to veer off to one side. 'Chubby' said the director really ate him out. Leo wasn't accustomed to being chewed out, because he always gave really more than was asked for. He was really good. He would figure things out and he did an excellent job of motion picture flying.

"Then he went back a little bit farther than the railroad, and spun down, came out of the spin and rolled right up to the camera and stopped. The director had his picture right there, but he ate Leo out again, and 'Chubby' said Leo was white and shaking. Leo was the most imperturbable human being I ever knew. Nothing ever ruffled him. If he hadn't had that damned automobile accident he would have been in better control of himself. He went back over the railroad tracks, spun down and came out of the spin, but it was so close that he mushed into the ground. He recovered from the spin with his nose up, but he mushed into the ground."[226]

Harry Crandall was also killed about this time. He never joined the Associated Motion Picture Pilots because he went to work for United Air Lines when "Hell's Angels" was finished. Crandall and Al Gilhausen flew the mail with Boeing Mailplanes between Burbank and San Francisco. Fog covered the United Airport one night when Harry Crandall came in from San Francisco. He was killed at the edge of the field while they were trying to talk him in by radio.

Associated Motion Picture Pilots members missed a few small jobs during the next few months and no action was taken. When Paul Mantz, who was not a member, underbid all of the Associated Motion Picture Pilots and used nonunion pilots for Universal's "Air Mail," the American Federation of Labor entered the conflict. Howard Batt tells his view of the situation:

"The studios were practically all union and they honored our union. There was a lot of dissension in the organization about letting Paul Mantz in. We held him out for quite a while because he was doing a lot of under cutting of our fees, which none of us did. He got this picture and took some non-union pilots to Bishop. We went to the head of the union, and the union went to the studio. What happened is that we sent an equal number of our pilots up there, and they sat on the ground—got paid—and Mantz and the other pilots did the flying. That was the last time that ever happened."[227]

Florence "Pancho" Barnes wrote an article for "The Airline Pilot," a publication of the airline pilots organiza-

tion, that reflected the view of Howard Batt and other members of the Associated Motion Picture Pilots. According to this article, three union officers from the motion picture industry, along with one from the California State Federation of Labor, flew to the location at Bishop, California, where the studio soon came to terms. The previously hired pilots continued to fulfill their contract, but the studio had to hire an equal number of Associated Motion Picture Pilots members who did no flying, but reported for work each day and were paid.[228]

The camaraderie and spirit of brotherhood that bound the motion picture stunt pilots together showed itself again. Those pilots most in need and with families received the "Air Mail" jobs, and the more affluent pilots flew them to the location in their own airplanes.

Paul Mantz fulfilled his contract with skill and courage. He spent many precarious hours in the rarified air of the Sierra Nevada Mountains, flying heavy camera equipment. While stunting over the Bishop Airport, he lost his engine, but was able to make a safe dead-stick landing. The most spectacular scene of the picture was furnished by Paul Mantz when he flew through a hangar open at both ends.

Western Air Express furnished three Boeing Mailplanes and a Ford Tri-Motor, which were photographed

The pilots who flew for the aerial bridal party scene in "Sky Bride" pose by a Travelair at Metropolitan Airport. From the left standing: Jack Rand, Clinton Herberger, "Robby" Robinson, Ira Reed and Earl Gordon. Kneeling from the left: Oliver LeBoutillier and cameraman Charles Marshall. Courtesy: Frank Tomick

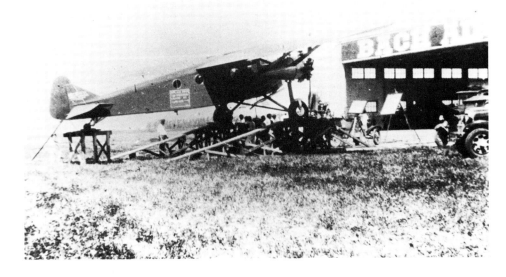

A Bach Trimotor in front of the Bach hangar at Metropolitan Airport, Van Nuys, for the filming of "Sky Bride." The airplane is placed on an elevated platform for the camera to get an upward shot of action supposed to be in the air. Courtesy: Jimmy Barton

Garland Lincoln crash lands a Fokker Universal for the Paramount picture "I'm From Missouri." Courtesy: Garland Lincoln

The Associated Motion Picture Pilots at the Wilson Airport in the early part of 1932. From the left: Tave Wilson, Jack Rand, Earl Gordon, Howard Batt, Frank Clarke, Florence Barnes (secretary), Earl Robinson, Oliver LeBoutillier, Roy Wilson, Dick Rinaldi and Joe Touhey, a public relations man. Courtesy: Tave Wilson

From the left: Leo Nomis, actor Tom O'Brien, Roy Wilson, actor William Boyd, unidentified, Frank Clarke and Dick Rinaldi. Photograph was made at Metropolitan Airport during the filming of "The Flying Fool." Courtesy: Tave Wilson

at Metropolitan Airport. Mantz took a Travelair, a Stearman and a Buhl Air Sedan to the Bishop location.

"Air Mail" depicts the risks and hazards faced by air-mail pilots in heavy rain and snowstorms. Pat O'Brien is a bragging, but daring and skilled flyer, who flirts with the wives of other flyers. Ralph Bellamy plays the level-headed and modest manager of the Desert Airport, the locale for most of the story. When Pat O'Brien turns his back on duty to run away with Lillian Bond, whose husband has just been killed, Ralph Bellamy is forced to fly the mail in Pat O'Brien's place. Bellamy crashes in the mountains during a violent snowstorm. He is eventually sighted alive, but injured, in a precarious location where everyone believes it is impossible to land. The dishonored pilot played by Pat O'Brien scoffs at the other pilots and steals a plane for the rescue. He is able to bring it down near the injured airport manager, though the rough landing causes damage to the wing and landing gear. After repairing the damage, he places Bellamy aboard, barely takes off, and is redeemed by the rescue.

Roy and Tave Wilson signed a contract with Columbia at this time for "War Correspondent," a story influenced by the work of contemporary news correspondents covering the civil war raging in China at this time. Jack Holt plays a soldier of fortune—an ace American air fighter who is flying for the Chinese national army. Ralph Graves is cast as a war correspondent of great reputation who is boastful but far from courageous in dangerous situations. Graves falls in love with Lila Lee, a girl of tarnished reputation who returns his love, though she shares an apartment with Jack Holt. When she is captured by an enemy Chinese general, Graves proves his

courage by going to her rescue, though he is also captured. The lovers escape in an automobile, reluctantly, at first, aided by Jack Holt who shoots down the pursuing airplanes as they attack the fleeing car.

Studio set designers, carpenters and painters trans-

Roy Wilson, Frank Clarke and Earl Robinson at the Wilson Airport during the filming of "Central Airport." Courtesy: Tave Wilson

Roy Wilson and Jack Holt pose for a picture at Wilson Airport while waiting for the next scene in "War Correspondent." Courtesy: Tave Wilson

Sid Saylor stands up in the cockpit of a Travelair for a scene in the comedy short, "Plane Crazy," at the Wilson Airport. Courtesy: Tave Wilson

Jack Holt and Roy Wilson stand by Roy Wilson's Speedwing Travelair at the Wilson Airport. The airplane is painted up for "War Correspondent." Courtesy: Tave Wilson

Preparations at the Wilson Airport for a scene in Columbia's "War Correspondent." Courtesy: Tave Wilson

Roy Wilson checks the remote camera installation on his Speedwing Travelair at the Victorville location for the Columbia picture "War Correspondent." Courtesy: Tave Wilson

formed the Wilson Airport into a military air field somewhere in China. After several days of photographing Speedwing Travelairs in Chinese markings as they taxied and took off from the set, the crew moved to Dry Lake, twenty miles east of Victorville, California in the Mojave Desert.

On June 25, 1932, Roy Wilson went up in his Speedwing Travelair for a scene in which he was to strafe military vehicles on a road, and then spin down from 3,000 feet, leveling off at thirty feet above the desert floor. Leo Nomis, Frank Clarke and Roy Wilson had thrilled crowds at many air shows with this same stunt, which had resulted in the death of Leo Nomis a few months before. Roy Wilson kicked the Travelair into a beautiful power-on spin and headed for the floor of the dry lake. After many revolutions he opened the throttle to gain more power for the recovery, but the engine failed to respond immediately. He crashed in a manner similar to the final flight of Leo Nomis. He lived for a while, but died soon after he was taken to the nearest hospital, despite the best efforts of army surgeons flown up from March Field.[229] The thin hot air and deceiving whiteness of the desert floor were thought to have been contributing factors to the tragedy.

Roy Wilson was popular with his fellow pilots, and his sense of humor always added a little more fun for those who worked with him. His skill and courage as a stunt flyer was equal to that of any other motion picture stunt pilot. A few weeks before his death, he had signed a contract for a week of stunt flying at the soon-to-be-held Cleveland Air Races.[230]

Roy Wilson was buried three days later at Forest Lawn in Glendale. The funeral procession was more than three miles long, and even the increasingly secretive Howard Hughes arrived to pay his respects. Three army planes, provided through the efforts of "Robby" Robinson, flew patrol over the area throughout the ceremony. With a sky-writing plane, Earl "Chubby" Gordon made a cross and wrote "Our Pal" in the skies above Forest Lawn.[231]

Almost as if to bear out the superstitious belief of bad news coming in threes, Al Wilson soon followed Leo Nomis and Roy Wilson in death. While appearing at the National Air Races in Cleveland, his Curtiss Pusher was drawn into the vortex of an autogyro's blades, and both planes fell from one hundred feet altitude to crash in front of the grandstand. The two occupants of the autogyro escaped injury, but Al Wilson suffered lacerations, a crushed rib cage and a fractured skull. He lingered for a few days in a Cleveland hospital, but died of his injuries on September 5, 1932.[232]

Al Wilson was probably involved in more precarious aviation stunts than any other pilot in the world. His courage was matched by his piloting skill, and he was thoroughly professional in his work. In the words of Frank Tomick, who worked with him for several years:

"If Al Wilson says he's gonna do a stunt—risk his neck—you could always depend on it. No backing out."[233]

In addition to his motion picture flying and other aviation accomplishments, Howard Batt made an important non-aviation contribution to the motion picture industry, and tells of an invention that eliminated the crude fog machines in use at the time.

"Sometimes you are too close to the forest to see the trees. I came from the outside, and the reason I made the device is that I walked in on a set. They had pots all over the sound stage, all over the floor, with a garden hose from each one to regular water faucets on a chamber with a big flexible pipe to a compressor somewhere on the lot. All it was doing was vaporizing this nu-jel into the air. It was greasy. They had the camera all covered up, and all the actors had on rain slickers. When they were ready for a shot everybody took off the slickers, and then the nu-jel would condense back into oil. The thing made a terrible hissing noise and they couldn't record while that was going on. I watched this and I thought there must be something to beat that.

"I used to sky write, and we'd put carbon tetrachloride and oil into the exhaust under pressure. The carbon tetrachloride would keep the fire out, and the

-128-

oil would make the smoke. I knew I couldn't use carbon tetrachloride in the studio because it was poisonous.

"It was two years before I got the machine so it would work. First I was blowing it up like a blow torch. I'd hit it and all I had was a flame coming out. So I went to a chemist and I asked him what oil would vaporize at a low temperature. He told me a vegetable oil would come off at a very low temperature. So I wound these coils in there, just like an iron, only I used pipe and isinglass. I used a certain size wire for a certain amount of heat. You can leave it on and it only gets so hot, just like an iron. Well, I wound it so it would be about 500 degrees more than this oil would vaporize. It worked out fine. I had a squirrel cage blower so it wouldn't make any noise. I could hook it up and put a section of pipe in and use dry ice, and you could make that stuff do anything you wanted. It would stay on the floor, or stay up on the wall, just like you plastered it there.

"It got a big play when they used it in 'Midsummer Night's Dream' at Hollywood Bowl. They cut holes in the stage floor and piped it onto the stage about so high and it was quite a sensation.

"When Warner Brothers made 'Midsummer Night's Dream' into a movie, they had to have it. That's when it began to pay off. It was a wonderful thing for me because it was a meal ticket in 1933 when things were tough. They all use it now, but I didn't renew my patent."[234]

Mascot Studios made another aviation serial, "Mystery Squadron," in 1933. Starring cowboy actor Bob Steele, and Guinn 'Big Boy" Williams, the story revolves around the efforts of the Black Ace and his squadron of airplanes, trying to prevent the construction of a dam. Bob Steele and Guinn Williams, as ace flyers, eventually capture the mysterious Black Ace and bring his criminal flyers to justice.

Universal cast another western star, Tom Tyler, as a border patrol pilot in its twelve-chapter serial, "The Phantom Of The Air." The plot is concerned with attempts to steal a new invention, "Contragrav," which overcomes the effects of gravity and will revolutionize aviation. With the aid of the Phantom, a pilotless airplane controlled from an underground headquarters, the inventor of "Contragrav" is barely able to avoid the crooks in each chapter.

Garland Lincoln's three Nieuports deteriorated through age and use, and became unreliable in the air. He decided to build a new one, and tells of his first special movie stunt plane, the LF-1.

"After flying my original Nieuports in several motion pictures, I decided to build a completely new airplane and incorporate some engineering changes to have a truly safe aircraft for acrobatic flying. It was necessary to keep the monosoupape rotary engine because the studios liked its distinctive sound, and I could find no better or more reliable engine at this time.[235] The fuselage was made of steel tubing and covered with fabric. The ailerons, stabilizer, flippers and the rudder were also steel tube and fabric covered. I installed metal 'N' struts for additional strength in the wings.

"The upper and lower wings were wood spars and ribs, fabric covered. I changed the upper wing by moving all the leading edge ribs four inches closer to the front spar. I did this to obtain more strength as I thought the upper wing had too much overhang. This change gave more speed and climb which I wanted.

"I replaced the landing gear struts with metal, but I used the original Nieuport axle and wheels. I also replaced the tail skid with a metal one, and this, of course, required new metal brackets attached to the four metal longerons, for the landing gear as well as the tail skid. One half inch rubber shock cord was used on both the tail skid and landing gear brackets.

"On August 10, 1932, I made my first test flight from the Sprott Airport, located at Atlantic Avenue and Firestone Boulevard in East Los Angeles. After a normal takeoff I climbed to 5000 feet and tried various maneuvers. I then did a few mild climbing turns and some stalls, two spins to the right and two to the left, some steep turns and spirals, and then an Immelmann turn. The airplane performed well. The reaction and recovery was very smooth and fast, and gave me a lot of confidence in my new airplane.

"I decided to try a tight outside loop. When I reached the top of the loop, the airplane started to shake violently. It flipped upside down and fell out of control. I gave it full power, nosed it down and then gradually got it right side up again. I had some control, but it was very slow and sloppy.

"I began to examine the aircraft. All of the controls looked all right, and then I noticed the leading edge of the solid upper wing—no center section—was pushed back and I could see the fabric bulged the entire length of the wing. I did not know just how serious the damage was, and if the struts would hold the upper wing in place until I could land.

"As I have always done when flying, I had an emergency field picked out below, and I throttled down as slow as possible. The monosoupape engine does not have a carburetor and the only throttle control is a blip switch on the control stick. If I held the switch down constantly, the engine would have quit. I had to time it just so the engine kept on running and slowed the airplane down. Working the blip switch, I gradually lost altitude and made a good landing in an open field approximately two miles from the Sprott Airport.

"I carefully examined my airplane and was amazed that the construction was that good. My only mistake in engineering was the leading edge of the wing which was not strong enough to fly or maneuver at high speeds.[236]

"No one was in sight, so I walked back to the airport. The first thing I heard was, 'Where is your airplane?' The upper wing was rebuilt with closer and stronger ribs and I never had another forced landing. It is always heartbreaking to build an airplane and have some part of it collapse, but after beefing up the top wing it proved to be a perfect acrobatic airplane."[237]

Columbia's "Air Hostess" was one of the first motion

pictures to use the airlines as a background for the story. Evelyn Knapp plays an airline hostess, the daughter of a flyer who died in France, and the pet of the commercial pilots who look after her as a kid sister. The airline pilots disapprove of her romance with James Murray, an impetuous and reckless stunt flyer with plans for a flight over the Pacific. Their relationship deteriorates after marriage, and reaches a climax when Murray becomes romantically involved with wealthy Thelma Todd, who promises financial backing for the Pacific flight. Evelyn Knapp packs her bags and boards a train for home after discovering the extramarital romance. Unknown to the engineer, the fast passenger train is headed for a washed-out bridge. Murray, who has turned his back on Thelma Todd, flies to warn the engineer. His wild stunting over the train is misunderstood and he finally crashes the airplane in front of the train to make the engineer stop. Only slightly hurt in the crash, he embraces his wife and all is forgiven.

Many of the exterior scenes were made at Grand Central Air Terminal in Glendale. Frank Clarke flew Bob Boone's Speedwing Travelair for the train buzzing sequence,[238] and "Boots" LeBoutillier performed the crash in front of the train. Jimmy Barton tells how that scene was finally made:

"We took an old Fisk biplane and fixed it up so's it could be crashed. It was an airplane Ed Fisk built before he started manufacturing the International biplanes. It originally had the 'I' struts and a Hisso 150 engine. I took the Hisso out and put in a Wright J-4 on an engine mount I got from a Ryan M-1. These changes were made so the ship would more near fit the script. They thought the old water cooled Hisso would make it seem too old. It wouldn't run worth a damn, anyway.

"It was being shot down near Redlands or Hemet, where a railroad track spur runs along a ridge. We rented the spur and a locomotive and cars from the Southern Pacific. The script called for an airplane to be piled down on the track, blocking it so's the engineer would have to stop the train. They was supposed to be a trestle washed out ahead which he couldn't see.

"The ship had to be put down at just the right spot—stalled in so the wing tip would catch a post, stopping it right on the tracks. The unit director was pretty much of a lush, and when he showed up in town he got picked up by the local gendarmes on a speeding charge. The court was handled by a justice of the peace. It seems that was the way most local law was in those days out in the sticks. Most times we had no trouble at all with them. They bent over backwards because we spent money freely. When we went out on location like that, the local bootleggers declared open season, raising their prices. Some of 'em made a pile of money.

"Well, this J.P. had a nephew that wanted to be a stunt man so bad he could taste it. When the old boy found out he had a real Hollywood tycoon in his clutches, he pulled out all the stops—told the director he would drop the charges if he gave the kid a job in the film.

"The nephew showed up on location, and right away he wants to do the crash job. He claimed he had done a lot of flying as well as motorcycle and car jobs. He had maybe jumped a cycle at county fairs some, but we could tell he was green as hell. The director was fit to be tied. He went back to the old J.P. and told him that Speedy, that's what the nephew called himself wasn't qualified to do anything, and he'd probably wind up killing himself. This got him nowhere at all with the J.P. Either Speedy did the crash or he'd go to jail on not only speeding, but drunken driving charges . . . and being charged in that court meant sure conviction.

"The net result was that he decided to let Speedy have a try at it, hoping that if he killed his self, the director could get out of town before they got him to the morgue. Speedy went out somewhere and got himself a couple of hours of dual instruction, and showed up on location. We all tried to get him to give up on it, but he wouldn't listen to any of us. We went to the unit director, but he had that six months in the hoosegow staring him in the face, so he had to go along and hope the whole thing would turn out all right, which was like wishing for a miracle.

"Speedy managed to get the old Fisk off the ground and pointed in the right direction. When he came in for the take, he chopped the throttle too soon and flopped it down in a wash four hundred yards from the spot. It wasn't busted up too much. The wing tips was tore up some and one side of the gear was bent. The prop tips was all busted so we patched it up, welded in some new streamline tubing and mounted a new prop over night.

"The next morning Speedy showed up on location with two girls in tow, to see him do his stuff. The director hadn't had a good night—looking like he'd been hitting the jug some. Speedy climbed in the airplane and wobbled into the air. He come around in a big circle at about two hundred feet heading the wrong way—went over the camera crew and hit the ground behind the set up. The director grabbed a piece of two-by-four and started for Speedy, who was just climbing out of the airplane, where it had stopped with the landing gear spraddled out and one tip bent up. Speedy saw him coming and got the idea—so he took off for the car where his two girl friends were waiting. They got out of there about two leaps ahead of the director, who got the last word by throwing the two-by-four at them as they went by.

"We went out to the ship after the dust settled. It was pretty well beat, but still fixable, at least for one more time. The director had holed up in his tent and wouldn't come out. We didn't know what to do—whether to go ahead with the work or not. Just after dark he come out and got into his car—he had an old 1927 Kissel roadster—and tore out of there.

"The chief cameraman called the studio and gave them the story, and asked if they wanted us to go on. After a few minutes of thunder and lightning that almost melted the wires, the producer asked him if we could salvage things and complete the crash scene—the only part of the footage that still had to be shot. He called me over and I told him I could fix the ship up good enough by day after next, and told him what we

Garland Lincoln's first LF-1 is ready for its test flight at Sprott Airport in East Los Angeles. Courtesy: Garland Lincoln

The wing fabric on Garland Lincoln's first LF-1 failed in almost the same manner as several wartime Nieuport 28's failed when pulling out of a dive in combat. The LF-1 wings were either from one of Mr. Lincoln's Nieuports, or were built and covered in the same manner as the original Nieuport 28's that suffered top wing failure in 1918. Courtesy: Garland Lincoln

needed. They got it out to us and we started to work.

"Then about noon the old J.P. showed up and told us we had to get out of there—we were trespassing. The chief cameraman had called the Southern Pacific meanwhile, and they assured him that all the land around there was railroad property. While we was arguing with the old man and his constable, who was toting a shot gun, two Southern Pacific railroad dicks drove up and took over. We never had no trouble with the J.P. again.

"They sent out 'Boots' LeBoutillier. We took a landing gear from a Travelair and rebuilt it onto the Fisk. I fixed the one wing tip and straightened the bad prop tip and engine mount. 'Boots' took it around the area once—then did the scene. He put it down exactly where it had to touch to catch the post. It swung around and stopped across the tracks. Took us over a week to shoot footage that should have been wrapped up in less than two days.

"Never ran into Speedy or the director again. None of us ever went back to that part of the country again if we could help it—always took a detour around if we had to go out that way."[239]

Warner Brothers used a variety of aviation services for the Wellman produced picture, "Central Airport." Paul Mantz received the overall aviation contract; Howard Batt flew a Ford Tri-Motor; and the Wilson Airport furnished the setting for a crash scene.

The absence of union problems on the picture may indicate that Paul Mantz had been admitted to membership in the Associated Motion Picture Pilots by this time. Even though the other pilots did not like Paul Mantz or his competition, he always rendered a highly professional service to the studios. Members of the Associated Motion Picture Pilots recognized his flying skill and professional abilities. They saw that he was not going to disappear from the motion picture scene, as many less-capable flyers had done. According to Frank Tomick, they eventually decided that it was better to have him inside the organization, instead of competing from the outside.[240]

"Central Airport" opens with Richard Barthelmess as

Oliver LeBoutillier crash lands for a scene in Columbia's "Air Hostess." In the story the pilot deliberately crashes in front of the train to warn the unsuspecting engineer of a washed out trestle ahead. Courtesy: Tave Wilson

the expert pilot of a crashed airliner in which several passengers are killed. Even though the crash was unavoidable, he is discharged by the airline. Later he rescues exhibition parachute jumper Sally Eilers when her chute is caught in a tree. When her pilot is killed, Barthelmess fills the position and they become partners in a barnstorming air circus. They fall in love and the girl wants to get married, but after seeing the problems suffered by the widow of another pilot, Barthelmess takes the position that pilots should never get married. After he is injured in a crash, his younger brother, Tom Brown, who is also a pilot, takes his place and falls for Sally Eilers. While convalescing, Barthelmess changes his mind and buys a ring. In the meantime the younger brother has married the girl and Barthelmess is too late. He drifts from one flying job to another, and eventually meets Sally Eilers by chance. She sees the wedding ring he now wears as an amulet, and confesses that she still

loves him the most. Before they can make any decisions, a message comes that his younger brother is down at sea. Barthelmess flies to his rescue, bids his sweetheart goodbye, and returns to his wandering. John Wayne appeared in a bit part as a co-pilot.

Howard Batt recalls an incident that took place at United Airport during the filming of "Central Airport:"

"I hit the east side of the Burbank airport with a tri-motor Ford. I had a load of passengers which I never take up as a rule. I had been taxiing all night into these lights, and at two o'clock in the morning Billy Wellman said, 'I want you to make this flight—come in and land.' I don't know why I stood for it, but they loaded me up with twelve extras. I was supposed to come in and land, and they were to get out.

"This old Ford I was using—you know how Ford glass used to turn amber. Well, they had changed the glass on the pilot's side, but not on the co-pilot's side. For me to fly it and be seen from the door side of the airplane—I was in an airline pilot's uniform—I had to fly it from the co-pilot's side. I was flying it with the amber glass. Paul Mantz was in there to give me a hand.

"I came around—and there were two lights on these power poles—we found out later they were out. I never sued the power company. I could have collected. I hit this power pole right on the cross arm with the center engine. I took twenty feet of the pole with me. I knocked all the 60,000 volt lines down, and there were ground fires up and down the street, wherever the wires touched the ground. I had six or seven feet of pole in my center engine. It didn't go all the way through—just stuck there. I brought it in—it was just one of those things. Paul didn't see it and I didn't see it."[241]

An old American Eagle and a worn-out Eagle Rock provided the crash scene at Wilson Airport. In the story, an inexperienced pilot taxies into another airplane that is parked with its engine idling. When Wellman gave the signal, Paul Mantz, who was in the cockpit of the American Eagle, opened the throttle and headed for the Eagle Rock. When it was well on its collision course, he leaped from the cockpit and tumbled on the ground, receiving a broken collarbone when the tail passed over him. The airplanes met and the scene was a success as the wooden propellers shattered in a shower of wood and fabric.

Pathe's, "The Flying Fool," also dealt with contemporary aviation, though the film opens with a short dog fight sequence in France. The next scene shows an American ace flyer, William Boyd, being decorated by the French and receiving the admiration of local French girls. The setting then shifts to the Los Angeles Metropolitan Airport where Boyd is now a stunt flyer known as The Flying Fool. The rest of the story revolves around the love of Boyd and his flying younger brother for Marie Prevost. After several incidents of competitive stunt flying, William Boyd wins the girl and the younger brother wishes them well. Two Travelairs, flown by Frank Clarke and another unidentified pilot, provided the stunt flying.

M.G.M. returned to World War I for "The White Sister" and "Today We Live." Aviators were leading characters in both pictures, but as far as can be determined, no flying was done by the motion picture stunt pilots in either picture. Most of the flying sequences that did appear on the screen came from "Hell's Angels."

In "The White Sister," Italian aviator Clark Gable falls for Helen Hayes, already promised to another man in a family arranged marriage. When the war comes, Gable is shot down in combat. Thinking he is dead, Helen Hayes enters a convent. After two years in a prison camp, Gable escapes by stealing an Austrian airplane. After a long search he finds his sweetheart in the convent. She refuses his pleas because of her vows. Fatally wounded in an Austrian bombing raid, Clark Gable dies

in her arms, reconciled to her decision.

In "Today We Live," Joan Crawford is an aristocratic English girl who rents the family home to an American student, Gary Cooper, while her father is away at war. On the same day she receives news that her father has been killed, her brother, Franchot Tone, and childhood sweetheart, Robert Young, are ordered into combat. Gary Cooper consoles her, and by the time she joins an ambulance unit to be near her brother and childhood sweetheart, she realizes that she is in love with the American. When the United States enters the war later, Gary Cooper joins the Air Service.

All four meet at the front where Gary Cooper flies a bomber, and Robert Young operates a torpedo boat along with Franchot Tone. Joan Crawford believes Gary Cooper to be dead after his plane is wrecked on a mission, and she gives herself to Robert Young. But the American flyer is alive, and returns to find Joan Crawford and Robert Young living together. In his frustration, he accepts a suicide mission to blow up an important ship. Robert Young is blinded on a torpedo boat mission, and not wishing to be a burden, he and Franchot Tone undertake the suicide mission. They destroy the ship with their torpedo boat, but both are killed, leaving the lovers to be re-united.

In the spring of 1933, Tave Wilson furnished the airplanes and his airport for Columbia's "Soldiers Of The Storm." Frank Clarke did the stunt flying in a Speedwing Travelair.

The title, "Soldiers Of The Storm," is only barely related to the story, in which Regis Toomey is a flying border patrol agent. In order to apprehend a gang of smugglers, he is ordered to a border resort where he poses as a stunt flyer at the dedication of the local airport. Here he meets and falls in love with Anita Page, the daughter of a local politician. Unknown to the girl, her father is indirectly, but financially involved with the gang leader in the smuggling of narcotics and illegal aliens across the Mexican border. When the undercover border patrol agent befriends a local bar girl in order to obtain information about the gang, his romance with Anita Page is jeopardized. Unable to reveal his identity to Miss Page, Toomey joins the gang as a flyer. He gathers evidence by making several flights between the resort and a remote location across the border. Facing arrest and conviction, the gang leader kills the girl's father in a confrontation, and escapes in an automobile with his confederate. Toomey pursues the pair in his airplane armed with a machine gun. The airplane dives on the car, eventually causing it to crash. The lovers are reunited and the picture ends as they leave on a flying honeymoon.

While Columbia crews shot airport scenes for

"Soldiers Of The Storm," Tave Wilson's maintenance crew restored five Thomas Morse Scouts for use in Paramount's "Eagle And The Hawk." A D.H.4 and D.H.9 also appeared in the picture. Garland Lincoln's records indicate that the Lincoln Air Service furnished two D.H.s, one Jenny and four Nieuports to Paramount in April 1933.

Paramount built a British air field set for takeoffs, landings, taxi scenes, and several dramatic scenes that take place on the field. The location for the air field set is unknown. It appears to have been filmed at the Triunfo location on the Russell Brothers Ranch, but Paramount had its own ranch at Agoura, just a few miles from Triunfo. The hills and trees in the background look the same in both locations.

The story for "The Eagle And The Hawk" came from John Monk Saunders. Frederic March plays the role of the best pilot in a Royal Flying Corps observation squadron. After losing several observers, and seeing some of this fellow pilots die, he is demoralized and becomes disgusted with his role in the war. In the meantime, Cary Grant, bitter at having been washed-out in pilot training by March when he was an instructor, is assigned to the squadron as an observer. The commanding officer sends March to London for a restful leave. Here he has a brief romantic encounter with Carole Lombard, but he returns to the squadron with very little improvement. Returning to combat, he brings down a famous German ace, but his observer is killed in the fight. During a wild squadron party to celebrate his victory, Frederic March retires to his room and commits suicide. Cary Grant discovers the tragedy before anyone else, and though still resentful of the man who prevented him from completing his pilot training, he recognizes the sincerity and dedication of his former flight instructor. Before dawn, Grant loads the body into the front seat of a D.H., and takes off, flying the airplane with dual controls from the observer's cockpit. When he reaches the front lines, he turns his machine gun on the dead pilot in the front seat. He then shoots up the wings, going to his own death in the crash, in order to hide the suicide and preserve the heroic image of March.

Air scenes came from "Wings" and "Dawn Patrol." Process photography, where an airplane is set up on a sound stage and photographed against a screen on which previously shot background scenes are projected, provided closeup scenes of the actors in the air.

The crash scene from "Young Eagles" was tied into "The Eagle And The Hawk" with painstaking detail. Studio technicians carefully placed a dummy airplane in the same location on the field, and in the same position as the one crashed by Dick Grace three years previously. Careful examination of the crash scene, and the airplane

that appears in "The Eagle And The Hawk," reveals minor differences in the landing gear, radiator and other details. The crash scene appeared in the part of "The Eagle And The Hawk" where Frederic March lands and taxies up to the German airplane he just shot down.

While Paramount completed "The Eagle And The Hawk," R.K.O. shot the final scenes for "Flying Devils." Metropolitan Airport served as the location for the air field scenes, and Frank Clarke did most of the stunt flying. Garland Lincoln and Tave Wilson furnished airplanes for the picture, which contained several good flying scenes.

The background for the story is Speed Hardy's flying circus, a group of daredevil flyers who perform at county fairs. Arline Judge has the leading role as a daring parachute jumper who is not-too-happily married to Ralph Bellamy, the villainous leader of the barnstorming group. Bruce Cabot and Cliff Edwards are flyers in the air circus that functions well until Eric Linden, Cabot's younger brother, joins the act. When he performs a series of double parachute jumps with Arline Judge, they fall in love. Bellamy's jealousy reaches a climax when his wife and Linden are forced to spend a night together in a deserted cabin after an airplane crash. He devises a new stunt for his rival where two airplanes crash head on in the air, just after the pilots have bailed out. Cliff Edwards sees Bellamy cut Linden's parachute just before time to

"Boots" LeBoutillier on location by a Thomas Morse Scout for "Eagle And The Hawk." Courtesy: Howard Batt

Tave Wilson checks the progress of Thomas Morse Scouts being prepared for "Eagle And The Hawk" at the Wilson Airport.
Courtesy: Tave Wilson

Paul Mantz has just jumped from the moving airplane, nearest the camera, as it taxied into the other airplane for a scene in "Central Airport."
Courtesy: Howard Batt

Garland Lincoln's first LF-1 as it appeared in "Ace Of Aces." Courtesy: Garland Lincoln

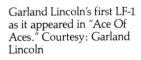

The aerial crew of "Ace Of Aces" at Metropolitan Airport before going aloft for a dogfight scene. From the left: Harry Perry, Oliver LeBoutillier, Howard Batt, Frank Tomick, Earl Gordon, Garland Lincoln, Frank Clarke and Earl Robinson. Courtesy: Frank Tomick

Hisso powered Travelair "Wichita Fokkers" that were rented from Caddo Productions for use in "Ace Of Aces." The Wacos used for the Allied formation can be seen in the background. Courtesy: Garland Lincoln

Filming a scene for "Ace Of Aces" at the Triunfo location. The airplane is a mockup originally made to resemble an S.E.5. It has been fitted with a ring cowling to make it resemble the Wacos used for the Allied airplanes. Courtesy: Garland Lincoln

take off for the stunt. Cabot goes up and warns his brother, but then Bellamy chases Linden through the air trying to make him crash. Cabot saves his brother by crashing into the jealous leader, but both are killed in the flaming crash. The lovers are then married and Edwards goes to work as an airline pilot.

Even before "Flying Devils" was released to the theaters, R.K.O. carpenters constructed an air field set on the Russell Brothers Ranch at Triunfo for another aviation motion picture. Shooting for "Ace Of Aces" began in the mid-summer of 1933.

Garland Lincoln obtained the aviation contract, for which he assembled a fleet of thirteen airplanes. In addition to his LF-1, Stearman camera plane, Kinner-powered Fleet and Hisso Travelair, he leased four more Travelairs, and five Waco Fs from private owners. R.K.O. provided two dummy S.E.5s that later appeared in "Flying Down to Rio." Why the studio did not use the two authentic S.E.5s that were purchased for "The Balloon Buster" is unknown. At least one of these airplanes appeared in more than one subsequent R.K.O. movie.

The LF-1 and the Waco Fs served as the American airplanes, while the Travelairs, some of which still retained their "Hell's Angels" markings, served as the German formation. Flying the airplanes were Garland Lincoln, Howard Batt, Frank Clarke, Earl Gordon, "Boots" LeBoutillier, "Robby" Robinson and Frank Tomick. Harry Perry did the aerial photography.

The LF-1 performed well as Lincoln flew it to double for Richard Dix. Dogfights, takeoffs, landings and taxi scenes kept the crews busy for two weeks at the Triunfo location.

In "Ace Of Aces" Richard Dix portrays an idealistic sculptor whose moral scruples in regard to the war are misinterpreted as cowardice by his fiancee. Shamed into enlisting, he shows up in France as a pursuit pilot in the U.S. Air Service. In the course of compiling 42 victories, he becomes not only the leading ace, but a ruthless killer, despised by his own squadron mates. On leave in Paris he meets his former fiancee who is now a Red Cross nurse. After a love affair he returns to the front and is wounded in combat. Making his way back to his field, he recovers enough to shoot down a young German pilot who appeared over the field at the same time to drop a note informing the Americans that one of their pilots made a safe landing behind the German lines. The German boy occupies the hospital bed next to Dix, who is overwhelmed by conscience when the German dies. When Dix returns to duty, he allows himself to be shot down rather than kill another victim. The final scene shows the convalescing ace reunited with his fiancee, Elizabeth Allen, in a resumption of their pre-war romance.

Hollywood's next aviation movie was "Night Flight" by MGM. Paul Mantz won the aviation contract, but other members of the Associated Motion Picture Pilots also worked on the picture. The studio leased two Douglas Mailplanes from Garland Lincoln. Frank Clarke did the stunt flying, while Elmer Dyer and Charles Marshall did the aerial photography.

Airfield scenes were made at Culver City Airport, and location crews went to the Rocky Mountains in Colorado for air scenes that were supposed to take place over the Andes Mountains in South America.

Frank Clarke demonstrated his exceptional flying skill and courage in a flying stunt over the Rocky Mountains that Charles Marshall said was the best flying he ever saw. With 14,600-foot Long's Peak as a background, Clarke put an old Curtiss Falcon into a stall at the top of a solid rock wall that rose 2,500 feet above its base. With nothing but snow, ice and rock outcroppings below, Clarke rode the airplane straight down for 2,000 feet before pulling out of his dive, with only 500 feet to spare.[242]

Herb White and Ivan Unger made parachute jumps over the Rockies to double for the actors, but, as with all of the flying, it was done in the daytime. Elmer Dyer utilized infrared film and filters for the first time in aerial photography to achieve the effect of night flying.[243]

The setting for "Night Flight," based on the novel by Antoine de Saint-Exupery, is South America, where pilots of the Air Express Company are pioneering night flying over the Andes Mountains. John Barrymore is the strict general manager who enforces military-type discipline on the airmail pilots. The flyers are fined for any infraction of the rules, even if they miss a flight because of bad weather conditions. He severely rebukes his chief inspector, Lionel Barrymore, for familiarity with a subordinate by having dinner with one of the pilots. He forces the chief inspector to restore the superior-subordinate relationship by finding some lapse of discipline for which the pilot can be punished.

Tragedy enters the story when one of the pilots, Clark Gable, is lost in a storm. After running out of fuel, he and a colleague parachute to their deaths at sea. Though he can't show his feelings, the general manager feels the loss deeply, and lest fear infect the system, he adopts a cold attitude when he has to inform the widow, Helen Hayes.

Robert Montgomery is cast as a happy-go-lucky pilot, while William Gargan is another pilot who flies through a severe storm when the general manager suggests that he might be a coward. Myrna Loy has a lesser role as Gargan's wife.

John Barrymore insists that the pilots maintain their schedules, even during violent weather conditions. Dedication to duty is justified when one of the pilots flies through a storm to deliver life-saving serum to a stricken city. The night flights continue and the general manager must continue with his heavy responsibility.

Garland Lincoln landed a Monocoupe in the surf at Palos Verdes for a scene in R.K.O.'s non-aviation picture, "The Right To Romance." He flew this same airplane for a minor scene in "Flying Down To Rio."

A few months later Lincoln disassembled a Stearman at his Metropolitan hangar and trucked it to R.K.O. Studios in Hollywood where it was used in closeup shots for the sequence where airplanes attack the giant ape atop the Empire State Building in "King Kong."

Universal released the twelve-chapter serial "Tailspin Tommy" with actor Maurice Murphy (not to be confused with the pilot Maurice "Loop Loop" Murphy) in the leading role. Based on the comic strip character, the story revolves around Tommy, a pilot for Three Point Airlines, and many encounters with a rival flyer and his aerial pirates who try to destroy the new airline. The aviation scenes include Tommy's prevention of a runaway plane from taxiing into a group of children; his dangling from a refueling hose in the air; a crash in the sea; prevention of a railroad disaster, and other peril situations that occur before the aerial outlaws are brought to justice.

Frank Clarke, Earl Robinson, Frank Tomick and Tave Wilson flew the camera and stunting airplanes using the Wilson Airport as a base of operations.

Warner Brothers awarded the aviation contract for "Ceiling Zero" to Paul Mantz. Mantz then hired Frank Tomick to fly the camera ship. Both pilots performed their work in a highly professional manner.

In the story, Pat O'Brien is the soft-hearted boss pilot of Federal Airlines who gives a job to his war-time flying buddy, James Cagney, an able flyer but irresponsible and preoccupied with the pursuit of females. When Cagney feigns sickness to keep a date, his replacement pilot is trapped in the fog with ceiling zero and crashes to his death. Heartbroken and feeling responsible, Cagney decides to atone for the tragedy. Taking the place of a pilot assigned to test new safety equipment for severe weather conditions, Cagney takes off in a blizzard and keeps O'Brien informed of his progress with the apparatus. The airplane becomes overloaded with ice and Cagney crashes to his death, but not before he has conveyed enough information to make blind flying safer for the future.

In the story of Columbia's "Speedwings," Tim McCoy and Billy Blakewell are the last of a group of flyers who have been killed while trying to develop a racing airplane that will bring the speed trophy back to the United States. Evelyn Knapp, as Blakewell's secretary, is kidnapped by a rival air firm who also steal the plans for the new racing plane. After a chase between a plane and a

train, Blakewell wins the race and then rescues the girl.

Frank Clarke, Frank Tomick and Garland Lincoln performed the stunt flying with Travelair and Waco biplanes. Frank Tomick recalls a scene where three airplanes race around a pylon:

"We go around the pylon low. I'm down on the ground, and Clarke next and Garland on top. This director—I say, 'You want us to go around left to right or right to left.' He say, 'Left to right.' We go around almost touching wings, and we have to do it over again because it was supposed to be right to left. I say to him, 'I ask you which way!' He said, 'Don't worry about it. You got a parachute!' I got a parachute, and I'm right down on the ground."

Monogram used many of the leftover "Hell's Angels" scenes in the low-budget feature, "A Crimson Romance," which starred Ben Lyon. Several new scenes that showed the actors in and around airplanes were shot at the Wilson Airport.

The story has an unusual twist in that two Americans join the German Air Service in 1916. When the U.S. enters the war, one young man returns to America while his German-descended friend chooses to remain. The young German is killed in combat leaving the American to return to Germany after the war and marry the pretty German nurse whom both had courted.

Tave Wilson remembers how the studio got its full value from Ben Lyon:

"We were out there making a picture for one of those independents. They didn't have too much money to throw around anyhow, and they had to make each nickel count. We used to call it Candlelight Service. They would come out there the minute the sun was up and they'd shoot till the sun went down. So we got out there early in the morning for this Candlelight picture, and poor old Ben Lyon, he was out there in the hangar, and they were working him the night before till about two o'clock in the morning. He wanted to get some sleep, so I told him to go in there in the office and use the bed where the mechanic sleeps. He went in there and about the time he falls off to sleep, in comes the assistant director to run him out. They had to get some shots with him in the scene. He came out there fit to be tied and said, 'What do you guys want? A limousine for the price of a Model T!' He was so dern mad. I never laughed so much in my life. That was the way it was sometimes."

Paul Mantz was awarded another contract for Warner Brothers "Parachute Jumper," a story of two ex-Marine pilots who become involved with gangsters in smuggling narcotics into the U.S. by air from Canada. Douglas Fairbanks, Jr., Bette Davis and Leo Carrillo played the leading roles.

At this same time Garland Lincoln rented his D.H.9 and three Orencos to Warner Brothers for a brief scene in

Frank Clarke, Garland Lincoln, Tim McCoy and Frank Tomick pose for a picture at Metropolitan Airport during the filming of "Speedwings." Courtesy: Garland Lincoln

The "Hollywood Trio," led by Frank Clarke flying upside down, performs at an unidentified air show. Courtesy: Howard Batt

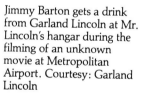

Jimmy Barton gets a drink from Garland Lincoln at Mr. Lincoln's hangar during the filming of an unknown movie at Metropolitan Airport. Courtesy: Garland Lincoln

The "Hollywood Trio" flies over the Los Angeles Basin in Speedwing Travelairs. Courtesy: Howard Batt

the non-aviation picture "Captured."

Frank Clarke, Howard Batt and Paul Mantz formed a stunt team to perform at major air shows. Sponsored by Phillips Petroleum and calling themselves the Hollywood Trio, they flew Speedwing Travelairs while performing acrobatic maneuvers in tight formation. Each airplane was equipped with a skywriting device to trail "smoke" during the execution of various maneuvers.

They appeared at the National Air Races in September 1933, held at Chicago in conjunction with the Century of Progress World's Fair. The program listed Frank Clarke as "veteran movie stunt pilot and leader of the Phillips 66 Hollywood Trio."[244] Other events of the show included the looping of an autogyro, delayed parachute jumps, formation flights by the First Pursuit Group and the Marine Corps, and individual acrobatic flying by Ernst Udet and Lt. Tito Falconi of the Royal Italian Air Force.

Howard Batt tells how he gave up smoking the day before the Hollywood Trio's first performance at the 1933 World's Fair:

"Clarke, Mantz and I did a show at the Curtiss-Wright-Reynolds Airport in Chicago during the World's Fair and International Air Races. We were known as the Hollywood Trio sponsored by Phillips 66. We used Speedwing Travelairs. We had two ships of our own, but the third one was a local plane rented for the show.

"Our smoke device was a mixture of oil and carbon tetrachloride sprayed into the exhaust under pressure. We had this installed on the local ship and I took it up for a trial flight on the day before we were to perform. When I turned it on there was a leak somewhere and the cockpit was filled with carbon tetrachloride. I was almost overcome by the fumes. I practically stood up in the cockpit, but I was able to get the ship down. I lit a cigarette after I got out of the airplane and was terribly nauseated. I couldn't smoke for a year after that, so I gave up cigarettes."[245]

"Hell In The Heavens" was the next big air picture and Garland Lincoln, who maintained the only group of World War I airplanes, was awarded the contract by Fox. The Triunfo location was the airfield setting again, but this time it was the base for a group of American flyers serving in the French Air Service. While the similarity with the Lafayette Escadrille was obvious, and the airplanes even carried the famous Indian Chief insignia, the characters and plot were all fictitious. Edwin C. Parsons contributed to the screenplay, acted as technical advisor and performed as an actor in a bit part.

Flying a Speedwing Travelair, Frank Clarke makes a three point touchdown for the Warner Brothers picture "Devil Dogs Of The Air." Courtesy: Dick Grace

Garland Lincoln and one of his modified Nieuports at the Triunfo location for "Hell In The Heavens." Courtesy: Garland Lincoln

From the left: Jack Rand, Howard Batt, Frank Tomick, Edwin C. Parsons, Warner Baxter, Earl Gordon, Garland Lincoln and Herbert Mundin pose by one of Lincoln's Nieuports during the filming of "Hell In The Heavens." Courtesy: Frank Tomick

The story opens when a group of replacements arrive at a battered French squadron stationed opposite a tough German ace, referred to only as the Baron. As one of the new pilots, Warner Baxter's ambition is to get the Baron. The girl in the story, Conchita Montenegro, lives with her mother at the chateau where the pilots are housed. Frequently getting in the way of the pilots, she sets her sights on Warner Baxter. Torn by fears and dreaming of falling in flames, Baxter eventually conquers his fears and succeeds in bringing down the Baron alive, whom he discovers is haunted by similar dreams and fears.

The contract between Fox Film Corporation and Garland Lincoln gives a good picture of the responsibilities involved in furnishing airplanes for an aviation picture. The compensation rates are tiny by today's standards,

but were considered as good pay in 1934.

The contract lists the following airplanes to be furnished by the Garland Lincoln Air Service for use in connection with the photographing of scenes and sequences in the motion picture "Hell In The Heavens" commencing August 20, 1934.

1. Nieuport #2539—Motor Type: Monosoupape
2. Nieuport #10415—Motor Type: Monosoupape
3. Nieuport #4—Motor Type: Monosoupape
4. Nieuport #75W—Motor Type: Monosoupape
5. Travelair #3947—Motor Type: Hisso E 180 H.P.
6. Travelair #NC2538—Motor Type: OX-5
7. Travelair #NC3621—Motor Type: Hisso E 180 H.P.
8. Travelair #NC4958—Motor Type: Hisso E 180 H.P.

A "Wichita Fokker" strafes the French airfield set at Triunfo for a scene in "Hell In The Heavens." Courtesy: Jerry Phillips

Two of Mr. Lincoln's Nieuports can be seen in this photograph of strafing action for the Fox picture "Hell In The Heavens." Courtesy: Jerry Phillips

9. Travelair #NC6417—Motor Type: Hisso E
   180 H.P.
10. (Baby) Travelair #NC434W—Motor Type:
    Warner Scarab 110 H.P.
11. Waco F #NC617Y—Motor Type: Kinner B-5
12. Waco F #NC619Y—Motor Type: Kinner B-5
13. Waco F #NC644Y—Motor Type: Kinner B-5
14. Nieuport #NR12237—Motor Type: Monosoupape
15. DeHaviland #NR3228—Motor Type: Liberty
    #2838

The contract further bound Lincoln Air Service to furnish four pilots, specifically Frank Tomick, Earl Gordon, Howard Batt and Jack Rand, to be used as pilots and actors.

As compensation Fox agreed to pay Lincoln the following:

A. $250.00 for transportation of the airplanes to the location site at the Russell Brothers Ranch near Triunfo, California

B. $20.00 a day for each airplane listed as 1 to 13.
C. $35.00 a day for airplane listed as 14.
D. $30.00 a day for airplane listed as 15.

Compensation to include one hour flying time for each airplane listed. Additional flying hours per day in excess of one hour, shall be paid in the same amount as the daily compensation for each airplane.

E. Pilots to receive $66.00 per week plus $50.00 per hour flying time.

Terms of the contract required Lincoln to furnish mechanics for maintenance of the aircraft, workmen's compensation for pilots and mechanics, public liability and property damage insurance, and insurance covering fire, theft, windstorm, land damage and perils of the air for the airplanes. The cost of such insurance and the pay for mechanics was to be reimbursed to Lincoln by the studio.

Further paragraphs of the contract required the airplanes to always be in proper working order, and all airplanes except those listed as 1 thru 4 to be in proper flying condition. The studio agreed to furnish oil and gasoline while Lincoln agreed to operate the airplanes in compliance with all federal, state and local laws, and agreed to remove the airplanes immediately from the location site upon completion of filming.

Lincoln also had to obtain permission to depart from various Air Commerce regulations, which was granted in the form of a letter from the Department of Commerce, Aeronautics Branch, to Garland Lincoln Air Service, containing the following items:

1. Waiver to the regulations requiring display of license numbers to permit camouflage as military aircraft.

2. Waiver to the 300 foot proximity rule to permit formation flying.

3. Waiver to the prohibition of dropping of objects to permit the dropping of messages over the field being used as a movie set.

4. Waiver of minimum altitudes to permit low flights over open territory adjacent to the airport.

5. Waiver to minimum altitude of 1500 feet for acrobatics to permit the execution of a single acrobatic maneuver in the film which constitutes a signal in one scene.

6. Waiver to prohibition of the transporting of explosives to permit the carriage of machine guns and ammunition therefor.

The letter of waiver lists the names of the pilots working on the picture and notes the airplanes to be flown as the LF-1 (NR12237), three Wacos, the DeHaviland, six Travelairs as listed in the contract, plus Orenco ID-2145.

The Hollywood Trio. From the left: Howard Batt, Frank Clarke and Paul Mantz. Courtesy: Howard Batt

One of Garland Lincoln's Nieuports as it appeared in "Hell In The Heavens." Lincoln's D.H.9, two Waco F's and an Orenco can be seen in the background. Courtesy: Jimmy Barton

CHAPTER FIVE
THE CLOSING OF AN ERA

Three Ryan ST's fly formation for a publicity shot for
Howard Batt's photographer who is in a fourth Ryan ST.
Courtesy: Howard Batt

IMPROVEMENTS IN aircraft design brought more sophistication to the field of aviation in the 1930s. Flying pictures continued to be popular, and while Hollywood produced more big aviation movies, the motion picture stunt pilots faced the paradox of less and less work.

Passenger transportation by air was now an established industry, and screen writers turned to the airlines for story backgrounds. Eager to gain advertising benefits, the new airlines allowed the studios to photograph their airplanes in flight, during landings and takeoffs, and in any other situation that did not interfere with safety or the normal method of operations. The fuselage mock-ups used to train airline personnel were readily made available for interior shots.

Continued use of military aviation facilities, with large numbers of airplanes for lineup and formation shots, further reduced the need for movie pilots. The Associated Motion Picture Pilots lodged an official protest with the military authorities in Washington, but the army and navy continued to cooperate with the studios, because the release of a military aviation movie always resulted in an increase of young men at the recruiting offices.

An increasing use of models and miniatures in aviation movies took away a few more flying jobs, but the market did not close completely. Scripts still called for a stunt or a crash now and then, and a camera pilot was always needed, even when Uncle Sam's military airplanes provided the action.

Dick Grace, who had already retired from motion picture flying, was joined by some of the other pilots. No longer able to maintain an airport and a fleet of airplanes on the few pictures that came his way, Tave Wilson gave up his lease and sold the airplanes and equipment. Jack Rand went to work for Pacific Airmotive, and Ira Reed joined Hughes Aircraft Co. as a security guard. "Boots" LeBoutillier became a wholesale distributor for pharmaceuticals, and "Robby" Robinson devoted his full time to the California Air National Guard.

Howard Batt turned to the business side of aviation, and was very successful as the manager of Clover Field, and the distributor for Beechcraft and Ryan airplanes. He owned a Ford Tri-motor and still obtained motion picture contracts from time to time.

Garland Lincoln continued to maintain a small fleet of movie airplanes, but his maintenance and modification facility at the Los Angeles Metropolitan Airport in Van Nuys, and later at Grand Central Air Terminal, was his main source of income.

Soon after moving to Grand Central Air Terminal, Lincoln designed and built two additional movie stunt planes. Powered with 200 h.p. Wright J-4-B engines, and having an outward appearance similar to the Nieuport 28, they proved to be outstanding acrobatic airplanes.

Lincoln could climb to 6,000 feet in sixty seconds, and could outmaneuver any aircraft of the time. In spins he could make eighteen turns in 1,000 feet, and could do snap rolls about the horizontal axis of the airplane, instead of the usual cork screw maneuver.[246]

Paul Mantz supplemented his motion picture work with charter flights, instruction and weekend joy rides at Union Air Terminal in Burbank. For a while he operated what he called the "Honeymoon Express" and flew several Hollywood personalities to Las Vegas for quick weddings.

Warner Brothers awarded the aviation contract for "Murder In The Clouds" to Frank Clarke, with Howard Batt, Frank Tomick, Clinton Herberger and Dick Rinaldi as additional pilots.

The story is centered on a new high explosive that will revolutionize warfare, and the rivalry of two fliers, Lyle Talbot and Gordon Wescott, who are after the same girl, airline stewardess Ann Dvorak. Lyle Talbot is assigned, with Dvorak's brother as co-pilot, to fly the scientist inventor and a sample of his explosive from the west coast to Washington. Detained by a gang trying to steal the formula, Talbot fails to reach the airport in time, and Wescott, secretly in league with the gang, takes his place on the government-chartered airliner. Setting a time bomb, Wescott jumps with the container holding the explosive sample and the airliner explodes, crashing in the Sierras. Dvorak travels to the crash site looking for her brother but is captured by the gang who have come to pick up Wescott and the explosive. After an air fight between the gang and Talbot, with the help of machine gun firing planes from the Sheriff's Aero Squadron, the girl is rescued and the sample is recovered.

Frank Clarke did most of the acrobatic flying in his Speedwing Travelair. Howard Batt rented and flew his own Ford Tri-Motor as the airliner. All pilots flew in the air fight, which operated from a field at Big Bear Lake, California.

When "Murder In The Clouds" was finished, Clinton Herberger accepted a position with Universal Pictures in the Special Effects Department. Dick Rinaldi went to work for one of the airlines.

Fluent in three European languages, Frank Tomick joined Metro Goldwyn Mayer where he translated dialogue into foreign language subtitles for films to be released in Europe.

Howard Batt, Garland Lincoln and Paul Mantz, with their fixed bases of operation, did most of the aviation contracting for the remainder of the 1930s, along with Frank Clarke. Even though Frank Clarke did not maintain a hangar or a group of airplanes, he contracted for pictures on his own merits, and was the only pilot who continued to make a living almost exclusively from motion picture work.

Paul Mantz submitted the low bid for "West Point Of The Air" and immediately received a contract from Metro Goldwyn Mayer. Wallace Beery, who had the leading role, flew his own airplane from the Union Air Terminal in Burbank to the location site at Randolph Field, Texas.

The story is built around Wallace Beery's efforts, as a sergeant at Randolph Field, to see that his son, Robert Young, becomes a good army pilot. After graduating from West Point and saddled with conceit gained as a star football player, Young is sent to Randolph Field for flight training. Further handicapped by the attentions of a shallow society girl, Young ignores his sweetheart, Maureen O'Sullivan, and violates army regulations. After a friend is burned to death in a crash, Young loses his nerve. In an effort to prevent nearby high-ranking officers from overhearing his son's heated remarks against flying, Beery socks Young and is cashiered from the service for striking an officer. Assigned to fly at night and drop flares for army maneuvers, Young loses his nerve again. Beery, flying an unreliable civilian plane, secretly fills in for his son. When Young learns of this he takes off and risks his own life to rescue Beery after the old airplane loses a wing and crashes in flames. Young now realizes he is not yellow and completes his training. Beery is reinstated and at graduation pins the wings on his son, who is now reformed and back with Maureen O'Sullivan.

Paul Mantz hired Otto Timm to build a replica Curtiss Pusher for a scene at the beginning of the picture where Wallace Beery is an army flyer in the early days of military aviation. Timm also reconditioned a Fokker D.VII, which had been used in "Hell's Angels," as the civilian aircraft Wallace Beery used to drop flares.

Frank Clarke again demonstrated his exceptional flying ability in Warner Brothers "Devil Dogs Of The Air" which was filmed at the San Diego Naval Air Station. Paul Mantz won the contract, but according to Frank Tomick, Frank Clarke did the stunt flying in Clarke's own Speedwing Travelair.

Flying as James Cagney, the cocky civilian stunt flyer who shows off his ability when reporting for duty at the San Diego Naval Air Station, Clarke repeatedly buzzes the field. When a Navy ambulance, in the story, drives onto the field, Clarke makes a three-point touchdown about one hundred feet from the vehicle, bounces over the ambulance and touches down about one hundred feet away on the other side, and then bounces back into the air under full power to resume his buzzing of the field.

In the story, James Cagney joins the Marines to be with his boyhood idol, Pat O'Brien, who is a flight instructor. Quickly moving to the head of the class, Cag-

ney alienates everyone with his conceit and contempt for military regulations. When Cagney goes after O'Brien's girlfriend, Margaret Lindsay, their friendship dissolves. During fleet maneuvers, in which the camera records many good scenes of naval air and sea power of the time, the two fliers share an emergency and are reconciled. O'Brien accepts a long-ago-applied-for transfer, leaving the way open for the developing romance between a mellower Cagney and Margaret Lindsay.

Garland Lincoln signed a contract with Universal Pictures for the aviation work in "Storm Over The Andes." Lincoln's hangar at Metropolitan Airport served as a Bolivian air base. In addition to Lincoln's rotary engine powered LF-1, two Wacos with Kinner engines, one Continental-powered Waco and two Wright J-6 powered Stearmans appeared in the air fighting scenes. Lincoln, Frank Clarke and "Chubby" Gordon flew in the picture, but the identities of the other two pilots is uncertain.

In the story, Jack Holt is a philandering professional soldier aviator who joins the Bolivian Air Force during its war with Paraguay. Injured in an air fight, he frets over the inactivity at the hospital and mingles with a fiesta crowd where he meets and seriously falls in love with Mona Barrie. When Holt's commanding officer, Antonio Moreno, flies him back to the air base after recovery, Holt discovers that his lover is Moreno's wife. Aware of Holt's reputation with the ladies, Moreno tries to get himself killed when he discovers the triangle situation. Holt rescues Moreno after a crash in the jungle and their conflict is resolved. Wounded in a subsequent air fight, Holt makes a gentleman's exit, leaving Moreno and his wife to reconcile.

Paul Mantz received the contract for Metro Goldwyn Mayer's 'Suzy.' A French airfield set was erected at the Triunfo location. Six Thomas Morse Scouts, painted to resemble French pursuit planes, appeared briefly in the film as part of a squadron lineup. As a pilot who is strafing a fleeing car with escaping spies, Mantz dived on the speeding car with a Populaire, while a string of previously placed dynamite caps explode in sequence along the road to simulate machine-gun fire from the airplane. For the next sequence, where the strafing plane lands and taxies into a tree, the camera shows Mantz landing the Populaire, but then the scene cuts to an S.E.5 taxiing into a tree. The damage to the S.E.5 appears to be extensive, but the crash was accomplished with spring loaded "breakaway" wings.

"Suzy" begins with Jean Harlow as a show girl in prewar London who marries Franchot Tone, an Irish inventor who unwittingly works for a German spy ring. When he is shot by the spies, who make the crime to appear as if the wife is guilty, Harlow flees to Paris as the war breaks out. Believing her husband is dead, she meets and marries Cary Grant, a famous French flyer who continues to have affairs with other women. After recovering and now an aircraft designer for the British government, Franchot Tone comes to Paris, where Cary Grant is to test Tone's new airplane. The inventor meets his bigamist wife and accuses her, but she finally convinces him that she thought he was dead. Shirking a mission, Grant goes to a chateau with his current flame who Jean Harlow recognizes as the same German female agent who shot her first husband. Harlow and Tone go to the chateau to warn Grant, but he is killed by the spies, who escape in an automobile. Tone takes off in his new airplane and machine guns the car, killing the occupants. He then runs into a squadron of German fighter planes. After shooting down three (in leftover "Hell's Angels" scenes), he lands at the chateau and crashes into a tree. Before the military authorities arrive, Harlow and Tone place Grant's body in the airplane to appear that he died from wounds suffered in the air fight, thus preserving his family's honor. Realizing that Harlow is sincere, Tone forgives her completely and they start a new life.

Paramount's "Thirteen Hours By Air," Universal's "Flying Hostess," RKO's "Without Orders," and Warner Brothers' "China Clipper" had airline settings, and except for camera flying there was no work for the motion picture stunt pilots. All pictures contained good scenes of United Boeing 247's and Pan American's China Clipper.

Garland Lincoln recalls an interesting flying experience apart from his career as a motion picture stunt pilot:

"In November 1936 I was employed by a mining company to fly three of their engineers on a survey of the company's Alaskan properties in my nine passenger Bach. I had no radio or navigational aids, only the basic instruments.

"We took off from Grand Central Airport in Glendale and had bad weather all the way to Seattle. The next stop was Vancouver, B.C. where we waited one day for weather. Then we flew to Prince George for refueling and on to Vanderbilt and Hazelton. The weather was still bad and I tried to get through, but we had to return to Hazelton where we were grounded for four days.

"When the weather lifted I took off and flew for more than three hours absolutely blind. Finally I saw a small clearing through the clouds near Telegraph Creek and landed. Before trying a takeoff I hired some local Alaskan Indians to cut down small trees and use their dog teams to drag these trees over the clearing to smooth out a runway. We filled any crevices with small limbs, debris and packed snow until we had a fairly smooth runway. All of this took about one week and then we took off. When I got airborne I found that I had no flipper control so I came back and landed. I discovered a broken stabilizer brace which happened while one of the Indians was holding the tail down for

me to warm up. I had most of our load too far forward and the brakes would not hold on the icy ground while I warmed up the engine. The strut was streamlined metal and broken at the bottom where it was attached to the fuselage.

"I found an Indian in the village whose business was making dog sleds out of metal. He had a hand-operated forge and suggested that I look over a nearby wrecked Fairchild 71 which had been abandoned a year or two before. We were lucky as I found a similar brace but it was 10 inches too long. The sled builder cut the excess with a hack saw, then heated and hammered the cut end into a crow foot which I attached to the stabilizer and the fuselage.

"Before I could take off the next day, a Canadian mail plane, a Ford Tri-Motor with mail and passengers aboard, landed on our runway, but he ran out of runway and went up on his nose in a snowbank. The pilot said he usually landed at the nearest level clearing which was about 30 miles to the north, and his passengers and mail then came to Telegraph Creek by dog sled. When he saw my plane, which was just as long as his, sitting on a nice looking runway, he decided to try it.

"With ropes and several local men we pulled the tail down. The three engines and propellers were undamaged but there was a buckle in the fuselage. I took the pilot and his remaining passengers and mail to the nearest town, Atlin, where the pilot waited for mechanics and equipment to come from Vancouver.

"From Atlin we flew to Carcross, to Burwash and then to Fairbanks, where we were weathered in. While waiting I had some skis made for the airplane so we could fly on to Nome and Ft. Yukon.

"During the layover I stayed at a hotel and enjoyed talking to the manager, the postmaster and other guests. One afternoon we were sitting in the lobby when a tall young man staggered in. He knew the postmaster but he was emotionally upset and kept trying to tell us something. We helped him to a chair. After some coffee and a short rest he regained his composure and told us what he had been through. He said, 'I am going home because I cannot live in such a lonely place in the kind of storm we just had. I have been very sick and depressed so I decided one day to go to a trading post four miles from my cabin to see if I had any mail, hoping that it would cheer me up. I harnessed my five dogs to the sled and started out. About a mile from my cabin there is a river to cross. When I was about a half mile beyond the river a sudden storm came up. It soon became impossible to see in any direction through the blowing snow and it got very cold. I decided that since I was shaky from my illness I had better go back to the cabin before the snow got so deep that I and my dogs would be unable to get back, and freeze to death. The snow was getting deeper and powdery—dangerous to walk in as it has no bottom. I could not see ahead and the dogs kept falling into holes. I could not find the usual crossing place and I kept going along the bank trying to find a safe place to cross. I finally got across the river but we couldn't get up on the bank on the other side. The dogs would slip back and the sled would turn upside down. I don't know how long we we were trying to get up the bank. I only remember my poor dogs and their little frozen feet and their fur covered with ice. I laid down and tried to hold all my dogs and I cried. I kept saying my dogs are the only things that love me and now I am causing them to freeze and die. I prayed and asked God to please allow me to get my dogs back to the cabin and get them warm. I don't care about myself, I only have my dogs and I don't want them to freeze.

"My prayer must have been answered, because the next thing I can remember is waking up in my cabin with my five dogs, some on my bed and some under the covers with me. My sled was in the cabin too. How I ever got my dogs, and especially the long sled, into my small cabin, built a fire and went to sleep will always be a miracle to me. I have had all I want of this rough, lonely life. I am going home.'

"All of the people in the lobby were crying with him and I will never forget this young man's ordeal. I later learned from the postmaster that the young man was well educated and from England with no close relatives. His fiancee had been killed in an automobile accident about two weeks before their wedding. He was so broken up that he decided to come to a remote part of the world to forget his troubles. The postmaster had tried to talk him out of living alone in a cabin, but the young man wanted to try it. He gave his dogs and sled to the postmaster and returned to England. I never heard any more about him.

"After the weather cleared I flew the mining engineers on their survey and then we returned to Los Angeles."[247]

Paul Mantz provided several Stearmans and R.K.O. built a French airfield set for "The Woman I Love," but the air action in the final release of the film was minimal.

The story, which had originally been filmed in France as "L'Equipage," follows Paul Muni as a jinxed pilot in the French Air Service whose observers always get killed. When no one will fly with him, Louis Hayward finally volunteers. After meeting Muni's wife, Miriam Hopkins, a triangle situation develops. When Muni is wounded and Hayward is killed in an air battle, Muni discovers a picture of his wife on his observer's body. The unfaithful wife nurses the wounded pilot back to health and he forgives her in the process.

Paul Mantz was the aviation contractor for Metro Goldwyn Mayer's next major aviation picture, "Test Pilot." United Airport in Burbank, which was now known as the Union Air Terminal, was the setting for most of the flying scenes. Camera crews also photographed excellent scenes of Boeing B-17-Cs, Douglas B-18s and Northrop attack planes at Hamilton Field, California for the military side of the picture.

Mantz flew Charles Marshall in the Lockheed Sirius twenty to fifty feet above orchards, gullies and fields in the San Fernando valley to obtain background scenes to be used in process work on a sound stage.[248]

The Drake Fighter in the picture, being tested for acceptance by the army, was actually a Seversky P-35 flown by Mantz.

As the airplane became more sophisticated with increased speeds, a number of unlikely peril situations appeared on the screen that sometimes reached the point of incredibility. While "Test Pilot" was an excellent movie as a whole, it contained its share of technical errors that seemed to always appear in aviation movies. When Clark Gable used the questionable method of testing a new army fighter by diving at full speed to see how much it could take, a wing neatly folded and flapped on the wing stub, just as if it were a mock-up on a sound stage. In the reality of a 400 m.p.h. dive, the wing would have been ripped away. The forces resulting from such an imbalance of stability at that speed would have thrown the airplane into violent rotation, making it impossible for Clark Gable to calmly remove the instrument panel, in order to bring the performance figures back to the manufacturer, and then bail out in a mild breeze created by an obvious wind machine somewhere off camera.

When Gable and Spencer Tracy are testing a four-engine bomber, the fuselage is loaded with sand bags to simulate bomb loads. While testing the aircraft the securing straps break and the bags shift forward to pin Tracy in the cockpit, but some mysterious force prevents the bags from reaching the other half of the cockpit where Gable sits. When the airplane crashes the now unsecured

Frank Clarke. Courtesy: Garland Lincoln

bags remain in their first shifted position instead of moving forward at the time of impact, thus denying the basic laws of physics.

But "Test Pilot" was a good story and opens with Clark Gable as a famous test pilot for the Drake Airplane Company. Spencer Tracy is his faithful friend and mechanic. On a cross-country flight with the new Drake Fighter, Gable has engine trouble and lands on a Kansas farm where he meets, courts and marries Myrna Loy. When Lionel Barrymore, the head of Drake, refuses to give him time off for a honeymoon they quarrel and Gable is fired. Going on a long drunk Myrna Loy leaves

him, but Spencer Tracy patches things up with the company and the girl and Gable is rehired. Spencer Tracy is killed while he and Gable are testing a new bomber. Deeply affected by the death of his friend, Gable gives up test flying and goes into the army as an instructor where he finds happiness with his wife and new son.

Garland Lincoln, Howard Batt and Paul Mantz furnished and flew airplanes for short scenes in many non-aviation films during the 1930s. Some of these scenes consisted of nothing more than an airplane taxiing up to the camera for an actor to deplane. But these small jobs helped to pay the bills, and an examination of the follow-

Garland Lincoln and Elmer Dyer in Lincoln's Stearman camera plane. Courtesy: Garland Lincoln

Remote camera Mount on Garland Lincoln's Stearman camera plane. Courtesy: Garland Lincoln

An S.E.5 and the similar Populaire at the Triunfo location for "Suzy." Courtesy: Carter/Mantz collection

Paul Mantz bounces a Travelair for the Warner Brothers film "Dive Bomber." Courtesy: Jimmy Barton

ing partial list of Garland Lincoln's "credits" for these lesser flying jobs will give one some idea of that part of motion picture flying.

Studio	Film Title	Aircraft
Republic	"Bengal Lancer Patrol"	Stinson R Lycoming 220
Paramount	"I'm From Missouri"	Fokker Universal J-5
Columbia	"Life Is Cheap"	Stearman J-5, 2 LF-1s, Stearman J-6 9
Republic	"Drums Of Fu Manchu"	Fairchild J-6 9, Stinson R Lyc 220
R.K.O.	"Border Patrol"	Stearman J-5
R.K.O.	"Arise My Love"	Stinson A Tri motor
Paramount	"Illegal Traffic"	D.H.9 #10587
Republic	"Dick Tracy Vs. Crime Inc."	Stearman J-6 7
Columbia	"Roaming Lady"	LF-1, Bach #NC219H
Paramount	"Safari"	DeHaviland Moth
Fox	"Sundown"	Stinson A Tri motor
Condor	"Looking For Trouble"	Curtiss Condor
Fox	"Bright Eyes"	Stinson R Lycoming 220
Fox	"Great American Broadcast"	Curtiss JN-1 OX-5
Fox	"Happy Landings"	Stinson A Tri motor
Columbia	"Mistaken Identity"	Stearman J-6 7 #N668K
Condor	"Roundup"	Fairchild 42 #N106M
RKO	"Right To Romance"	Monocoupe #N192K
RKO	"Lost Patrol"	Stearman

Garland Lincoln didn't own all of the airplanes in this list. The group he maintained for motion picture work during the 1930s varied from time to time. In spite of past references to a large number of Lincoln's Nieuports, no more than four can be documented. The fifth Nieuport listed in the Fox contract for "Hell In The Heavens" was Lincoln's first LF-1 which looks almost exactly like a modified Nieuport 28. If his two later LF-1's can be called "Nieuports," as they frequently were in the motion picture industry, then Lincoln's fleet of Nieuports can be said to total seven, four modified Nieuport 28's and three LF-1's.

Paul Mantz and Howard Batt always owned two or three airplanes each for motion picture work, while the Wilson brothers usually had two or three Travelairs, a couple of Stearmans and a Waco or two at their airport. Frank Clarke kept a Speedwing Travelair for some time and some of the other stunt pilots owned an airplane now and then. But the contractor for aviation movies usually had to rent airplanes from other owners as it would have been prohibitively expensive to maintain fleets of all existing types of aircraft that could fit any script situation. Jimmy Barton gives an insight into the procurement of aircraft for motion pictures:

"After you worked in the business for several years you got to know who had what and where it was. We rented armament from Otto Steimrich at Paramount, airplanes from Garland Lincoln and some others, and where we had to make anything special we went to Arrigo Balboni who had the big junk yard out in El Monte. He had more wrecked and junked ships than you could shake a stick at. I think he got his start back about the middle 1920s. He bought a Standard and for some reason stuck a big 300 Hisso in it—made it nose heavy as hell. It got off the ground pretty good, but it took nearly all the back stick he could hold on it to keep it straight and level. One day he busted it and put the pieces up for sale. Brought in more than he had in the ship originally. That gave him the idea of going into the aircraft junk trade. He was ahead of everybody else in that line—the first one to make it a business.

"Lots of times someone mentioned that they'd been out to so and so's place late the night before, and ran into Arrigo and his old truck, bringing in a wrecked ship. He'd hear about a crash at Visalia or out at Hemet, and be there practically before the dust settled, dickering for the leftovers. You could pick up anything you wanted. He had some stuff surplus from the World War. I bought LeRhone and Gnome cylinders, still in factory grease, for six and eight bucks.

"If the script called for a certain type of airplane, say an old cabin monoplane for a bush pilot story or something that could be reworked to look like a foreign job, we could usually rent or lease a ship from several people around Southern California who owned old jobs—kept 'em squirreled away in the back of a hangar somewhere. I did that myself when I was living out in the San Fernando Valley in the thirties, before it was built up. It was nothing like it is now—nothing but dirt and gravel roads, except for the main highways. Most of the houses were pretty shacky. A lot of 'em had junk piled around—old bathtubs, toilets, pipe and other crap. Mine was a different kind of junk pile, though. At one time I had three ships disassembled and stored on the lot, covered with tarps. I picked them up from people that had gone broke, moved away and sold them for eating money. Or in a couple of cases from estates—guys that had died and their widows wanted to get rid of anything that reminded them of the old man.

"A lot of these ships wasn't even flown—just used on location for background atmosphere. On these movies where there was only a minimum of flight footage—where the action called for only a forced landing in bad country, the prop department made up models and they faked it. Sometimes we'd film outside shots for intercutting, using the real thing.

"One film we needed an old cabin monoplane for this scene where they had to put down in the Alaskan bush in mid-winter. I had a line on a Bellanca up in San Luis Obispo, but it got burned in a hangar fire a week before we were to shoot the scene. Then we found a Travelair 6000 in Ventura that was okay for the script.

"We flew it over to Van Nuys and trucked it into the back lot where they had a refrigerated big building. The set crew brought in background stuff to simulate a pine forest. We brought in the 6000 and I took the bolts out of one side of the landing gear so's it could be laid down like one side of the gear had folded. I rigged up an old bent up gear with a broken wheel in place of the one I took off, and it looked pretty real. They piled up fake underbrush around the ship, turned on the refrigeration, and sprayed water over the whole thing occasionally.

"In two days they was icicles two feet long on the fake trees and bushes. They brought in the gaffers, lights and camera crew and shot the one scene supposed to be right after the forced landing—then used a snow machine and wind generator to blow snow over the ship itself for the rest of the scenes.

"One part of the deal for the airplane was that the old boy who owned it insisted that he come along and stay with the ship. They sort of detailed me to keep him out of the way while they was shooting.

"It was colder'n hell in there and the fabric on the 6000 was pretty old. The action called for one guy to come to in the cabin, push the door open, crawl out into the snow, then try to pull the other fellow out. When he pushed on the door it wouldn't open, so he gave it a whack and the door fell off. Both hinges had crystallized. When he got out he slipped and put his arm through the fabric of the fuselage, leaning on it like he was weak and groggy. When the door came off, the old boy who owned the airplane jumped up and I had to haul him down and shush him. When the one guy finally hauled the other out of the cabin they had pocked a batch of holes on both sides of the frame, and the wind machine had ripped off a big section of the fabric off the side—peeled it right back. The old boy started to howl like a goosed moose, so I put my hand over his mouth and held him down until they finished the take.

"When the day's shooting was finished we opened the big doors and hauled the 6000 out into the sun. It sat there and sweated—every once in a while it would give a pop and sort of shake itself while it warmed up.

"By next morning more fabric had fallen off. The old boy was fit to be tied—said we'd ruined his ship. Well we hauled that 6000 back out to Van Nuys, drained the tanks, changed the oil, and got it started to run the moisture out of the mags and ignition harness. The studio had a new cover job done on it before it was returned to him, so he really got paid twice."[249]

During the summer of 1937 a four-engine Russian land plane with a crew of five was lost on a Polar flight from Moscow to Los Angeles. Jimmie Mattern was one of several American flyers who searched for the missing Russian aviators. Gasoline was extremely limited at Point Barrow, Alaska, the base for the various search flights, due to unseasonal ice in the harbor and numerous icebergs in the surrounding sea. An American oil company financed a refueling expedition for Jimmie Mattern and the company president engaged Garland Lincoln to fly the tanker airplane.

Under Lincoln's directions, the passenger cabin of a Ford Tri-Motor was stripped and filled with tanks capable of holding 1,800 gallons of gasoline and 450 gallons of oil. After a successful test flight, in which a hose was passed from Lincoln's Tri-Motor to Mattern's Lockheed Electra, the search expedition was launched.

Mattern flew to Alaska, and Lincoln followed with Frank Tomick as co-pilot. Charles Marshall was also on board with an assignment to photograph the expedition for a newsreel company. With the fuselage full of gasoline and oil tanks, the occupants had to enter the airplane through the emergency hatch above the pilot's cockpit. The refueling tanks were not yet filled as Lincoln planned to load up at Fairbanks, Alaska, the last place where fuel and oil was available.

They landed at Burwash, an Indian village known to Lincoln from previous trips to Alaska and were fogged in. But the emergency nature of their mission caused them to make a decision to continue on to Fairbanks.

With the aid of the few instruments available in those days, and with his ability at dead reckoning, Lincoln set his course. After several hours of blind flying they arrived at what Lincoln thought was their destination. There was no break in the cloud and fog cover making visibility zero. The radio had ceased to function in the meantime. It was later discovered that the ice buildup on the antenna had caused it to shear off.

After two more hours of flying around looking for a break in the clouds, the fuel gauge read empty and they decided to let down to the altimeter setting of Fairbanks. With a crashlanding almost certain, Tomick and Marshall threw all loose pices of equipment overboard and lashed down whatever remained. As an emergency signal to the ground, and also to drain any remaining fuel in the tanks to avoid fire, Lincoln put the Tri-motor in a power-on dive while they were still at a safe altitude. After cutting the master switch he levelled off at 65 m.p.h. Approaching the ground he saw three spruce trees directly ahead, with a brown field beyond. He missed the trees and skidded across what turned out to be tundra. The Ford turned up on its nose and then over on its back. As the airplane settled into the muck the three occupants smashed the windows and climbed out with no injuries.

Several men appeared and informed them that they were only a half mile from the edge of Fairbanks and that the whole city had been listening to their engines for the last two hours.

Lincoln, Tomick and Marshall remained in Fairbanks for several days, until they learned that the Russian plane had crashed into an iceberg with no survivors. After the engines were removed the Ford settled into the tundra and may still be there today.[250] The search was widely reported in newspapers all over the United States and Canada, and in many parts of Europe.

Six weeks later Garland Lincoln was again in the news. He had gone to St. Louis to pick up another Ford Tri-Motor that he and Buck Jones purchased together.

Their plan was for Lincoln to fly Buck Jones to various football games around the country on weekends, with Lincoln having use of the airplane for commercial and movie work during the week.

After a stop at Albuquerque, New Mexico, on the return trip from St. Louis, Lincoln, his co-pilot Earl Hobson and mechanic H.B. Taylor failed to arrive at their next destination, Winslow, Arizona. The missing flyers were the subjects of headlines in both the Los Angeles Examiner and the Los Angeles Times. After several days they were discovered to have made a forced but safe landing in the wilds of New Mexico.[251]

The Ford Tri-Motor refueling plane as it ended up in the tundra at Fairbanks, Alaska. Courtesy: Garland Lincoln

Garland Lincoln, Frank Tomick and Charles Marshall show the strain of their crash landing at Fairbanks, Alaska. Courtesy: Garland Lincoln

Garland Lincoln is welcomed by his wife, Pauline, after returning from a forced landing in New Mexico. Courtesy: Garland Lincoln

In February 1938 Los Angeles Metropolitan Airport was the location for the largest gathering of working motion picture pilots since the "Hell's Angels" crew flew from Caddo Field ten years before. Now they were working on Paramount's "Men With Wings."

Paul Mantz had the main aviation contract, but according to an interview with the flyers at the time and according to Paramount's publicity releases, Frank Clarke was the leader and king of the stunt pilots.[252] A fierce competition developed between Frank Clarke and Paul Mantz that was to reach a climax during World War II. According to one newspaper writer, William Wellman the director looked to Clarke's twenty years of stunt flying experience as credentials, and relied on his counsel throughout the picture.

"Men With Wings" begins with the beginning of aviation. Inspired by the Wright brothers flight, Walter Abel builds a plane in 1904, but his wife and young daughter see him killed when he tries to fly it. Ten years later the daughter, Louise Campbell, and two neighborhood pals,

Ray Milland and Fred MacMurray, build an airplane that leads to jobs for the two men in an aircraft factory. After a quarrel at the factory MacMurray goes to France and becomes a famous fighter pilot with the French. Miss Campbell goes to France as a telephone operator where she and MacMurray renew their friendship which leads to marriage. Back home Milland is prevented from going to war when America enters the conflict because he is now an aircraft designer and valuable test pilot. After the war Milland becomes an airmail pilot while MacMurray, bored with home life, leaves his wife to fly in the war underway in Morocco. Upon his return to the United States, MacMurray attempts a trans-Atlantic solo flight but fails just before Lindbergh succeeds. MacMurray goes off to another war in China while Milland's factory produces a successful bomber. When MacMurray returns, Milland's factory is a big success and Louise Campbell has now turned to Ray Milland. MacMurray departs, realizing their future will be better off without him.

Garland Lincoln poses by one of his LF-1's at Grand Central Air Terminal after it was flown in "Men With Wings."
Courtesy: Garland Lincoln

Garland Lincoln's two LF-1's at Grand Central Air Terminal in Glendale in the process of being painted for use in "Men With Wings." Courtesy: Garland Lincoln

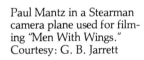

Paul Mantz in a Stearman camera plane used for filming "Men With Wings." Courtesy: G. B. Jarrett

Paul Mantz in the Spad VII that was used for still photographs but did not fly in the dogfight scenes of "Men With Wings." Courtesy: G. B. Jarrett

Several new pilots came into the Associated Motion Picture Pilots organization for the dogfight scene in "Men With Wings." William Wellman and the Paramount publicity department organized a studio luncheon at which the pilots dined with Paramount starlets and were presented with silk scarves. From the left: Frank Clarke, Jerry Andrews, Earl Gordon, "Robby" Robinson, Walt Quinton, Stan Hicks, Paul Mantz, Howard Batt, Jerry Phillips, Herb White and "Tex" Rankin. Other flying jobs prevented Dick Rinaldi and "Ace" Bragunier from attending. Courtesy: Howard Batt

Garland Lincoln readies one of his LF-1's for a scene in Columbia's "Roaming Lady." Courtesy: Garland Lincoln

Garland Lincoln's three modified Nieuport 28's sit on the flight line at Metropolitan Airport while being overhauled for use in the 1938 remake of "Dawn Patrol." "Men With Wings" aircraft appear in the background. Courtesy: Carter/Mantz collection

Paul Mantz gathered or had built most of the airplanes in the picture, and except for the dogfight scene and an air field buzzing sequence, did all of the flying. Jerry Phillips recalls the dogfight scene:

"Assembling at the Van Nuys airport were Frank Clarke, Paul Mantz, Tex Rankin, Dick Rinaldi, Earl Gordon, Robby Robinson, Ace Bragunier, Howard Batt, Herb White and myself. In one of the dogfights at 8,000 feet over the San Fernando Valley, I was flying a Nieuport[253] in an upper formation of five ships, and below at 5,000 feet was the German formation led by "Robby" Robinson.

"At a rocking of the wings signal from Paul Mantz in the camera ship, we dove down through the German formation with machine guns firing. After we passed through we chased each other all over the sky. In one instance Chubby Gordon was diving on me when I pulled up sharply to get a German plane in my sights, and his right wheel punctured a hole in my upper wing. There were several other near misses as we tried to confine the aerial combat within the camera range.

in front of an actual dog fight with French and German planes in terrific combat. His first reaction was to grab the controls and dive at the closest Fokker. Then he thought he was dreaming, but after the co-pilot shouted, 'What the hell's going on here?', he fully awoke and turned the plane away from the action, remarking to the co-pilot, 'It's those motion picture pilots playing war again'."[254]

Charles Marshall photographed the mock combat from the Lockheed Sirius camera plane flown by Paul Mantz. As Mantz circled the general melee at 160 miles per hour, Marshall shot whatever action seemed best at the moment.[255]

A Spad VII that Mantz said he had located in the basement of a hotel in Brawley, California, and a modified Nieuport 28 were painted with appropriate markings for the picture, but they couldn't keep up with the more powerful Travelairs, Wacos, two LF-1's and one Fokker D.VII used in the dog fight sequence. The Spad and

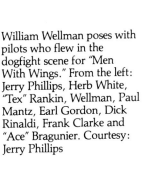

William Wellman poses with pilots who flew in the dogfight scene for "Men With Wings." From the left: Jerry Phillips, Herb White, "Tex" Rankin, Wellman, Paul Mantz, Earl Gordon, Dick Rinaldi, Frank Clarke and "Ace" Bragunier. Courtesy: Jerry Phillips

"A couple of days later I heard a story about a Western Airlines pilot who was flying from San Francisco to Los Angeles. In the last part of his flight, approaching the Los Angeles Airport, he happened to cross the San Fernando Valley at the height of our dog fighting. The pilot had a rough night before and was really bushed. He said that after passing Bakersfield he turned the controls over to the co-pilot, loosened his seat belt and slid down in his seat to take forty winks. This man, I later learned, had been a fighter pilot flying S.E.5's with the British in World War I. He was an ace with seven German planes to his credit. He said he did not know how long he had been dozing, but when he awoke still in a slight daze, the airplane was passing through large fluffy cumulous clouds. Emerging through one rather large cloud bank, he came out right

Nieuport appeared at several publicity events planned by the studio to advertise the picture. In another publicity stunt, Paramount hired Garland Lincoln to fly an S.E.5 to San Francisco to coincide with the opening of the picture at San Francisco theaters.

Frank Clarke made several high-speed passes over and between the hangars at Metropolitan Airport for the sequence where Ray Milland is supposed to be testing a new fighter. Paul Mantz bravely followed right behind the daring Clarke, and photographed the action with a camera mounted on top of his Stearman camera plane.

A defect was discovered in the controls of the Boeing 100 that Clarke flew for this incident, and there was

The only accident in "Men With Wings" occurred when Dick Rinaldi had engine trouble and had to make a forced landing in this Travelair. Courtesy: Jerry Phillips

speculation about the possibility of sabotage. Since he was the owner of the Boeing, Mantz called for an official investigation by federal aviation authorities who found no evidence to indicate that anyone had tampered with the controls.[256]

All of the air action in the 1938 re-make of "Dawn Patrol" came from the original version made eight years before. Some of the air field scenes had to be re-shot in order to show Errol Flynn and David Niven with the airplanes. Four Nieuports appeared in the new version, two with "N" struts and two with "I" struts. All had the shortened wings which apparently originated in 1926 when someone cut approximately two feet from each wing tip of a Nieuport 28 to gain more speed in racing. One of the "N" strutted Nieuports was the same one used for publicity shots for "Men With Wings." The original location for the British airfield had now disappeared under real estate development. The new scenes were made at Warner Brothers Ranch in Calabasas. Technicians carefully duplicated the airplane markings from the 1930 picture, and even placed a duplicate Thomas Morse Scout in what appears to be the same location and position, so a closeup could show Errol Flynn firing a signal flare into the cockpit as Richard Barthelmess had done in 1930.

Howard Batt flew an S.E.5 for "The Story Of Vernon And Irene Castle," and furnished and flew airplanes for a number of aviation and non-aviation movies including "Women In The Wind," "Five Came Back," "Flying Irishman" and many others.

Paul Mantz did the same for "Too Hot To Handle," "The Bride Came C.O.D.," "Love On The Run," "Country Doctor," "The Dictator" and many more.

Long before the attack on Pearl Harbor, the federal government encouraged the motion picture industry to produce a series of films designed to encourage a buildup of the armed forces, particularly in the area of air power. "I Wanted Wings," "20,000 Men A Year," "Flying Cadets," "Thunderbirds," "Give Us Wings" and "Keep 'Em Flying" reflected the spirit of the times and encouraged many young men to volunteer for flight training.

The airplanes in these films were all military aircraft or else civilian flight school aircraft leased to the military. Except for the camera flying, there was little work for the motion picture stunt pilots. Paul Mantz won all of these contracts and also did the camera flying for "Wings Of The Navy," "Flight Command" and "Dive Bomber." Elmer Dyer was the aerial photographer for most of the military films that came out just before World War II.

The last movie in which the Associated Motion Picture Pilots worked together as a team was Warner Brothers "Captains Of The Clouds." Frank Clarke received the main contract as chief pilot for Warner Brothers.

In the semi-documentary story of training flyers for the Royal Canadian Air Force, James Cagney is a cocky but skilled bush pilot who steals flying jobs from his competitors and competes with Dennis Morgan for the love of Brenda Marshall.

When the bush pilots join the R.C.A.F., Cagney is too

Shooting a scene for "Captains Of The Clouds." Courtesy: Howard Batt

Taking a break during the filming of "Captains Of The Clouds." Front row from the left: Garland Lincoln, Dennis Morgan, James Cagney and Frank Clarke. Howard Batt sits between Morgan and Cagney, and Jimmy Barton stands on the extreme left. Courtesy: Howard Batt

old for combat and is assigned as an instructor. Accustomed to flying by instinct he is unable to comply with all the regulations and is mustered out. Joining again later under an assumed name, he is assigned to ferry Lockheed Hudsons to England. Just before a group of bombers reaches England they are attacked by a German fighter and Cagney gives his life by crashing into the fighter to save the formation.

Jerry Phillips recalls his experiences on "Captains Of The Clouds":

"Frank Clarke, Howard Batt, Herb White, Garland Lincoln and myself were put under contract to Warner Brothers and flew to Canada to do the flying sequences and to double for the stars.

"The first scenes were photographed at the Royal Canadian Air Force station in Uplands, Ontario. We were scheduled to do some formation flying in North American Harvards, the forerunner of the AT-6. The C.O., a very distinguished and proper individual, was a little concerned about our abilities in flying the Harvards, because he knew nothing of our past experience. In a very dignified manner he asked Michael Curtiz, the director, if we were qualified to fly the aircraft. Mike replied, 'My boys can fly anything.' Turning to me he said, 'How about you, Jerry—you fly Harvards?' I said, 'It just happens that during the last year I ferried about 100 of them to six different R.C.A.F. stations in Canada. Some of these airplanes here are ones I flew up from Los Angeles last winter.' We flew the Harvards without any further indoctrination.

"We went to North Bay to fly floatplanes off of Lake Nipissing and Caribou Lake, near Chandler, Ontario. While we were there we visited the Dionne Quintuplets. That is where they were born.

"One day I was flying a Norseman on floats, doubling for James Cagney. The shot called for me to land on the lake in front of the pier, then taxi up to the pier, cut the engine and let the plane coast the last few feet into the pier. In the meantime I was to duck down out of sight and Jimmy was to climb out onto the float nearest the pier and throw a rope to Brenda Marshall who was on the pier. During the rehearsal the director wanted Brenda to show anger because she was supposed to be mad at Jimmy for two-timing her. In his broken English, Mike Curtiz said, 'Brenda, I want for you to be mad at Jimmy like the bitch you are!' What he meant was her character in the picture. We all had a laugh, even Brenda.

"Another item came up shortly thereafter. We had a large raft anchored out in front of the pier where they would put the cameras for reverse shots from the water back to the pier. They used a little launch to go back and forth from the pier to the raft. On this morning things were going pretty well. Mike was getting a lot of closeup scenes with no re-takes and he was going full speed right past the normal lunch hour. Now in the movies you are not supposed to work more than four hours without a meal break. The assistant director was looking at his watch, and the crew was waiting for the call, 'Lunch!' The director wanted one more scene, a shot from the raft in front of the pier, back to the pier. With intentions of going out to the raft, Mike yelled, 'Launch! Bring the launch!' Everybody immediately broke and went to the lunch wagon, and no more work was done until we had 'launch'."[257]

This Certifies

that_____

IS A MEMBER OF

ASSOCIATED MOTION PICTURE PILOTS

CHARTERED BY

Airline Pilots Association

By such association has contributed to the pictorial history of aeronautical development and left for posterity a replica of aviation achievements and progress for the pleasure and enlightenment of the world.

Signed_____

Certificate issued to members of the Associated Motion Picture Pilots. Courtesy: Howard Batt

When the location work for "Captains Of The Clouds" was completed, the Associated Motion Picture Pilots joined the war effort in many capacities. Howard Batt went to work for North American Aviation as an acceptance test pilot, flying B-25's and P-51's on their final test flights before being released to the army. Jerry Phillips and Earl "Robby" Robinson were called to active duty with the Army Air Corps. Frank Tomick worked as a civilian ferry pilot. Garland Lincoln trained pilots for the Eagle Squadron at Grand Central Air Terminal, then ferried Lockheed Hudsons from Canada to England, before being called to active duty with the Army Air Corps. He served as staff pilot, flying officers of general rank to various theaters of operations, and ended the war as a lieutenant colonel. Earl Gordon worked as a civilian pilot flying C-42's for paratroop training at Ft. Benning, Georgia. Dick Grace joined the Army Air Corps and flew several missions with the 8th Air Force as a B-17 co-pilot. Paul Mantz, Frank Clarke and Clinton Herberger joined the Army Air Corps and served with the First Motion Picture Detachment, making training films. Elmer Dyer also served with this unit and eventually flew on many 8th Air Force missions over Germany as a combat cameraman.

As an organization, the Associated Motion Picture Pilots passed from the scene along with the pilots. In addition to their superior flying abilities, the Associated Motion Picture Pilots loved this country and were outspoken in their patriotism. Many of them possessed a kind and gentle nature that would not seem to fit their dangerous profession. Leo Nomis was loved by all who knew him. Unselfishness, and genial hospitality apply equally to Howard Batt and Jerry Phillips. Garland Lincoln was very tender-hearted and a proper gentleman. Frank Tomick's soft heart and geniality was apparent when he was around children. Wally Timm was a cultured, refined gentleman of the old school. Roy Wilson brought a smile to everyone who knew him, and Tave Wilson would give you the shirt off his back if you needed it. All members of the Associated Motion Picture Pilots didn't fit the same set of specifications, but each flyer had his own positive character traits that set him apart from the average.

Many people who knew these daring men consider the two Franks as fitting the popular conception of the movie stunt pilot. Jimmy Barton adds his recollections to those previously quoted:

> "Clarke and Tomick was practically a team—leastways during the earlier years. They hung out together most of the time, but once Tomick was supposed to have been forced down somewhere with some movie actress. They was missing for four or five days, and Clarke nearly flew his head off searching for

them from the air over the area they was supposed to have been in. Then they showed up and Tomick was clean shaven. The whole thing was a publicity stunt. Clarke was fit to be tied and was mad as hell at first, then later laughed about it too.

> "They were a pair. Tomick was more quiet, and some steadier than Clarke, but they was both practical jokers from way back—always thinking up some trick.

> "Clarke was a handsome son of a gun too. He had more girls gaga over him than some of the actors. One of the gossip columnists in Hollywood ran a story on him and described him as 'Satanically good looking—a real hunk of man beauty.' He had a hard time living that one down. Some of the boys started calling him 'Lucifer' or just 'Loose.' He finally put a stop to that. He could be rough when he had to."[258]

Frank Clarke was killed in a flying accident on June 12, 1948. With Mark Owens in the back seat of Clarke's war surplus BT-15, Clarke buzzed Frank Tomick at the trio's mining claim near Lake Isabella, as a signal to be picked up at the nearby Kernville Airport. Frank Tomick said that when the plane climbed from its dive the engine failed. It floundered for a second or two at 500 feet and then spun into the rocky slopes of Dutch Flats near Lake Isabella.

Richard Arlen delivered the eulogy at Clarke's funeral, which was widely attended by people from aviation and motion pictures. Broken up over the accident, Frank Tomick gave up flying and turned in his license. With the help of Mark Owens' brother and Jimmy Barton, Tomick erected a permanent monument at the site of the crash.

Spending his last years with his wife, Ruth, in their Lake Isabella home, Frank Tomick enjoyed working his mining claims and passed away at the Motion Picture Country Home and Hospital in 1966.

Reaching the rank of brigadier general in the Air National Guard, "Robby" Robinson had already passed away at the Veterans Administration Hospital in Sawtelle in 1958. Dick Grace died at this same hospital in 1965. Jack Rand passed away in San Pedro sometime in 1967. Clinton Herberger lived in Florida until his death in 1977. Tave Wilson died in Glendale the next year. "Boots" LeBoutillier passed away recently in Las Vegas. "Chubby" Gordon died soon after World War II and Ira Reed spent his last years in New Mexico or Arizona. Recent efforts to locate Garland Lincoln have proved fruitless.

Howard Batt, who enjoys life at his home in San Clemente, California, and Jerry Phillips who does the same thing in Hawaii, seem to be the only members of the old group of pilots who still remember the pioneering days of motion picture stunt flying.

The original motion picture stunt pilots and their colorful times are now in the realm of history. After

Four Ryan ST's wait for customers in front of Howard Batt's hangar at Clover Field. Courtesy: Howard Batt

Frank Tomick, on the left, and the brother of Mark Owens stand by the monument they built on the spot where Frank Clarke and Mark Owens were killed. The inscription on the BT-15's propeller reads: "A monument to Lt. Col. Frank L. Clarke, age 49, and Mark Owens, age 51, killed here in an airplane crash June 12, 1948. This monument is erected to their memory by their life long pals." Courtesy: Frank Tomick

World War II major changes affected society, aviation, and the motion picture industry. The business of contracting with the film companies for aviation work entered a new phase. Paul Mantz continued his distinguished career in aviation[259] and was the exclusive motion picture stunt pilot until the daring Frank Tallman, ably assisted by Frank Pine, appeared on the scene. Their stories, along with that of Jim Appleby and others, can be found in other publications.

Most of the air fields and location sites where the Associated Motion Picture Pilots worked have almost disappeared. The Venice Aviation Field is covered with streets and small houses. Clover Field exists as the Santa Monica Municipal Airport, but it no longer resembles the grass field on which open cockpit biplanes dragged their tail skids. Caddo Field is now a residential area in Van Nuys. Grand Central Airport in Glendale gave way to economic pressures to become an industrial park. Garland Lincoln's hangar still stands at Van Nuys Airport, but the field has changed radically and the hangar is now an industrial building. The Wilson Airport is covered by the western end of the Glendale-Burbank Airport, but the hangar used by Paul Mantz when Glendale-Burbank was the Union Air Terminal is still in use

today.

The Triunfo location, where Nieuports, Travelairs, Wacos, Stearmans and various other aircraft types lined up and took off for "Dawn Patrol," "Heartbreak," "Ace Of Aces," "Hell In The Heavens," "Suzy" and others is now covered by the affluent residential community of Thousand Oaks. The little stream into which Dick Grace made his most violent crash, for "Young Eagles," was dammed and is now under Lake Sherwood.

The German airfield location for "Dawn Patrol" is about the only site that remains untouched. You can still walk on the ground where two Pfalz D.XII's and a conglomeration of other aircraft types sat on the line for Leo Nomis and "Robby" Robinson to strafe. The underbrush on the hills behind the field is thicker, but the hills themselves haven't changed and can still be recognized by a comparison with still photos from the movie. When nearby freeway traffic slackens and a jet approaching LAX has passed over, one can almost hear the now unfamiliar but thrilling sounds of roaring engines, whirling propellers and singing wires that once filled the air in these locations as highly skilled professionals flew the biplanes and felt the air from their open cockpits.

Although the organization no longer functioned in motion picture work, the Associated Motion Picture Pilots presented a special trophy to Captain Chuck Yeager after he broke the sound barrier. From the left standing: Hank Coffin, Kirk Kerkorian, Paul Franklin, "Robby" Robinson, unidentified, Chuck Yeager, Frank Tomick, Geraldine Nomis, and Jerry Phillips. Seated from the left: Unidentified, Roy Pignet, Paul Mantz, Dick Grace, Howard Batt, Florence Barnes, Ira Reed and unidentified. Courtesy: Howard Batt

NOTES AND REFERENCES

1. The Library of Congress has two short newsreel type films made in 1905. "Ludlow's Aerodrome" shows a biplane being carried onto a field where a rope is hooked to an automobile that tows the plane into the air. A closeup of the airplane in the air and on the ground is shown. The film ends when the airplane cracks up. "Ludlow's Aeroplane No. 2" opens with a crowd watching the preparations for a man-laden biplane to be flown with the use of a long rope, kite fashion. The biplane is shown in the air, and another camera position shows it gliding into the water. The rest of the film shows rescue attempts with motor boats and a tug.

2. Hollywood Citizen, Dec. 31, 1915.

3. Historical Society of Southern California Quarterly, Dec. 1961.

4. Venice Daily Vanguard, Jan. 25, 1912.

5. Hollywood Citizen, Dec. 31, 1915.

6. In his autobiography, General Henry H. Arnold, mentions that while participating in an air meet in the New York area in 1911, he took time off to fly as a "double" for a motion picture being made at that time. Pioneer motion picture producer J. Stuart Blackton, was awarded a prize by the Aero Club of America for his use of aircraft in motion pictures.

7. Venice Daily Vanguard, Mar. 25, 1911.

8. Venice Daily Vanguard, Apr. 10, 1911.

9. Venice Daily Vanguard, May 25, 1911.

10. Venice Daily Vanguard, Oct. 9, 1911.

11. Venice Daily Vanguard, Jan. 31, 1912; Feb. 9 & 10, 1912; Mar. 7, 1912.

12. Venice Daily Vanguard, Mar. 29, 1912.

13. Venice Daily Vanguard, Apr. 20, 1912; Apr. 27, 1912.

14. Venice Daily Vanguard, Apr. 29, 1912.

15. Venice Daily Vanguard, Apr. 29, 1912.

16. Venice Daily Vanguard, May 8, 1912.

17. Venice Daily Vanguard, May 20, 1912.

18. Venice Daily Vanguard, Sep. 4, 1912.

19. The land was owned by the Machado family, descendants of the Machados who established the Rancho Machado with a land grant from the King of Spain.

20. Venice Daily Vanguard, Feb. 21, 1913.

21. Venice Daily Vanguard, Mar. 16, 1914.

22. Venice Daily Vanguard, Apr. 27, 1914; May 18, 1914.

23. Venice Daily Vanguard, May 21, 1914.

24. Venice Daily Vanguard, Jul. 30, 1914.

25. "Stunt—The Story Of The Great Movie Stunt Men"—John Baxter. Doubleday & Co. Inc., Garden City, N.J. 1974.

26. "Adventures With D.W. Griffith"—Kal Brown. Farrar, Straus & Giroux, New York 1973.

27. Los Angeles Examiner, Mar. 17, 1915. Los Angeles Times, Mar. 17, 1915.

28. Venice Evening Vanguard, Sep. 4, 1920. Saturday Evening Post, Sep. 19, 1925.

29. Venice Evening Vanguard, Sep. 4, 1920. Saturday Evening Post, Sep. 19, 1925.

30. Venice Evening Vanguard, Jan. 8, 1918.

31. Saturday Evening Post, Sep. 19, 1925.

32. Notes on Mercury Aviation by Cecil B. DeMille. Cecil B. DeMille Trust.

33. Venice Evening Vanguard, Aug. 12, 1918.

34. Venice Evening Vanguard, Mar. 4, 1918.

35. Venice Evening Vanguard, Apr. 11, 1918.

36. Venice Evening Vanguard, Jul. 2, 1918.

37. "Locklear, The Man Who Walked On Wings"—Art Ronnie. A.S. Barnes & Co. 1973.

38. From the show business term used to describe the traveling theatrical groups of the late 19th century, who often used barns for their one night performances in the rural areas of the nation. Contrary to popular opinion, the term was not related to the use of barns by touring aviators. Barns were built economically with many posts inside to support the structure above, thereby precluding the use of their interiors for the overnight storage of airplanes, unless the wings were removed.

39. "Locklear, The Man Who Walked On Wings"—Art Ronnie. A.S. Barnes & Co. 1973.

40. Personal interview with Garland Lincoln, 1961.

41. Personal interview with Garland Lincoln, 1961.

42. Personal interview with Garland Lincoln, 1961. Mr. lincoln distinctly recalled that Frank Clarke and Jeannie MacPherson, Mr. DeMille's secretary, were the first students taught by Al Wilson at DeMille Field.

43. Los Angeles Examiner, June 1, 1919. Taped interview with Robert E. Kennedy, conducted by Arch C. Wallen.

44. Taped interview with Robert E. Kennedy, conducted by Arch C. Wallen, and Los Angeles Times, May 22, 1966.

45. "Locklear, The Man Who Walked On Wings"—Art Ronnie. A. S. Barnes & Co. 1973.

46. Originally from Minnesota, Otto Timm was an early flyer and an aeronautical engineer. He came to San Diego in 1916 as a flying instructor at the naval flying school. When the U.S. entered the war, he designed and built naval training planes, aided by his brothers Wally and Reuben.

47. "Squadron Of Death"—Dick Grace. The Sun Dial Press, 1937.

48. An "E" appeared in his last name in the news accounts of his first aviation stunts.

49. Venice Evening Vanguard, Oct. 4, 1919. Los Angeles Examiner, Oct. 5, 1919.

50. Personal interview with Wally Timm 1977. Venice Evening Vanguard, Nov. 8, 1919.

51. Personal interview with Wally Timm, 1977.

52. Personal interview with Wally Timm, 1977.

53. Venice Evening Vanguard, Dec. 24, 1919.

54. Personal interview with Leo Stratton Nomis, 1980.

55. "The Parade's Gone By"—Kevin Brounlow. Alfred A. Knopf, 1969.

56. Personal interview with Leo Stratton Nomis, 1980.

57. Venice Evening Vanguard, Jan. 14, 1920.

58. Los Angeles Examiner, Feb. 6, 1920. Los Angeles Times, Feb. 6, 1920.

59. Personal interview with Frank Tomick, 1965.

60. Personal interview with Frank Tomick, 1965.

61. Personal interview with Howard Batt, 1976.

62. Venice Evening Vanguard, Feb. 15, 1920.

63. Venice Evening Vanguard, Feb. 12, 1920.

64. Venice Evening Vanguard, Apr. 23, 1920.

65. Venice Evening Vanguard, Mar. 16, 1920.

66. Venice Evening Vanguard, May 7, 1920.

67. Popular Aviation, Jan. 1940.

68. Venice Evening Vanguard, Jan. 4, 1920 & Jun. 28, 1920.

69. "Locklear, The Man Who Walked On Wings"—Art Ronnie. A.S. Barnes & Co. 1973.

70. "Locklear, The Man Who Walked On Wings"—Art Ronnie. A.S. Barnes & Co. 1973.

71. "Locklear, The Man Who Walked On Wings"—Art Ronnie. A.S. Barnes & Co. 1973.

72. Los Angeles Examiner & Los Angeles Times, Aug. 3, 1920. "Locklear, The Man Who Walked On Wings"—Art Ronnie. A.S. Barnes & Co. 1973.

73. Los Angeles Examiner and Los Angeles Times, Aug. 3, 1920.

74. Personal interview with Gloria Dyer Seaver, 1979.

75. Venice Evening Vanguard, Aug. 21, 1920.

76. Venice Evening Vanguard, Nov. 29, 1920.

77. Personal Interview with Howard Batt, 1976.

78. Venice Evening Vanguard, Sep. 20, 1920.

79. Personal interview with Wally Timm, 1977.

80. Personal interview with Wally Timm, 1977.

81. Personal interview with Wally Timm, 1977.

82. Personal interview with Wally Timm, 1977.

83. Personal interview with Wally Timm, 1977.

84. Motion Picture Exhibitors Herald, Jan. 22, 1921.

85. Venice Evening Vanguard, Jul. 7, 1921.

86. Notes On Mercury Aviation, by Cecil B. DeMille. Cecil B. DeMille Trust.

87. Venice Evening Vanguard, Sep. 10, 1921.

88. Personal interview with Moye Stephens, 1981.

89. Venice Evening Vanguard, Nov. 27, 1921. Personal interview with Moye Stephens, 1981.

90. Venice Evening Vanguard, Dec. 5, 1921.

91. Venice Evening Vanguard, Feb. 11, 1922 & May 12, 1922.

92. Venice Evening Vanguard, Jul. 21, 1922.

93. Venice Evening Vanguard, Oct. 9, 1922.

94. Venice Evening Vanguard, Dec. 17, 1921.

95. Venice Evening Vanguard, Feb. 1, 1922.

96. Venice Evening Vanguard, Oct. 6, 1922.

97. Personal interview with Wally Timm, 1977.

98. Venice Evening Vanguard, Nov. 3, 1922.

99. Venice Evening Vanguard, Nov. 6, 1922 & Nov. 13, 1922.

100. Venice Evening Vanguard, Sep. 21, 1922.

101. Los Angeles Examiner, Dec. 24, 1922. Hollywood Citizen News, Dec. 27, 1922.

102. Films In Review, Mar. 1960, article "Aerial Photographer Harry Perry" by Oscar G. Estes.

103. Venice Evening Vanguard, Mar. 14, 1923 & Mar. 19, 1923.

104. Venice Evening Vanguard, Apr. 17, 1923.

105. Venice Evening Vanguard, Mar. 17, 1923.

106. Personal interview with Tave Wilson, 1976.

107. Santa Monica Evening Outlook, Jul. 5, 1923. Venice Evening Vanguard, Jul. 6, 1923. Personal interview with Moye Stephens, 1981.

108. Los Angeles Examiner, Jul. 16, 1923.

109. Personal interview with Jerry Phillips. 1978.

110. "Squadron of Death"—Dick Grace. The Sun Dial Press, 1937.

111. Venice Evening Vanguard, Nov. 13, 1923.

112. Venice Evening Vanguard, Dec. 28, 1923.

113. Personal interview with Howard Batt, 1976.

114. Personal interview with Jerry Phillips, 1978.

115. Personal interview with Tave Wilson, 1976.

116. Personal interview with Leo Stratton Nomis, 1980.

117. Personal interview with Harry and Fern Perry, 1976.

118. Saturday Evening Post, Sep. 19, 1925.

119. Personal interview with Frank Tomick, 1965.

120. Photoplay, Aug. 1925.

121. Los Angeles Examiner, Apr. 19, 1925.

122. Personal interview with Frank Tomick, 1965.

123. Personal interview with Howard Batt, 1976.

124. Personal interview with Howard Batt, 1976. Los Angeles Times, Mar. 2, 1926.

125. Personal interview with Jerry Phillips and Howard Batt.

126. Interview with Jimmy Barton, conducted by James Dunavent.

127. Reprinted from Popular Aviation, copyright © 1939, CBS Magazines, with their kind permission.

128. "Wings" program notes by John Monk Saunders.

129. Personal interview with Frank Tomick, 1965.

130. "The Lafayette Flying Corps," Vol. I, pg. 483, Nordhoff and Hall.

131. Personal interview with Frank Tomick, 1965.

132. Films In Review, Mar. 1960. Article "Aerial Photographer, Harry Perry" by Oscar G. Estes.

133. Films In Review, Mar. 1960. Article "Aerial Photographer, Harry Perry" by Oscar G. Estes.

134. Interview with Jimmy Barton, conducted by James Dunavent.

135. Saturday Evening Post, Apr. 13, 1929. Interview with Jimmy Barton conducted by James Dunavent.

136. Interview with Jimmy Barton, conducted by James Dunavent.

137. Saturday Evening Post, Apr. 13, 1929.

138. Personal interview with Frank Tomick, 1965.

139. Personal interview with Tave Wilson, 1976.

140. Saturday Evening Post, Apr. 13, 1929.

141. "The Birth Of The Talkies"—Harry M. Geduld, Indiana University Press, 1975

142. Personal interview with Tave Wilson, 1976.

143. Western Flying, May 1927.

144. Personal interview with Frank Tomick, 1965.

145. Los Angeles Examiner, Aug. 24, 1927.

146. Personal interview with Moye Stephens, 1981.

147. Personal interview with Frank Tomick, 1965.

148. Article in International Photographer by Harry Perry, unknown date.

149. Personal interview with Moye Stephens, 1981.

150. Personal interview with Frank Tomick, 1965.

151. Personal interview with Wally Timm, 1977. Los Angeles Examiner, Dec. 31, 1927.

152. Personal interview with Frank Tomick, 1965.

153. "Visibility Unlimited"—Dick Grace. Longmans, Green & Co., 1950.

154. Personal interview with Howard Batt and Tave Wilson, 1976. Western Flying, Sept. 1927.

155. "The Birth Of The Talkies"—Harry M. Geduld, Indiana University Press, 1975.

156. Personal interview with Clinton Herberger conducted by Robert G. Elliott.

157. Western Flying, Apr. 1928.

158. Personal interview with Garland Lincoln, 1960.

159. "From Jennies to Jets"—Vi Smith, Sultana Press, 1974.
On page 44 the author states that three Nieuport 28's became available in Southern California, and that J.O. York obtained one. Each wing tip was shortened by 2'-3', and the parallel wing struts were replaced with "I" struts, giving it an increase of speed to 150 m.p.h. Eddie Martin of Santa Ana then obtained this airplane and flew it at many air shows.
Garland Lincoln says he obtained four Nieuport 28's from Clarence Prest in Riverside, cannibalized one for parts and ended up with three flyable airplanes. A note on the back of the original photograph that appears on page 120 states, "Built by Garland Lincoln. Test flown Jan. 6, 1930, Metropolitan Airport L.A. by Garland Lincoln T2051."
Page 17 of Issue No. 75, World War I Aeroplanes, shows pictures of the York modified Nieuport after it was owned by Eddie Martin.

160. Personal interview with Garland Lincoln, 1960.

161. Personal interview with Frank Tomick, 1965, and personal interview with Howard Batt, 1976.

162. Personal interview with Frank Tomick, 1965.

163. Personal interview with Frank Tomick, 1965.

164. Hollywood Daily Citizen, Mar. 24, 1928.

165. Interview with Jimmy Barton, conducted by James Dunavent.

166. Personal interview with Barney Korn, 1970.

167. Personal interview with Tave Wilson, 1976.

168. Interview with Clinton Herberger conducted by Robert G. Elliott.

169. Personal interview with Tave Wilson, 1976.

170. Los Angeles Examiner, May 27, 1928.

171. Personal interview with Frank Tomick, 1965.

172. Personal interview with Frank Tomick, 1965.

173. Personal interview with Frank Tomick, 1965.

174. Personal interview with Howard Batt, 1976.

175. Personal interview with Frank Tomick, 1965.

176. Personal interview with Frank Tomick, 1965.

177. Personal interview with Frank Tomick, 1965, and interview with Jimmy Barton conducted by James Dunavent.

178. Popular Aviation, Mar. 1940.

179. Personal interview with Frank Tomick, 1965, and interview with Jimmy Barton conducted by James Dunavent.

180. Personal interview with Frank Tomick, 1965.

181. Interview with Jimmy Barton conducted by James Dunavent.

182. Interview with Jimmy Barton conducted by James Dunavent.

183. Interview with Jimmy Barton conducted by James Dunavent.

184. Personal interview with Frank Tomick 1965, and Tave Wilson 1976.

185. Personal interview with Frank Tomick, 1965.

186. Personal interview with Frank Tomick, 1965.

187. Los Angeles Examiner Mar. 23, 1929. Los Angeles Times, Mar. 23, 1929.

188. Personal interview with Frank Tomick, 1965, and Tave Wilson 1976.

189. Los Angeles Examiner Apr. 22 & 23, 1929. Los Angeles Times Apr. 22 & 23, 1929.

190. Look magazine, Letters To The Editor, Mar. 23, 1954.

191. Personal interview with Howard Batt, 1976.

192. Personal interview with Frank Tomick, 1965.

193. Los Angeles Examiner Jan. 3 & 4, 1930. Los Angeles Times Jan. 3 & 4, 1930.

194. Personal interview with Tave Wilson, 1976.

195. Personal interview with Howard Batt, 1976.

196. Personal interview with Frank Tomick, 1965.

197. Western Flying, Nov. 1928.

198. Popular Aviation, date unknown.

199. Interview with Jimmy Barton conducted by James Dunavent.

200. Personal interview with Howard Batt, 1976, and Moye Stephens, 1981.

201. Personal interview with Garland Lincoln, 1960, and copy of contract between Garland Lincoln and Warner Brothers.

202. Personal interview with Garland Lincoln, 1960.

203. New York Times Nov. 21, 1930 and Sep. 6, 1931.

204. Warner Brothers was in the process of buying First National at this time.

205. "Warner Brothers"—Charles Higham. Chas. Scribner & Sons 1975.

206. Personal interview with Tave Wilson, 1976.

207. American Cinematographer Oct. 1930 and Aug. 1931.

208. Personal interview with Tave Wilson, 1976.

209. Interview with Jimmy Barton conducted by James Dunavent.

210. Personal interview with Garland Lincoln, 1960.

211. Popular Aviation, Mar. 1940. Article by Charles Marshall.

212. Personal interview with Howard Batt, 1976.

213. "Hollywood Pilot" - Don Dwiggins. Doubleday, 1967.

214. "Hollywood Pilot" - Don Dwiggins. Doubleday, 1967.

215. New York Times, July, 1930.

216. Personal interview with Frank Tomick, 1965.

217. Personal interview with Tave Wilson, 1976.

218. Union Oil Co. Bulletin, date unknown.

219. Interview with Jimmy Barton conducted by James Dunavent.

220. "von Stroheim"—Thomas Q. Curtiss. Farrar, Straus & Giroux 1971.

221. Personal interviews with Howard Batt, Dick Grace, Garland Lincoln, Frank Tomick and Tave Wilson.

222. Article in The Airline Pilot titled "Motion Picture Pilots Formed By Necessity," by Florence "Pancho" Barnes. The article was clipped and the date is unknown, but references within the article indicates that it was written soon after the formation of the Associated Motion Picture Pilots.

223. Personal interview with Howard Batt, 1976.

224. Article in The Airline Pilot by Florence "Pancho" Barnes.

225. Los Angeles Times Feb. 6, 1932. Los Angeles Evening Herald Express Feb. 5, 1932.

226. Personal interview with Moye Stephens, 1980.

227. Personal interview with Howard Batt, 1976.

228. Article in The Airline Pilot by Florence "Pancho" Barnes.

229. Los Angeles Examiner and Los Angeles Times Jun. 26, 1932. International Photographer, July 1932.

230. International Photographer, Jul. 1932.

231. Personal interview with Tave Wilson, 1976.

232. Los Angeles Times, Sep. 8, 1932.

233. Personal interview with Frank Tomick, 1965.

234. Personal interview with Howard Batt, 1976.

235. Sound tracks of Garland Lincoln's rotary powered Nieuports and LF-1 went into sound libraries and their distinctive flat roars can be recognized in current motion pictures.

236. It seems that Mr. Lincoln either used the original Nieuport 28 wing, though shortened, or else built a new wing structure following the original pattern and method of covering. Almost identical wing failures happened to Eddie Rickenbacker, James Meissner, Waldo Heinrichs and other American pilots in 1918 while flying Nieuport 28's in combat. The problem was finally traced to the way the fabric was attached.

237. Personal interview with Garland Lincoln, 1960.

238. Personal interview with Tave Wilson, 1976.

239. Interview with Jimmy Barton conducted by James Dunavent.

240. Personal interview with Frank Tomick, 1965.

241. Personal interview with Howard Batt, 1976.

242. Popular Aviation, March 1940.

243. International Photographer, July 1933.

244. Program for 1933 National Air Races, courtesy of Howard Batt.

245. Personal interview with Howard Batt, 1976.

246. Popular Aviation, date unknown.

247. Personal interview with Garland Lincoln, 1960.

248. Popular Aviation, March 1940.

249. Interview with Jimmy Barton conducted by James Dunavent.

250. Personal interview with Garland Lincoln, 1960, and Popular Aviation April 1939.

251. Los Angeles Examiner and Los Angeles Times, Sep. 30, 1937, and personal interview with Garland Lincoln, 1960.

252. Los Angeles Times, Feb. 21, 1938 and undated clippings from Paramount Studios publicity department.

253. Garland Lincoln's two LF-1's, used in the picture, were often referred to as "Nieuports."

254. Personal interview with Jerry Phillips, 1979.

255. Popular Aviation, March 1940.

256. Undated news clipping in Garland Lincoln's scrap book, and personal interview with Garland Lincoln and Dick Grace.

257. Personal interview with Jerry Phillips, 1979.

258. Interview with Jimmy Barton conducted by James Dunavent.

259. See "Hollywood Pilot," Don Dwiggins, Doubleday, 1967, for the many aviation accomplishments of Paul Mantz. The author has been told by more than one acquaintance that they witnessed an unusual act of courage and flying skill by Paul Mantz at one of the major Los Angeles air shows in the 1930s. Immediately after a fatal crash during an acrobatic demonstration, Mantz took off and continued the performance even though he was not on that part of the program.

Title	Studio	Year
ABOVE THE CLOUDS - Richard Cromwell	Columbia	1933
ACE OF ACES - Richard Dix, Elizabeth Allen	RKO	1933
ACROSS THE ATLANTIC - Monte Blue	Warner Bros	1928
ADVENTURE IN DIAMONDS - George Brent	Paramount	
ADVENTUROUS SEX, THE - Clara Bow, Herbert Rawlinson	Assoc Exhib	1925
AFLAME IN THE SKY - Sharon Lynn, Jack Luden	R-C Pictures	1927
AFTER YOUR OWN HEART - Tom Mix, Ora Carew	Fox	1921
AIR CIRCUS - David Rollins, Arthur Lake	Fox	1928
AIR DEVILS - Dick Purcell, Beryl Wallace	Universal	1938
AIR EAGLES - Lloyd Hughes, Norman Kerry	Big Productions	1931
AIR FURIES -	Columbia	1935
AIR HAWK, THE - Al Wilson	Film Booking Off	1925
AIR HAWKS - Ralph Bellamy, Wiley Post	Columbia	1935
AIR HOSTESS - Evelyn Knapp, Thelma Todd	Columbia	1933
AIR LEGION - Antonio Moreno, Ben Lyon	RKO	1928
AIR MAIL, THE - Warner Baxter, Billie Dove	Paramount	1925
AIR MAIL - Ralph Bellamy, Pat O'Brien	Universal	1932
AIR MAIL PILOT, THE - James Fulton, Earl Metcalf	Superlative Prod	1928
AIR PATROL, THE - Al Wilson	Universal	1928
AIR POLICE - Ken Harlan	Wide World	1931
AMAZING VAGABOND, THE - Bob Steele	Film Booking Off	1929
AMBUSH -	Paramount	
ANOTHER DAWN -	Warner Bros	1936
ARE ALL MEN ALIKE - May Allison	Metro	1923
ARISE MY LOVE - Claudette Colbert, Ray Milland	RKO	
ARM OF THE LAW, THE -	Universal	
AROUND THE WORLD IN 18 DAYS -	Universal	1923
ATLANTIC FLIGHT - Dick Merrill, Paula Stone	Monogram	1937
AVIATOR, THE - Edward Everett Horton	Warner Bros	1929
BEAUTIFUL - Ann Harding	RKO	1941
BEAU SABREUR - Gary Cooper	Paramount	1926
BENGAL LANCER PATROL -	Republic	
BIG HOP, THE - Buck Jones, Jobyna Ralston	Buck Jones Prod	1928
BODY AND SOUL - Charles Farrell, Myrna Loy	Fox	1931
BORDER FLIGHT - John Howard, Frances Farmer	Paramount	1936
BORDER PATROL -	RKO	
BORN TO LOVE - Joel MacRea, Constance Bennett	Pathe	1931
BRIDE CAME C.O.D., THE -		
BRIGHT EYES - James Dunn, Shirley Temple	Fox	1934
BROKEN WING, THE - Kenneth Harlan, Miriam Cooper	Paramount	1923
BROKEN WING, THE - Melvyn Douglas, Lupe Velez	Paramount	1932
CAPTAIN SWAGGER - Rod LaRocque, Sue Carroll	Pathe	1928
CAPTAINS OF THE CLOUDS - James Cagney, Dennis Morgan	Warner Bros	1942
CAPTURED - Leslie Howard, Douglas Fairbanks, Jr.	First National	1933
CEILING ZERO - James Cagney, Pat O'Brien	Warner Bros	1936
CENTRAL AIRPORT - Richard Barthelmess, Tom Brown	First National	1933
CHARTER PILOT - Lloyd Nolan, Lynn Bari	Fox	1940
CHINA CLIPPER - Pat O'Brien, Beverly Roberts	Warner Bros	1936
CHINA FLIGHT -	Ambassador	1936
CHRISTOPHER STRONG - Colin Clive, Billie Burke	RKO	1933
CLIPPED WINGS - Don Terry, Thurston Hall	Treo Prod'ns	1938
CLOUD DODGER, THE - Al Wilson	Universal	1928
CLOUD RIDER, THE - Al Wilson	Film Booking Off	1925

COAST GUARD - Randolph Scott, Ralph Bellamy	Columbia	1939
COCK OF THE AIR - Chester Morris, Billie Dove	United Artists	1932
CODE OF THE AIR -		
CONQUEST - Monte Blue, H.B. Warner	Warner Bros	1928
CRACK UP - Brian Donlevy, Peter Lorre	Fox	1937
CRIMINALS OF THE AIR - Charles Quigley, Rita Hayworth	Columbia	1937
CRIMSON ROMANCE, THE - Ben Lyon, Sari Maritza	Mascot	1934
CROWD ROARS, THE -		
CORPORAL KATE - Vera Reynolds	Paramount	1926
COWBOY ACE, A - Al Hart, Jack Mowyer	Westart Pictures	1921
COUNTRY DOCTOR -		
DANCE HALL - Olive Borden, Arthur Lake	RKO	1929
DANGER FLIGHT - John Trent, Marjorie Reynolds	Monogram	1939
DARING DEEDS - Billy Sullivan, Molly Malone	Rayart	1927
DAREDEVILS OF THE CLOUDS -		
DAWN PATROL, THE - Richard Barthelmess, Doug Fairbanks	First National	1930
DAWN PATROL, THE - Errol Flynn, David Niven	Warner Bros	1938
DEATH FLIES EAST - Conrad Nagel, Florence Rice	Columbia	1935
DEATH IN THE AIR - John Carroll, Leon Ames	Puritan Distr Co	1937
DEVIL DOGS OF THE AIR - James Cagney, Pat O'Brien	Warner Bros	1935
DEVILS SQUADRON, THE - Richard Dix, Lloyd Nolan	RKO	1936
DICK TRACY VS CRIME INC. -	Republic	
DICTATOR, THE -		
DIVE BOMBER - Errol Flynn, Fred MacMurray	Warner Bros	1941
DIRIGIBLE - Jack Holt, Fay Wray	Columbia	1931
DO AND DARE - Tom Mix	Fox	1922
DOG OF THE REGIMENT - Tom Gallery, Dorothy Gulliver	Warner Bros	1927
DOLLAR DOWN - Ruth Roland, Harry B. Walthal	Truart Pict	1925
DR. JUDITH CRANDALL -	Republic	
DRUMS OF FU MANCHU -	Republic	1940
EAGLE AND THE HAWK - Frederick March, Cary Grant	Paramount	1933
EDUCATING FATHER - Jed Prouty, Shirley Dean	Fox	1936
EMERGENCY LANDING - Forrest Tucker, Carol Hughes	Prod Releas Corp	1941
ETERNALLY YOURS -		
EXCUSE ME - Norma Shearer, Conrad Nagel	MGM	1925
FAST MAIL, THE - Charles Jones, Eileen Percy	Fox	1922
FIGHTING AMERICAN, THE - Pat O'Malley, Mary Astor	Universal	1924
FIGHTING PILOT, THE - Richard Talmadge, Gertrude Mess'r		
FIVE CAME BACK - Chester Morris, Lucille Ball	RKO	1939
FLIGHT - Jack Holt, Ralph Graves	Columbia	1929
FLIGHT ANGELS - Dennis Morgan, Virginia Bruce	Warner Bros	1940
FLIGHT AT MIDNIGHT - Robert Armstrong, Roscoe Turner	Republic	1939
FLIGHT COMMAND - Robert Taylor, Walter Pidgeon	MGM	1940
FLIGHT FROM GLORY - Chester Morris, Van Heflin	RKO	1937
FLIGHT INTO FAME - Charles Farrell, Jacqueline Wells	Columbia	1938
FLIGHT INTO NOWHERE - Jack Holt, Dick Purcell	Columbia	1938
FLIGHT LIEUTENANT - Glenn Ford, Pat O'Brien	Columbia	1942
FLOATING PLATFORM #1 - Conrad Veidt, Leslie Fenton	Fox	1933
FLY AWAY BABY - Glenda Farrell, Barton MacLane	Warner Bros	1937
FLYING BLIND - Richard Arlen, Jean Parker	Paramount	1941
FLYING BUCKAROO - Wally Wales	Pathe	1928
FLYING CADETS - Edmund Lowe, William Gargan	Universal	1941
FLYING COWBOY - Hoot Gibson	Universal	1928
FLYING DEVILS - Bruce Cabot, Ralph Bellamy	RKO	1933
FLYING DOWN TO RIO - Gene Raymond, Dolores Del Rio	RKO	1933
FLYING EAGLES -		
FLYING FLEET, THE - Ramon Navarro, Anita Page	MGM	1928
FLYING FOOL, THE - Gaston Glass, Dick Grace	Aywon Film Corp	1925
FLYING FOOL, THE - William Boyd, Marie Provost	Pathe	1929
FLYING G-MEN -	Columbia	1939

FLYING HIGH - William Fairbanks, Alice Calhoun	Lumas Productions	1926
FLYING HIGH - Bert Lahr, Charlotte Greenwood	MGM	1931
FLYING HOSTESS - William Hall, Judith Barrett	Universal	1936
FLYING IRISHMAN, THE - Douglas Corrigan, Paul Kelly	RKO	1939
FLYING LUCK - Monte Banks, Jean Arthur	Pathe	1927
FLYING MAIL, THE - Al Wilson	Associated Exhib	1926
FLYING MARINE, THE - Ben Lyon, Jason Robards	Columbia	1929
FLYING PAT - Dorothy Gish	Paramount	1920
FLYING ROMEOS - Charlie Murray, George Sydney	First Nat'l	1928
FLYING THROUGH - Al Wilson	Aywon Film Corp	1925
FLYING WILD - Leo Gorcey	Monogram	1941
FORCED LANDING - Onslow Stevens, Esther Ralston	Republic	1935
FORCED LANDING - Richard Arlen, Eva Gabor	Paramount	1941
FOUR ACES, THE -	Syn	1933
FUGITIVE IN THE SKY - Warren Hull, Gordon Oliver	Warner Bros	1936
GIRL FROM GOD'S COUNTRY - Neil Shipman, Edward Burns	Nell Shipman	1921
GIVE US WINGS - Dead End Kids	Universal	1940
GO AND GET IT -	First Nat'l	1920
GOING UP - Douglas MacLean	Associated Exhib	1923
GOING WILD - Joe E. Brown	First Nat'l	1930
GOLD - Jack Hoxie, Alice Day	Majestic Pictures	1932
GREAT AIR ROBBERY, THE - Ormer Locklear	Universal	1919
GREAT MAIL ROBBERY, THE - Theodore von Eltz	R-C Pictures	1927
GREAT PLANE ROBBERY, THE - Jack Holt, Stanley Fields	Columbia	1940
GREAT AMERICAN BROADCAST, THE - John Payne, Alice Faye	Fox	
GRIM GAME, THE - Houdini	Laskey Co.	1919
HAPPY LANDINGS - Sonja Heine, John Payne	Fox	1938
HARDBOILED HAGGARTY - Milton Sills, Molly O'Day	First National	1927
HEARTBREAK - Charles Farrell	Fox	1931
HELLDIVERS - Wallace Beery, Clark Gable	MGM	1932
HELL IN THE HEAVENS - Warner Baxter, Conchita Montenegro	Fox	1934
HELL'S ANGELS - Ben Lyon, James Hall, Jean Harlow	Caddo Productions	1930
HERO FOR A NIGHT, A - Glen Bryon, Patsy Miller	Universal	1927
HIGH FLYER, THE - Reed Howes, Etherl Shannon	Rayart	1926
HIGH FLYERS - Wheeler and Woolsey	RKO	1937
HIPS HIPS HOORAY - Wheeler and Woolsey	RKO	1938
HIS MASTER'S VOICE - George Hackthorne, Thunder	Lumas Productions	1925
HOLLYWOOD COWBOY - Buck Jones	Condor Productions	1937
HOUSE ACROSS THE BAY -	Walter Wanger	1940
ILLEGAL TRAFFIC -	Paramount	
I'M FROM MISSOURI - Bob Burns	Paramount	
INTERNATIONAL SPY -	Columbia	
I WANTED WINGS - Ray Milland, William Holden	Paramount	1941
KEEP 'EM FLYING - Abbott & Costello	Universal	1941
KISS BARRIER, THE - Edmund Lowe, Claire Adams	Fox	1925
LADIES CRAVE EXCITEMENT - Norman Foster, Evelyn Knapp	Mascot	1935
LADIES MUST LIVE - Robert Ellis, Mahlon Hamilton	Paramount	1921
LAST FLIGHT - Richard Barthelmess	First National	1931
LEGION OF LOST FLYERS - Richard Arlen, Andy Devine	Universal	1939
LEGION OF THE CONDEMNED - Gary Cooper, Fay Wray	Paramount	1928
LIFE IS CHEAP -	Columbia	1938
LILAC TIME - Colleen Moore, Gary Cooper	First National	1928
LIVE WIRES - Johnny Walker, Edna Murphy	Fox	1921
LONE EAGLE, THE - Raymond Keene, Barbara Kent	Universal	1927
LOOKING FOR TROUBLE - Buck Jones	Condor Productions	1937
LOST HORIZON - Ronald Coleman	Columbia	
LOST IN THE STRATOSPHERE - William Cagney, June Collyer	Monogram	1934
LOST SQUADRON - Richard Dix, Mary Astor	RKO	1932

LOST PATROL - Victor MacLaglen	RKO	1937
LOST ZEPPELIN - Ricardo Cortez, Virginia Valli	Tiffany Pictures	1929
LOTTERY BRIDE - Jeanette MacDonald, John Garrick	United Artists	1930
LOVE AFFAIR - Humphrey Bogart, Dorothy McKail	Columbia	1932
LOVE ON THE RUN -		
LOVE TAKES FLIGHT - Bruce Cabot, Beatrice Roberts	Grand National	1937
MAID OF THE WEST - Eileen Percy, William Scott	Fox	1921
MAN WHO FOUND HIMSELF, THE - John Beal, Joan Fontaine	RKO	1937
MARINES FLY HIGH, THE - Richard Dix, Chester Morris	RKO	1940
MARRIAGE - Allan Durant	Fox	1927
MEN AGAINST THE SKY - Richard Dix, Kent Taylor	RKO	1940
MEN OF THE SKY - Jack Whiting, Irene Delroy	First National	1931
MEN WITH WINGS - Fred MacMurray, Ray Milland	Paramount	1938
MERCY PLANE - James Dunn, Frances Gifford	Prod Releas Corp	1940
MIKE -	MGM	1926
MISTAKEN IDENTITY -	Columbia	1935
MIDNIGHT LOVERS - Lewis Stone, Anna Nilsson	First National	1926
MURDER IN THE AIR - Ronald Reagan, John Litel	Warner Bros	1940
NAVY BORN - William Gargan, Claire Dodd	Republic	1936
NEW TEACHER, THE - Shirley Mason, Alan Forest	Fox	1922
NIGHT FLIGHT - Clark Gable, John Barrymore	MGM	1933
NON-STOP FLIGHT, THE - Knute Erickson, Marcella Daly Emory	Johnson Prod	1926
NOW WE'RE IN THE AIR - Wallace Beery, Raymond Hatton	Paramount	1927
ONE WEEK OF LOVE - Elaine Hammerstein		1922
ONLY ANGELS HAVE WINGS - Cary Grant	Columbia	1939
OUR NEIGHBORS THE CARTERS -	Paramount	
OUTLAWS OF THE ORIENT - Jack Holt, Mae Clark	Columbia	1937
PARACHUTE JUMPER - Douglas Fairbanks, Jr., Bette Davis	Warner Bros	1933
PARADISE - Milton Sills, Betty Bronson	First National	1926
PHANTOM FLYER, THE - Al Wilson	Universal	1928
PIRATES OF THE SKIES - Kent Taylor, Rochelle Hudson	Universal	1939
PIRATES OF THE SKY - Charles Hutchison, Wanda Hawley	Pathe	1927
PLANE MISSING -	Republic	1940
POWER DIVE - Richard Arlen, Jean Parker	Paramount	1941
PUBLICITY MADNESS - Lois Moran, Edmund Lowe	Fox	1927
RAMPANT AGE, THE - James Murray, Myrna Kennedy	Continental	1930
REPORTED MISSING - William Gargan, Jean Parker	Universal	1937
RIDING ON AIR - Joe E. Brown	RKO	1937
RIGHT TO ROMANCE - Robert Young, Ann Harding	RKO	1934
ROAMING LADY - Fay Wray, Ralph Bellamy	Columbia	1936
ROOKIES - Karl Dane, George K. Arthur	MGM	1927
ROUNDUP -	Condor Prod	1937
SAFARI -	Paramount	
SECRET SERVICE OF THE AIR - Ronald Reagan, John Litel	Warner Bros	1939
SHIELD OF HONOR - Neil Hamilton, Dorothy Gulliver	Universal	1927
SILENT VALLEY - Tom Mix	Comm	1935
SKIRTS - Clyde Cook, Chester Conklin	Fox	1921
SKY BANDITS -	Monogram	1938
SKYBOUND - Lloyd Hughes, Lona Andre		
SKY BRIDE, THE - Richard Arlen, Virginia Bruce	Paramount	1932
SKY DEVILS - Spencer Tracy, William Boyd	United Artists	1932
SKY EYE -		1920
SKY GIANT - Richard Dix, Joan Fontaine	RKO	1938
SKY HAWK, THE - John Garrick, Helen Chandler	Fox	1930
SKY HIGH - Tom Mix	Fox	1922
SKY HIGH SAUNDERS - Al Wilson	Universal	1927
SKYLARKING - Joe E. Brown		

SKY PARADE, THE - Jimmie Allen, Katherine DeMille	Paramount	1936
SKY PATROL - John Trent, Marjorie Reynolds	Monogram	1939
SKY PIRATE, THE - Bryant Washburn	Aywon Film Corp	1926
SKY RAIDERS - Lloyd Hughes, Madeline Day	Columbia	1931
SKY RAIDER, THE - Charles Nungesser	Assoc Exhibitors	1925
SKY RIDER, THE - Alfred Heuston, Gareth Hughes	Chesterfield	1928
SKY SKIDDER, THE - Al Wilson	Universal	1929
SKY SPIDER, THE - Glen Tryon, Pat O'Malley	Action Pictures	1931
SKYWAY - Kathryn Crawford, Ray Walker	Monogram	1932
SKYWAYMAN, THE - Ormer Locklear	Fox	1920
SOLDIERS OF THE STORM - Regis Toomey, Anita Page	Columbia	1933
S.O.S. ICEBERG - Rod LaRocque, Gibson Gowland	Universal	1933
SPEED GIRL, THE - Bebe Daniels, Theodore von Eltz	Paramount	1921
SPEED WINGS - Tim McCoy, Evelyn Knapp	Columbia	1934
SPY 77 - Don Alvarado, Greta Nissen	Grand National	1937
STATE TROOPER -	Columbia	
STORM OVER BENGAL - Patrick Knowles, Rochelle Hudson	Republic	1938
STORM OVER THE ANDES - Jack Holt, Mona Barrie	Universal	1935
STORY OF VERNON & IRENE CASTLE - Fred Astaire, Ginger Rogers	RKO	1939
STRANGER THAN FICTION - Katherine MacDonald, Dave Winter	Kath MacDonald	1921
STUNT PILOT - John Trent, Marjorie Reynolds	Monogram	1939
SUZY - Franchot Tone, Jean Harlow	MGM	1936
SPEEDWAY -		
SUCH MEN ARE DANGEROUS - Warner Baxter	Fox	1930
SUNDOWN - Gene Tierney, Bruce Cabot		
TAILSPIN - Alice Faye, Nancy Kelly	Fox	1939
TEST PILOT - Clark Gable, Spencer Tracy	MGM	1938
THIRTEEN HOURS BY AIR - Fred MacMurray, Joan Bennett	Paramount	1936
THREE MILES UP - Al Wilson	Universal	1927
THUNDERBIRDS - Gene Tierney, Preston Foster	Fox	1942
TODAY WE LIVE - Gary Cooper, Joan Crawford	MGM	1933
TOO HOT TO HANDLE - Clark Gable, Myrna Loy	MGM	1938
TORCHY BLAINE IN PANAMA - Paul Kelly, Lola Lane	Warner Bros	1938
TRAPPED IN THE SKY - Jack Holt, Ralph Morgan	Columbia	1939
20,000 MEN A YEAR - Randolph Scott, Preston Foster	Fox	1939
WAR CORRESPONDENT - Jack Holt, Ralph Graves	Columbia	1932
WAR EAGLES -		
WEST POINT OF THE AIR - Wallce Beery, Robert Young	MGM	1935
WHITE SISTER, THE - Clark Gable, Helen Hayes	MGM	1933
WINGED HORSEMAN, THE - Hoot Gibson, Ruth Elder		1929
WIDE OPEN - Dick Grace, Grace Darmond	Shar	1927
WINGS - Buddy Rogers, Clara Bow	Paramount	1927
WINGS IN THE DARK - Cary Grant, Myrna Loy	Paramount	1935
WINGS OF ADVENTURE - Rex Lease, Clyde Cook	Columbia	1938
WINGS OF DOOM -		
WINGS OF THE NAVY - George Brent, John Payne	Warner Bros	1939
WINGS OVER HONOLULU - Ray Milland, William Gargan	Universal	1937
WINGS OVER THE DESERT -	MGM	1940
WITH WINGS OUTSPREAD - Fred Terry, Walter Franklin	Aywon Film Corp	1922
WITHOUT ORDERS - Robert Armstrong, Sally Eilers	RKO	1936
WOMAN I LOVE, THE - Paul Muni, Louis Hayward	RKO	1937
WOMAN WITH FOUR FACES - Betty Compson	Paramount	1923
WOMEN IN THE WIND - William Gargan, Kay Francis	Warner Bros	1939
WON IN THE CLOUDS - Al Wilson	Universal	1928
WORLDLY GOODS - James Kirkwood, Merna Kennedy	Continental	1930
WORLD ON PARADE - Paramount	1939	
WOLVES OF THE AIR - Johnnie Walker, Lois Boyd	Sterling Pictures	1927
YOUNG EAGLES - Buddy Rogers, Jean Arthur	Paramount	1930
YOUNG WHIRLWIND - Buzz Barton, Edmond Cobb	Film Booking Off	1928

SERIALS

ACE DRUMMOND - John King, Noah Beery, Jr.	Universal	1936
AIRPLANE EXPRESS -	RKO	
AIR MAIL MYSTERY - James Flavin	Universal	1932
BRANDED FOUR, THE - Ben Wilson	Select Pictures	
BURN 'EM UP BARNES -		
EAGLE OF THE NIGHT - Frank Clarke, Shirley Palmer	Pathe	1927
EAGLES TALONS, THE -		
FLYING G-MEN - Robert Paige, James Craig	Columbia	1939
GALLOPING GHOST, THE - Red Grange	Mascot	
GHOST CITY -	Universal	
HURRICANE EXPRESS - John Wayne, Shirley Grey	Mascot	1932
MYSTERIOUS AIRMAN, THE - Walter Miller	Artclass Pictures	1928
MYSTERIOUS PILOT, THE - Frank Hawks	Columbia	1937
MYSTERY PLANE - John Trent, Marjorie Reynolds	Monogram	1939
MYSTERY PILOT - Rex Lease	Rayart	
MYSTERY SQUADRON - Bob Steele, Guinn Williams	Mascot	1933
PHANTOM OF THE AIR - Tom Tyler	Universal	1933
SHADOW OF THE EAGLE - John Wayne, Dorothy Gulliver	Mascot	1932
SILENT FLYER - Malcom MacGregor	Universal	1927
SKY RAIDERS - Robert Armstrong, Denny Woods	Universal	1941
SKY RANGER, THE - June Caprice	Pathe	1921
SNOWED IN - Allen Ray, Walter Miller	Pathe	1926
SPEED - Charles Hutchison, Lucy Fox	Pathe	
TAILSPIN TOMMY - Maurice Murphy, Noah Beery, Jr.	Universal	1934
TAILSPIN TOMMY & THE GREAT AIR MYSTERY - Clark Williams	Universal	1935
TIMBER QUEEN - Ruth Roland	Pathe	1922

ABOUT THE AUTHOR

When an aviation movie was on the Saturday afternoon program at the "picture show" in a small Georgia town during the early 1930s, the author was one of the kids who arrived well before the doors opened and sat through repeated showings of the film, until concerned parents arrived to drag them home.

After serving four years in the Army Air Corps during World War II, Mr. Wynne attended the University of Southern California, graduating in 1951.

With a strong interest in the history of military aviation of the 1914-1918 War, the author contacted other enthusiasts and invited them to his home in 1959 where Cross and Cockade, The Society of World War One Aero Historians was founded. Serving as the first president, he was an editor of the society's journal for two years, remaining as a contributing editor for several more years.

Prompted by a large amount of misinformation about the original motion picture stunt pilots then circulating in aviation history circles, the author located and interviewed the surviving original members of the Associated Motion Picture Pilots in order to preserve their true story.

Now retired from practice as an architect, the author lives in Tustin, California, where he is an avid student of the Bible and is devoted to his family.